Philip Yorke I
(1743-1804)
Squire of Erthig

Philip Yorke I, (1743-1804) – Squire of Erthig
© 1995 Eric Griffiths

ISBN 1-872424-47-3

Published in Wales by
BRIDGE BOOKS
61 Park Avenue,
Wrexham, Clwyd,
LL12 7AW

I
'Nhad a 'Mam

CIP Data for this book is available
from the British Library

Printed and bound by
Amadeus Press Ltd
Huddersfield, West Yorkshire

CONTENTS

ILLUSTRATIONS & MAPS

ACKNOWLEDGEMENTS

I would like to thank the following institutions for their contributions to this book:–

The British Library, the Public Record Office, the Courtauld Institute of Art, the National Trust, the National Library of Wales, the libraries at Chester College, the North East Wales Institute, Cartrefle, and the University College of North Wales, Bangor, the Clwyd County Library and the public libraries at Shrewsbury, Oswestry and Wrexham, the Clwyd County Record Office (particularly the Hawarden branch where the Erthig papers are housed) and the Hertfordshire, Shropshire and Warwickshire Record Offices.

I would also like to thank a number of individuals who took the time and trouble to answer my queries and those who gave me the loan of material.

I owe special thanks to Alistair Laing, Adviser on Pictures and Sculptures to the National Trust, for permission to reproduce photographs of paintings from Erthig taken by the Courtauld Institute; Robert Dillon, the Administrator at Erthig, for allowing me to use the resources of the library; Lord Brownlow for giving me access to the then uncatalogued family papers at Belton House; Jeremy Cragg, the House Steward at Erthig, for his interest in the work and his help in ways too numerous to mention; Joan M. Hughes, my former colleague who read the manuscript and made many valuable and instructive comments and criticisms; and my wife for typing the text and providing constant support and encouragement while the work was in progress.

Eric Griffiths,
Wrexham,
March 1995

A NOTE ON SPELLING

To avoid confusion, the spelling ERTHIG, employed in Philip Yorke's day, has been used throughout.

The original spellings have been retained in the quotations from contemporary sources.

ABBREVIATIONS

Ag.HR	*Agricultural History Review*
Arch. Camb.	*Archaeologica Cambrensis*
BBCS	*Bulletin of the Board of Celtic Studies*
Brit.Mus.Add.MSS.	British Museum Additional Manuscripts
CRO	Clwyd Record Office
Ches.RO	Cheshire Record Office
DHST	*Denbighshire Historical Society Transactions*
DNB	*Dictionary of National Biography*
DWB	*Dictionary of Welsh Biography*
Ec.HR	*Economic History Review*
Glam.H	*Glamorgan Historian*
Herts.RO	Hertfordshire Record Office
JFHS	*Journal of the Flintshire Historical Society*
JMHRS	*Journal of the Merionethshire Historical and Record Society*
Mont.Colls.	Montgomeryshire Collections
Morg.	*Morgannwg*
NLW	National Library of Wales
NLWJ	*National Library of Wales Journal*
PRO	Public Record Office
SRO	Shropshire Record Office
Shr.PL	Shrewsbury Public Library
TAAS	*Transactions of the Anglesey Antiquarian Society*
TEHerts.AS	*Transactions of the East Hertfordshire Archaeological Society*
THSC	*Transactions of the Honourable Society of Cymmrodorion*
THSLC	*Transactions of the Historic Society of Lancashire and Cheshire*
WRO	Warwickshire Record Office

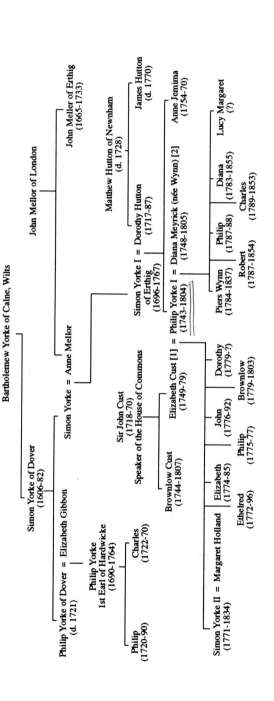

Philip Yorke's Family and 'Connexions'

PREFACE

There are only two descriptions of Philip Yorke by men who knew him. One was a brief obituary notice by the Rector of the church he attended, the Rev. Samuel Strong; the other was included in a book of reminiscences by C. J. Apperley, 'Nimrod', the son of one of Philip Yorke's tenants. Both depicted him as a paragon of eighteenth century gentlemanly virtues; he was benevolent, patriotic, cultured, generous even to a fault, a scintillating conversationalist and a classical scholar free of all taint of pedantry.

Similar qualities were attributed to a host of eighteenth century squires in their obituaries; they represent the stereotype on which the gentleman was expected to model himself, rather than the personality of an individual. Nimrod, it is true, added many colourful touches to his anecdotal portrait but he was writing forty years after Philip Yorke's death and his information can occasionally be shown to be inaccurate. For instance, he described Philip Yorke as a squire worth £7,000 a year who, ignoring economic realities, spent every penny of his income.

This portrayal of an extravagant landowner has been seized upon by later writers. Thus Richard Williams in the 1887 edition of *The Royal Tribes of Wales*, the *Dictionary of Welsh Biography* published in 1959 and R. G. Thorne in *The House of Commons, 1790-1820* (London, 1986) have accepted Nimrod's account. Even Albinia Lucy Cust's account written early in this century, the first to be based on unlimited access to family papers, was highly coloured by it, though she did modify the traditional picture somewhat by stating that, while he spent his income 'royally', he did expect value for money and kept a close eye on expenditure.

Nearer our own day, while Merlin Waterston in *The Servants' Hall* has presented a more balanced view of his character and attitudes, H.M.C. Jones-Mortimer in *A List of the Names and Residences of all the High Sheriffs of the County of Denbigh* (1971) called him "a dilettante squire of English origin".

In none of these instances, however, was Philip Yorke the main subject of study and, consequently, no attempt was made to write a comprehensive account of his life based on a detailed, critical examination of available sources. He was a man of many parts and interests: an 'improving' landowner, a member of Parliament and justice of the peace, a soldier and an author and, so far, his attitudes and conduct in these roles have not been subjected to a thorough analysis.

The scope of any such enquiry must necessarily be circumscribed by the nature and extent of the available source material and that on Philip Yorke has certain, in some cases considerable, limitations. Firstly, there is the dearth of comment on him by his contemporaries and of his on them. Secondly, he kept very few of his correspondents' letters, though they, fortunately, kept a great many of his. This will necessarily influence the final interpretation of Philip Yorke's actions, particularly in those areas where analysis is heavily based on correspondence. Thirdly, the source material is not equally representative of all Philip Yorke's activities; for instance, a great many more records are available for a study of estate matters at Erthig than of those at his 'peripheral' properties. This rules out a detailed examination of the situation at Newnham and Dyffryn Aled such as has been possible for Erthig. Nevertheless, though the Yorke papers contain many gaps in the documentary evidence concerning Philip Yorke's other activities, these can, fortunately, often be filled by material housed in other repositories.

Within these limitations, this study seeks to explore Philip Yorke's ideas and actions in his various spheres of interest with two aims in view: to discover how well the traditional generalisations about him stand up to close examination and to see what light it will throw upon his character and achievements, as well as upon the age in which he lived.

INTRODUCTION

The first member of the Yorke family to achieve some importance in his own locality was Simon Yorke of Dover (1605-1683), the eldest son of Bartholomew Yorke of Calne in Wiltshire. He was a prosperous wine merchant who invested his wealth in property in Dover and its neighbourhood and became a powerful figure in the municipal life of the town. He had six children, the fourth and fifth of whom, named Philip and Simon, were to become the founders of two socially mobile branches of the Yorke family.[1]

Philip, baptised in 1651, who flourished as a solicitor in Dover in the later years of the seventeenth century, acquired in the process influence and property, and a fearsome reputation as an "obstinate executor, well versed in the knavish part of the law, and very resolute to insist upon it."[2]

He fathered a son of the same name who would in due course become Lord Chancellor and the first Earl of Hardwicke.[3] Simon, younger by three years, became a wholesale grocer in London, and inherited from his father a large house in Dover and six acres of land in a neighbouring parish. Nevertheless, he seems to have been the least successful member of the family, and it is possible that he spent some time in a debtors' prison. In 1682, however, he married Anne, daughter of John Meller, a prosperous London draper. Anne's brother, also John Meller, had amassed sufficient wealth from his career as a Master in Chancery[4] to acquire land and gentry status. In 1716 he purchased from its bankrupt owner, Joshua Edisbury, the estate of Erthig, on the outskirts of Wrexham in Denbighshire, for the sum of £17,000.[5] Many estates changed hands in the Wrexham area in the late seventeenth and early eighteenth centuries. A number of them were bought by new arrivals in the area, and were not, as was often the case in other parts of the country, swallowed up by one of the great neighbouring estates, such as Wynnstay.[6] The replacement of the Edisburys by first the Mellers and then the Yorkes was one of many instances in eighteenth century Wales of the estate of a native family of the so-called 'lesser gentry' falling into the hands of prosperous, socially ambitious newcomers of the 'middling-sort'. The cause, however, in this instance, was bankruptcy and not the failure of male heirs which bedevilled so many of the Welsh gentry during this period.[7] This 'takeover' saved Erthig from the extinction which befell several of the country mansions of Wales.[8]

John Meller extended the mansion built by Joshua Edisbury and set out to furnish it with discrimination. Unlike many country gentry, he was not satisfied with the work of local craftsmen and employed his nephew, Simon Yorke, son of his sister Anne, to obtain fine furniture in London and arrange its transport to Erthig. Simon was also instructed to conduct important legal and financial transactions in the capital for him. Not surprisingly, therefore, Meller, a bachelor, bequeathed Erthig to his nephew who became squire in 1733.

The description of Simon on his memorial in the family church at Marchwiel as "a pious, temperate, sensible country gentleman of a very mild, just and benevolent character", suggests a worthy but colourless individual. Such obituaries have to be treated with caution, however, and other evidence, in any case, indicates a livelier, more interesting figure. His surviving letters to John Meller concerning his London interests, during the period May to August 1729 in particular, demonstrate a clear grasp of essentials and an ability to express his ideas with precision and style. He wrote a stream of letters, concentrated on a very narrow range of subject-matter,[9] a procedure which would be adopted by his son on occasion. A suggestion, by no means fanciful, has been made that Simon Yorke could have been a non-practising barrister.[10] Unfortunately, the surviving records are silent on this matter, as indeed they are on his education and most of his adult life. After he inherited Erthig in 1733, Simon Yorke's visits to the capital became much rarer and he depended increasingly upon letters from friends such as Owen Brereton[11] and Richard Wolfe,[12] both barristers, to satisfy his keen interest in the latest news about national and international events.

In 1739 he married Dorothy, the daughter of Matthew Hutton of Newnham in Hertfordshire. She was twenty years his junior, and was to outlive him by the same margin. There is no information about the education of either Simon or Dorothy but her signature is to be found inside the covers of three novels still housed in the library at Erthig.[13] Like Joseph Addison's Leonora, a wealthy widow, and countless other women of her class and period, Dorothy Hutton's reading had obviously "lain very much in romances".[14] At a time when a girl's education normally consisted of a mere smattering of the 3Rs and 'polite accomplishments', and a learned woman was an anachronism, Dorothy Hutton's reading habits were not unusual and her letter-writing, though at times uncertain on points of grammar and spelling, was no mean attainment.[15] Her surviving letters, a few to Simon and a large number to her son Philip after her husband's death, written in an untidy scrawl, reveal a lively concern for her family and servants, her own health, local gossip and 'excursions'. Between 1767 when Philip inherited Erthig and 1770 when he married, her letters were greatly concerned with estate matters and his marriage prospects.[16]

Simon and Dorothy Yorke had only two children. Philip was born on July 30th, 1743 and christened at Erthig on Friday, August 12th by the curate of Gresford, Simon Jones.[17] His sister, Anne Jemima, was born eleven years later, on June 28th, 1754, but died on April 6th, 1770.

The choice of Philip's godfathers, the first Earl of Hardwicke and Matthew Hutton, was significant. A key factor in the lives of the Yorkes of Erthig in the eighteenth century was the family connection with the more illustrious and influential Hardwickes, whose patronage would be vital to Philip Yorke's education and subsequent career. Also destined to play an important role was the Hutton family of Newnham in Hertfordshire. The manor of Newnham, together with its fifteenth century manor-house, had fallen into the hands of Matthew Hutton in 1716[18], and the inheritance of the property was ultimately to be a determining factor in the realisation of Philip's matrimonial plans.

CHAPTER 1: School and University

There are no records of Philip Yorke's life before he went to school. The views of Simon and Dorothy on the most desirable form of education for their son can only be inferred from the choice which they actually made. They may or may not have been aware of the controversy over whether home or school provided the better education for the sons of the aristocracy and gentry, about which so much was written in the eighteenth century[1], but it was the latter form which they chose for Philip, even from the early age of five.

He spent the period from 1748 to 1752 at a preparatory school at Wanstead. The identity of the headmaster is unclear, but the most influential persons so far as Philip was concerned would appear to have been Matthew Wymondesold of Lockinge and the Rev. John Shepherd, who, it has been suggested, was Wymondesold's domestic chaplain.[2] Matthew Wymondesold himself seems to have been a close friend of the Huttons. In 1762 he was one of the signatories of the will of James Hutton, Philip Yorke's uncle.[3] This friendship extended to the Yorkes and lasted over many years. In a letter to Simon Yorke in January 1755, Matthew Wymondesold called him "my old friend",[4] in August 1768 he visited Erthig,[5] while in the following year Dorothy Yorke stayed at his London home.[6]

The Rev. John Shepherd was Philip's special tutor at the school. "... he hath been some sort a tutor to my son from his early infancy ...", wrote Simon Yorke to his cousin Charles Yorke[7] on January 24th, 1755.[8] John Shepherd supplied Simon and Dorothy Yorke with regular reports on their son's progress. Allowing for a certain degree of anxiety to please the parents which might have coloured what he wrote, these reports, especially when they are considered in the light of the character and achievements of the mature Philip Yorke, seem to have been quite prophetic. For instance, on October 21st, 1749, he wrote:

> There is great occasion too to believe the Improvement of his Mind will keep pace with that of his Person; for he is very inquisitive about the meaning of every thing; and I doubt not but he will make up the lost time (if it be called lost) occasioned by the Small Pox etc. He told us on Sunday last he had now done with the Spelling Book, and was got into the Tables....[9]

Again on May 29th, 1750, when Philip Yorke was six years old, he stated:

> He has such a Desire of Knowing everything and such an Emulation of exceeding the other boys of the same standing with himself, that I think there is not the least Room to doubt his Progress in Learning.... He should read his Book every Day and so get before Jack Smith (whom he always speaks of as his Rival) when he comes back.[10]

Another correspondent was Richard Wolfe, a barrister from South Shields who at one time held the post of Deputy Clerk to the Duchy of Lancaster.[11] He noted Philip's equable, easy-going temperament and remarked shrewdly that he "... knows as well how to lay his schemes for perfecting his views as the most consomate politician...."[12] Philip Yorke spent part at least of his holidays with relatives or friends at Wanstead itself, at Lockinge, or at Newnham,[13] but the assertion that he did not visit his parents during his first two years at Wanstead rests on very slender evidence.[14]

His links with Wanstead were not severed when he ceased to be a pupil at the school. He spent his Christmas and parts of his summer holidays there when he was at the Hackney Academy. John Shepherd informed Simon Yorke that his son was a great favourite with the Wymondesold family, and added,

> He is what you yourself would chuse him to be.... His vivacity perhaps may prevent his attending so closely to his Book as Boys of less spirit, but I'm sure he has parts equal to anything suited to his Age, and as his years and Understanding advance he cannot fail of making great Improvements under proper Direction.[15]

A number of references were made to Matthew Wymondesold's generosity towards Philip. John Shepherd said that "Mr. Wymondesold is become extremely fond of him"[16] and that he treated Philip "as his own"[17] while Simon Yorke wrote that he treated his son like "an indulgent parent."[18] This close relationship had not passed unnoticed by Philip's fellow pupils. Richard Woolfe wrote to Simon Yorke on June 15th, 1749, "I ask't him what nick-name the Boys had given him. He replyed, gloating, Wymondesold."[19]

Such friendships, however, may not have been entirely dis-interested, for the Yorkes of Erthig had access to the patronage of their influential kinsfolk, the Hardwickes. Matthew Wymondesold wished to procure a living for John Shepherd and, as Lord Chancellor, the Earl of Hardwicke exercised patronage over ecclesiastical appointments which were in the gift of the Great Seal. He would exclude candidates known to be hostile to the Hanoverians [20] and would not "depart from his rule not to promise livings before they became vacant." [21]

In a letter written in January 1755, Matthew Wymondesold asked Simon Yorke to approach the Earl of Hardwicke with a view to procuring for John Shepherd "some prebend, those of Gloucester and Bristol are in his Lord's disposal, and are not considerable things in themselves, tho' one of them would be so to him." He added a warm recommendation, praising John Shepherd's "...learning, manners and steady affection to his Majesty and Government...."[22] After Simon Yorke had made the initial approach, the machinery of patronage was set in motion, and eventually a choice of livings in the Lockinge area was offered to John Shepherd.[23]

In 1752, aged eight, Philip Yorke went to Dr. Henry Newcome's Private Academy in Hackney, "the oldest, the largest and the most fashionable of all private schools of the eighteenth century."[24] Founded in 1685, it catered mainly for the sons of the upper and upper-middle classes, and was in the hands of the Newcombe family from 1721 to 1803.[25]

The Hardwicke connection smoothed Philip Yorke's path into the Academy. The two sons of the Earl of Hardwicke had preceded him there, and a place had been reserved for Philip himself.[26] In August 1764, perhaps as a result of Philip Yorke's recommendation, his friend in later years, Thomas Pennant, placed his son David in Hackney.[27] Philip Yorke's transition from Wanstead to Hackney was described by John Shepherd on April 25th, 1752.

> Dr. Newcome seems much pleased with his Scholar and I don't doubt but he will fill the vacant Place, which he tells him is reserved for him among the Yorkes, with credit to the Family. He will necessarily be retarded a little by the different method of teaching, but that will soon be got over as he seems to have a strong emulation to reach the goal the Dr. has set before him.[28]

The headmaster, as he wrote to Simon Yorke on April 28th, 1752, was clearly impressed by that combination of liveliness, intelligence and amiability noted by others.

> I find him of a very lively, active temper, capable of doing his business with little application. He plays with great vigour and courage. I think he is of a very tractable disposition, and I believe will not want any severity.[29]

The private academies of the eighteenth century were boarding schools which had developed from the courtly academies of an earlier age. They offered a broader curriculum and used more practical teaching methods than the traditional public and grammar schools.[30] It has been suggested that around twenty per cent of upper-class children were educated in private schools of one kind or another in the eighteenth century.[31] Proposals for educating the nation's ruling élite appeared in book after book during this period, the bulk of them being drawn up as alternatives to what was generally regarded as the narrow approach to the classics exhibited by the public and grammar schools.[32] The private academies gave practical expression to the idea that education was for action as well as conversation,to prepare for a career of public service as well as to ensure success in cementing social relationships. Hence, a general course of liberal studies, accompanied by a study of more obviously utilitarian subject-matter, was looked upon as a more effective preparation for a man-of-affairs.[33] Hans has described a number of private academies, including the one at Hackney, as "... mainly general secondary schools of literary-scientific education with an opportunity of studying some vocational subjects for those pupils who wished it."[34]

Not surprisingly, the first Earl of Hardwicke, himself a man who had fought his way through the ranks of the legal profession to the exalted position of Lord Chancellor and who had received his education at a private school in Bethnal Green,[35] opted to send his sons to the Hackney Academy in preference to one of the great public schools and, as we have seen, had a place reserved there for Philip Yorke.

The course for those students intended for Oxford or Cambridge, (and presumably this is what Philip Yorke's parents had in mind for their son) continued until they were sixteen or seventeen. The subjects were divided into four groups and, in the absence of documentary evidence and to judge from his later interests, it seems likely that he would have studied subjects from the literary group, namely English, Latin, Greek, French and History, and, in addition, Mathematics and Sciences. It is also likely that his studies included Dancing, Drawing, Music and Physical Training.[36]

In addition to a broad curriculum, the Hackney Academy would appear to have generated a lively atmosphere. According to Edward Burke, it was "the new arsenal in which subversive doctrines and arguments were forged",[37] though Dr. Newcombe himself, who was a Dissenting minister, has been described as "a Whig of the old stamp." His pupils, however, were not drawn exclusively from Whig families and in their later careers did not follow any one party line.[38] The atmosphere of debate would, perhaps, have encouraged the development of an independent spirit. It could also, along with other factors, have helped, perhaps, to kindle a desire for a career in politics. Between 1754 and 1790 twenty-six Members of Parliament, including Philip Yorke, had been educated at Hackney. A number of these attained very exalted positions: Charles Yorke, like his father, became Lord Chancellor, Lord John Cavendish, Chancellor of the Exchequer, and Lord Euston, Prime Minister.[39]

Philip Yorke's seven years at Hackney, completed in February 1759, were followed by just two terms at Eton. The suggestion has been made that what was termed the Secondary phase of his education was curtailed because

> Perhaps the family Exchequer was exhausted; Erthig was always an expensive place to keep up, and the rental at that time being less than £300 a year.[40]

These statements are open to question. Firstly, the Hackney Academy was regarded as a valid alternative to a public school and not as a preliminary to it.[41] As we have seen, many parents preferred to send their sons to a private academy, with its broader curriculum, rather than to a traditional public school. Secondly the marriage settlement of Simon Yorke and Dorothy Hutton had been fairly generous.[42] Thirdly, the estimate of £300 annual rental for the Erthig estate at this time was well below the figures provided by the rent rolls themselves. The accounts for 1759 and 1760 are not available, but those for 1744, 1756 and 1764 showed that the rentals were £1,169[43], £1,178[44], and £1,210[45] respectively. It is hard to believe that money problems were responsible for Philip Yorke's short stay at Eton.

The answer must be sought elsewhere. It would appear that at least one-fifth of the members in each Parliament during the period 1754 to 1790 were educated at either Eton or Westminster.[46] Research based on a sample of two thousand MPs has shown that the numbers attending these two schools had greatly increased in the second half of the eighteenth century, Westminster from 167 to 301, Eton from 162 to 331.[47] After 1760 Eton had become more popular with the nobility and gentry than Westminster, and it had begun to supplant the latter as the primary nursery of MPs and government officials.[48]

In many instances, boys were sent to Eton or Westminster for one, two, or three years only, after receiving their formal education at home or in some other institution. Although, for some unaccountable reason, Philip Yorke's stay at Eton was particularly restricted, there was nothing unusual in attending for a comparatively short spell. The reasons for doing so were more social than educational. Though some might wish to gain further knowledge of classical literature, for those who had been educated within the protected confines of home, a period spent at a public school would provide an opportunity to rub shoulders with other boys and, in the process, gain confidence and improve their social skills. But perhaps the primary motive for spending some time in a public school was, in the words of Eustace Budgell, because,

> We very often contract such friendships at school as are a service to us all the following parts of our lives.[49]

In a society and class in which connection, interest and influence were the *sine qua non* of social and political advancement, the cementing of early friendships of lasting value was all-important. They were certainly significant in the case of Philip Yorke. It was at Eton that he first made the acquaintance, amongst others, of Brownlow Cust, his future brother-in-law, and it was the alliance with the Custs which would open the door to a parliamentary career for him. Clearly, the value of attendance at Eton was not lost on Philip Yorke for he sent three of his sons there, Simon in 1780, Brownlow in 1791 and Piers in 1795. The school's increasing popularity as a training ground for a new generation of MPs was doubtless a contributory factor, particularly in the case of his heir, Simon, who was to succeed his father as MP for Grantham in 1792. Another could have been the fact that three members of the Cust family, Sir John, Francis and Richard, had been to Eton after attending the local grammar school in Grantham.[50] Nor should one discount the appeal of a classical education, however restricted its scope, to one of Philip Yorke's intellectual tastes.

Although he did not send any of his sons for their early education to the Academy at Hackney itself, he did ensure that they went to private classical schools whose approach tended to be more liberal than that of traditional establishments and which were thus reminiscent of the regime in Hackney. Simon Yorke spent two years, 1778 to 1780, at Cheam school,[51] a preparatory establishment renowned for its wide curriculum which yet retained the classics at its core, for its enlightened forms of punishment and its practical activities. All these were intended to provide for the boys what its famous headmaster, William Gilpin, termed "the miniature of the world they were afterwards to enter."[52] Perhaps the decision to send Simon to Cheam might have been influenced by the fact that Charles Yorke (1764-1834), the half-brother of the second Earl of Hardwicke, had also attended Cheam before going on to Harrow.[53] It seems clear that Philip Yorke's own education had not resulted in feelings of disillusionment, but led him to give his sons, at considerable expense,[54] the kind of school experiences which he himself had enjoyed and which he obviously considered educationally and socially beneficial.[55]

After leaving Eton in 1760, Philip Yorke spent the next two years at home, but the records are silent on this interlude. From 14 April 1762 until July 1764 he was a student at Bene't College (later Corpus Christi) in the University of Cambridge, attended considerably earlier by Philip and Charles Yorke, the sons of the first Earl of Hardwicke,[56] and by Sir John Cust, his future father-in-law.[57] Mathematics was an important element in the course at Cambridge, and Philip Yorke's education at the Hackney Academy would no doubt have given him an advantage over those undergraduates who had been educated in one of the traditional public or grammar schools. The two sons of Charles Yorke, for instance, who came from Harrow to Cambridge were very ill-equipped to cope with the mathematics element in the course.[58] As for his own studies, remarks in letters to his father suggest that Philip Yorke did not entertain a very high opinion of them.

> The publick lectures of our College which employ during the term only 3 Hours in the day, are neither extraordinary clever or Entertaining. Cicero's Tusculan Disputations, Saunderson's Algebra, employ the morning hours, 1 hour to each, one Hour of Logick in the Evening, these studies are indeed good enough in themselves but the whole or greater part of the College Attending but with no good Attention, are lightly skimmed over, and no great Improvement is to be attain'd... .[59]

At the same time he claims that "I have been endeavouring (to the Improvement of my Knowledge and Understanding) to wear with my steps the thresholds of the wise...."[60]

In the same letter he suggested to his father that it might be of advantage to engage a private tutor at £20 yearly to give him a lecture each day. Simon Yorke complied with his wishes, but how soon is not clear, since it was not until his letter of December l9th, 1763 that Philip Yorke referred to private one-hour lectures.[61] Among the Erthig papers, however, there is a very neatly-written exercise book containing concise notes by Philip Yorke on such diverse subjects as Greek and Roman history, medieval British history, Mathematics, John Locke on Education, a treatise on *The Art of Thinking*, Shakespeare and Milton.[62] This wide span of subjects indicates either the existence of a broader curriculum at the College than the one outlined in his letter, or that, in certain instances, he was pursuing his own interests. This activity, taken in conjunction with his critical comments on his lecture programme and reading, and his private lectures, would suggest that Philip Yorke should be classed with the small minority of his contemporaries who took their studies seriously.

His letter of December l9th, 1763 also contained comments on John Locke's *Essay concerning the Human Understanding*. These form a confident, highly critical analysis, quite remarkable in a twenty-year-old student. The following extracts give a flavour of his observations.

> When I consider Locke's subject as a subject in itself of a very daring, and new Nature, I also consider the very great merit of the Author for the lights he has

thrown upon it, but being open to Conviction am also conscious of many absurdities...I very much admire his Introduction altho' his Definition of an Idea (at the end of it) is very obscure and I think will be found false.... Mr. Locke by confounding together Ideas and Perceptions, and in some places using them as synonymous terms renders himself absolutely unintelligible.... His Definition of Harmony requires much unfolding.

He attributes alone to Memory what belongs to two other other distinct powers of the mind viz. Imagination and Reminiscens; Imagination revives the Idea, Memory recollects names and Reminiscens convinces us that which we perceive at any particular instant is the same with that which we perceived before.... Abstract Ideas (if there are any) proceed not either from Sensation or Reflection, but are produced by a power of the mind which may be called Abstraction; a power I cannot myself conceive as I can have no idea of a Genus without fixing on a Particular, nor think of Horses in general without annexing my Ideas to a particular Horse.[63]

Philip Yorke's own ideas on what he thought should constitute a typical University day were contained in a programme he submitted on April 6th, 1774 to the second Earl of Hardwicke, at the latter's request, as a guide for his son at Saint John's College, Cambridge.[64] This contrasted sharply in its intellectual demands with both the hours of study described in Philip Yorke's letters, and those that reportedly existed at Cambridge in the 1770s, which consisted of about four or five hours of study a day, and a very large number of hours spent socialising in rooms or coffee-houses.[65] His own proposals were a judicious, and probably idealistic, blend of intellectual and social activities.

Rise at six – Chapel, Walk, Breakfast till eight. Eight to nine, Prepare for lecture, Private tutor, rather, if within your expence/ nine to ten the College lecture. Ten to eleven, Revision of lecture. Eleven to Twelve, Logick or Mathematics, College Lecture. Twelve to three, Correspondence, Dress,

Dinner, coffee-house, or Friend's room, to drink wine. Three to five, Greek History and Translation. Five to Six, visits, Tea drinking. Six to Seven, Locke/or Private Tutor rather. Seven to Eight, Chapel, Hall, Classical part of Examination (College Exercise) extending sometimes beyond eight. Nine to Eleven, Friends' Rooms, or company at home. Eleven to six, Rest (seven Hours). Wash before Chapel, and take with you a small Greek Testament in your Pocket.[66]

Philip Yorke's own University course, like his period at Eton, was short. When he vacated his College rooms in July 1764, he had not completed the statutory ten terms of residence to qualify for a B.A. degree. This would not, however, be unusual. Sir John Cust, for instance, left Bene't College without taking his degree,[67] and so did Thomas Pennant after some years' residence at Oxford.[68] In fact, Oxford and Cambridge, according to one historian, "came to be attended mainly by sauntering young gentlemen filling their time with bagatelles," who paid little attention to their studies, and, for the most part, did not take the trouble to graduate.[69] The standard of the examination for a degree was in any case never very high in the eighteenth century; it has been described as "an informal and inadequate enquiry of undergraduate fitness for a degree."[70]

The reason why Philip Yorke left Cambridge after only seven terms is a matter for speculation. There was clearly then no expectation that every undergraduate would take a degree, and he might have been disillusioned with the course or the examination. On the other hand, it might have been that, as his father, Simon, was in his late sixties, he felt it better for Philip to proceed to the next stage of his preparation for the role of a landowner. He had already been admitted to Lincoln's Inn on November 12th, 1762. When he left the University he began immediately, in the July of 1764, to keep term there and was called to the Bar on July 4th, 1767,[71] shortly before his father's death.

Very few completed the seven or eight year course; a large proportion of the students admitted to Lincoln's Inn were never called to the Bar, and many called to the Bar never proceeded to practise law.[72] Someone like Philip Yorke, who was to inherit an estate on his father's death, had no need to expend his finances and energy in doing so. In company with many other eldest sons of gentry families, he was being trained not to practise law but to undertake the duties of a country gentleman as squire, JP, High Sheriff, militia officer and, possibly, MP. [73] As in the universities, standards in the Inns of Court were lax; "One qualified for the Bar by eating dinners at the Inns of Court".[74] There would be some, however, who would pursue their studies assiduously and profit from them. Unfortunately, no records are available for this phase of Philip Yorke's education but, perhaps, a number of reports on the Wilkes case which he was to write for the second Earl of Hardwicke[75] testify to the fact that he did more to qualify for the Bar than eat dinners at the Inns of Court.

Meanwhile the Yorke family took advantage of the procedure by which those with sufficient influence could be granted a degree without fulfilling the statutory requirements of residence or submitting to some kind of examination, however inadequate.[76] The Crown possessed the right, when petitioned by the Lord Chancellor, to issue letters mandatory for a degree to be conferred on a person not qualified under the statutes to receive it. Close supervision of the procedure ensured that it did not get out of hand, until the Duke of Newcastle became Chancellor of the University of Cambridge in 1748 and relaxed the rules. He was a fanatical believer in patronage and encouraged his supporters to ask for what they wanted.[77]

Once again the Yorke connection was called into play; the Earl of Hardwicke contacted his great friend the Duke,[78] and on June 8th, 1765, he wrote to Philip Yorke,

I mentioned on Saturday last to the Duke of Newcastle your Desire of a Mandamus Degree, his Grace most readily came into it, & I writ by the next Post to the Vice-Chancellor on the subject. I have just received his Answer, wh is, that He will prepare every Thing necessary for the Mandamus, & as soon as he receives the Chancellor's Instructions, will carry Them into Execution. I think my self Happy in this Opportunity (tho' a Trifle) of assuring you that I am

Sir

Your faithful humble servt Hardwick[79]

Philip Yorke received the degree of M.A. per Lit. Reg. by mandate in the summer of 1765.[80] On July 6th, he wrote a letter of thanks to the Duke of Newcastle.

Having had through your Grace's favour the degree of Master of Arts fully conferred upon me at Cambridge on Tuesday last, I cannot but acknowledge in the warmest manner my particular obligations to your Grace thereupon, and nothing but a grateful sense of them could apologize for their liberty.[81]

Can any conclusions be drawn at this stage about the lasting impact of such an education as has been described on someone who was, reportedly, naturally gifted in terms of intellect and temperament?

Philip Yorke's abiding love of history and his antiquarian interests might be said to spring from this formative period.[82] So might the pleasure he derived from the classical languages and literature, expressed in the occasional translation[83] and frequent quotations from Latin authors in letters to his more learned acquaintances, including members of the Hardwicke family. Charles James Apperley, better known as Nimrod, who, although he wrote about Philip Yorke and his contemporaries in 1842, had known him personally in the squire's latter years, claimed that he "... devoted a part of each day to the classics; and I really believe he had every line of his favourite author, Virgil, at his fingers' ends...."[84] Nimrod's assertion would appear to be supported by the remnant of a document in the Erthig papers in which Philip Yorke made several rough drafts of a critical comment on the sixth book of the Aeneid for his friend the Rev. Samuel Strong, the Rector of Marchwiel.[85] He called the Aeneid "this Divine Book" and added

The Sixth Book, on which I troubled you with some former very slight observations, concludes (I confess to me) most unintelligibly; I mean, in the manner of Aeneas's passage and dismission from the Infernal Regions; and no critic has yet cleared my Intelligence in that matter...(Remainder is indecipherable)[86]

It would be hard to believe that someone as intelligent and sensitive as Philip Yorke appears to have been would have remained unaffected by the sentiments and values enshrined in the Classics. Critics of a classical education, for the most part, directed their attacks against the uses to which the classics were being put by the schools and not against their content.

The books at school and college are full of incitements to virtue, and discouragements from vice, drawn from the wisest reasons, the strongest motives, and the most influencing examples.[87]

Educated Augustans admired the rational qualities of moderation, order, common-sense, stability, benevolence and restraint, and adopted as their models the great figures of the classical world in whom they chose to see these qualities best exemplified. They found in these authors, too, a dedication to service to the community and support for a balanced constitution like their own based upon the authority of a ruling elite. As Samuel Strong said of Philip Yorke,

> He loved his country and the constitution of its government, from a conviction of their excellence....[88]

Though the classics remained his main interest and source of inspiration, he was, claimed Samuel Strong, "well versed in most branches of polite literature, which an accurate and retentive memory enabled him to apply with great advantage."[89] In the age of Dr. Johnson the art of good conversation was the supreme social activity and the most widely cultivated; it was synonymous with good-breeding or "the art of pleasing or doing good to one another."[90] It called for the basic qualities of sense, restraint and good nature and, in addition, a large fund of knowledge acquired as a result of a broad, liberal education. In the words of one contemporary writer, a man needed "... a considerable stock of knowledge before he can be polite."[91] Good conversation or good-breeding sprang, therefore, from a combination of personal attributes of character, temperament and intellect, and Philip Yorke apparently scored highly on all three counts. "Mr. Yorke had a cultivated as well as benevolent mind," said Samuel Strong.[92]

Philip Yorke, according to Nimrod and Samuel Strong, was renowned as a conversationalist. Nimrod recalled his conviviality and stimulating talk at social gatherings at Erthig.

> ... but it was as a companion, at all times and on all occasions, that he shone above his fellows. He possessed a greater fund of anecdote than any other man that I have met with in life; in short, it may be said of him what Johnson said of Burke, that he possessed the affluence of conversation; and if a record of his sayings could have been preserved, they would have formed a large volume. It would have been seen by the character of them, that to the vivacity of the companion were added the wit and taste of the scholar, and the temper of a most benevolent man.[93]

Samuel Strong expressed similar sentiments:

> Of a character so respectable and amiable throughout, one of the most distinguishing traits was his talent for conversation. Few equalled him here. Whatever he advanced arose naturally from the occasion, and was expressed in such a happy manner and choice of words, as made him the very life and delight of society.[94]

It seems, in fact, that his conversation was appreciated not only locally but also that he introduced a welcome note of cultural refinement even to the London social scene, since one of his friends wrote to him,

No refined metaphysics are to be heard at Serles',till Phipp's arrival from the North. Nothing but Boroughs, mayors, Quo Warranto's and Elections are to be heard of.[95]

The 34th *Guardian* contained a definition of a gentleman as "a man completely qualified as well for the service and Good, as for the Ornament and Delight, of society."[96] Philip Yorke, it seems, revealed early signs of being able to meet the second requirement; a combination of innate good nature, high intelligence and a liberal education had equipped him for 'conversation'. To what extent he was also qualified for "the Service and Good of Society", in other words, to exercise the functions of a leader in the community, the following chapters will attempt to show.

CHAPTER 2: Marriage and Inheritance

Simon Yorke died on July 28th, 1767. Three days later, his son wrote to Charles Yorke,

> My dear Father's end, was, as his life, even and composed. He departed at nine o'clock on Tuesday night the 28th inst. lying on his Couch in his study, without a Groan. His decay was short and rapid since I came down the 11th, inst; no wishes have remained of his recovery, and I must confess, I enjoy more ease of mind now, than when I saw him daily labouring under an incurable distemper. [1]

Philip Yorke inherited an estate which in 1764 consisted of 1,801 acres, with a gross annual rental value of £1,210.[2] A fairly modest increase in acreage and rental value occurred during the first four years after he became squire of Erthig.[3] There is no evidence that Simon Yorke left his son a great burden of debt, the main encumbrance on the estate being Dorothy Yorke's jointure of £600 a year. Philip Yorke was, therefore, a moderately prosperous squire, who could be placed, along with 3,000 to 4,000 other landowners in England and Wales, in the class of lesser gentry.[4]

Philip Yorke, however, soon exhibited ambitions to be an 'improver', and he embarked on a programme of costly 'improvements' to his mansion and estate. The capital outlay would be considerable, calling for a substantial increase in his financial resources. The principal means of meeting this need in the eighteenth century were marriage and inheritance. It has been asserted that "the acquisition of wealth was becoming the primary object of an increasing number of marriages"[5] by the early part of the century, and that marriages to brides with large portions outnumbered marriages to heiresses. There was no guarantee that the properties of an heiress would become a permanent addition to her husband's family estate. Marriage to a bride with a large portion, however, usually resulted in a permanent accession of land which descended to the eldest son and heir.[6] The object of Philip Yorke's attentions fell into the latter category.

The efforts to conclude a profitable marriage were often prolonged and, in Philip Yorke's case, the negotiations were unduly protracted by the difficulties of ensuring a substantial inheritance from his uncle, James Hutton. Philip Yorke's experiences would seem to be worth relating in some detail because they provide a vivid, well-documented and, at times, amusing example of the tribulations attending the complex business of securing a suitable match and a favourable will.

He had set his heart on marrying Elizabeth Cust, the younger daughter of Sir John Cust, Speaker of the House of Commons, and a substantial Lincolnshire landowner, and sister of his Eton friend Brownlow Cust, of Belton House, near Grantham in the same county.[7] It was not unusual for an aspiring bridegroom to employ the services of an intermediary in this situation and who better in this case than his friend Brownlow? On September 2nd, 1767, Brownlow informed Philip Yorke that "... my father is now in possession of the secret", and described his reaction to the news. Sir John Cust felt that his daughter was too young to marry; he was perturbed by the news that James Hutton was opposed to the marriage of his nephew, but above all he feared that Philip Yorke lacked the financial resources to support his daughter adequately.[8] However, he was prepared to grant his daughter £5,000 on her marriage, and another £5,000 at a later date. The interest of £200 a year from the £5,000, together with his income from the estate would, thought Brownlow, leave Philip Yorke about £400 short of the £1,400 he would need to live on comfortably.

> Despite his reservations, however, Sir John...has such a very high opinion of you, that he wou'd rather marry his daughter to you than to a man with fortunes and honors five times as great; but this is provided his daughter's inclinations lead the same way, for those he will in the first place consult and attend to....[9]

Sir John Cust, by all accounts, was a kindly and considerate family man who, like a number of other landowners, would not allow material considerations to become the overriding factor in the choice of a husband for his daughter.[10]

> ... for solid lasting happiness is what he seeks for my sister, and not grandeur and great riches, such happiness as she may always find with a husband of your disposition, and your connections, the latter of no small consideration with him any more than with me....[11]

Philip Yorke's family connections with the politically and socially powerful Hardwickes appear to have counted in his favour.

Within a few days of this letter, Brownlow was exhorting Philip Yorke not to become despondent; his uncle's objections would soon disappear, his mother would give her approval, and there were no rivals for his sister's hand.[12] On November 6th, Brownlow urged Philip Yorke to pay his father a visit, at the same time warning him not to reveal that the suggestion came from himself. "Don't you in any letters to me say anything about following this advice of mine, for if I shou'd be under a necessity of shewing the letter you wou'd bring me into a scrape; but mention your coming to town as a resolution of your own for any reasons you think proper to give." He told him to bring "the new rental of your estate to lay formally before my father, and to talk over your new plan with him. He will then, I flatter myself, approve of your endeavouring to convince my sister of your attachment to her, and while you are either in Wales or Lincolnshire at Christmas she will be very cleverly disengaged for the free consideration of it...."[13]

There is no evidence that this projected meeting took place, but a few days later Brownlow wrote to say that his father would still like to see an improvement in Philip Yorke's financial position. Meanwhile, however, he did not object to his daughter's being informed of Philip's intentions, provided that, if she consented to marry him, the wedding would not take place until he had increased his savings.

As I know your disposition and your fears, I ventured to engage for you, that you wou'd very contentedly wait if he wou'd but consent to your making your addresses to her now, and by that, get the start of any one else.... [14]

Philip Yorke's situation was further complicated by the fact that his financial prospects were linked to the whims and life-expectancy of his uncle, James Hutton, who had no heir to succeed him. On the death of Philip's grandfather, Matthew Hutton in 1728, the manor of Newnham had fallen into the disreputable hands of his son James.[15]

His wild, reckless youth spent here at Newnham, in all manner of villainy, especially in the ducking of grave and honoured guests of his father in the moat, and his antique and devil-may-care order of life later in the outer world, earned for him the unchristian name of 'The Little profligacy'. The name pleased him, and he lived up to the utmost interpretation of it.[16]

His sister, Dorothy, Philip Yorke's mother, obviously took a poor view of his behaviour. She is supposed to have said in a letter, now unfortunately lost, that "my poor brother is dying slowly of drunkenness and debauchery, and when I remonstrate with him he damns my eyes".[17] Dorothy expressed her concern on many occasions. In a letter to her son dated July 1st, 1768, for instance, she gave him her complete support, and remarked,

I am very much grieved at your Uncle's oddity, proceeding from his dreadful excess in drinking. I do not for his whole fortune, wish you to be much with him lest it should taint your sobriety....[18]

Meanwhile, the tale had taken another turn when Philip Yorke wrote two letters to his prospective father-in-law. In the first written on January 7th, 1768, he begged that Elizabeth should not feel herself under any obligation to finalise her decision.

I ask (and I hope I ask not improperly) for your intervention with your Daughter that she will not hasten her final determination. I am most gratefully obliged to her that she hath considered me at all, and it is my warm request that you will point out to her (should the case require it) that it can be never necessary for her, through the consideration of me, to hurry her last Judgement. I beg this Sir! from you, through the right of the unalterable and most sincere attachment I feel towards your Daughter.[19]

In the second letter, written on February 3rd, he informed Sir John Cust that, as a result of two days spent at Newnham, including an interview with James Hutton, he was much more sanguine about his chances of boosting his finances. His uncle had assured him, he said, that "....my Fortune I have made to descend to you, and you will find that you may do as you best like with this place...."[20]

Philip Yorke I by Thomas Gainsborough .
[Erddig – The National Trust]

Encouraged by this, Philip's efforts to win the hand of Elizabeth continued unabated. In his letters to Brownlow he boasted about his attempts to 'improve' his Erthig demesne. For example, on September 24th, 1768, he informed his friend that,

> I was not out of my saddle or the dirt of overflowed fields, for 3 days but I look over all difficulties; I see nothing insupportable, if it but brings me in the end nearer to one I love dearer than myself ...[21]

His uncle's worsening illness was becoming an increasing source of worry to everyone concerned. Suspicion was rife, most of it falling on servants, James Hutton's illegitimate son, William Smith, and a 'friend' called James Chilton.[22]

Such people could take advantage of James Hutton's enfeebled state to make him change his mind and alter his will. Brownlow counselled,

> Even forging is what necessitous rogues will not stick at. You have often told me that you have fear'd lest your uncle shou'd lose his understanding before his life. What an advantageous situation wou'd that put a necessitous hanger-on in? You must be sure therefore at all events be upon the spot whenever your uncle is thought to be in danger, to watch every body about him as narrowly as a cat watches a mouse....

Brownlow went on to pressurize his friend to guard his interests diligently, for failure to do so would be an injustice to himself, his mother and his family. He added significantly, "I am very well aware that this business to a mind like your's will be very hateful...." [23]

The saga of James Hutton's decline continued to unfold over the ensuing months. On March 24th, 1769, his servant John Jones reported that "....He saw an angel at the feet of the bed which told him he shou'd die by 2 o'clock.... he had Mr. Finch to pray by him and shed some tears, but as soon as he was gone he talked as bad as ever...."[24]

Almost eight months later, however, Brownlow informed Philip Yorke that his uncle had arrived at Grosvenor Gate "...not without his Dulcinea...I am apt to think his strength will be exhausted before his purse...."[25] In the same letter he went on to say that his father was eager to finalise the arrangements for his daughter's marriage. Elizabeth would come of age in February 1770, when the vital decision on her fortune and that of her sister could be made. This might allay James Hutton's doubts. "By this your Uncle may see my Sister's fortune secured to Her upon parchment."[26]

Philip Yorke visited his uncle in January 1770. "... Poor James is now indeed very bad – He has voided, by the calculation of his Physician, ten ounces of blood – They have given him the last medicines – on their good effect, his miserable life now hangs...."[27] As a result of the medicines, or for some other reason, James Hutton survived until the end of July, 1770 [28] almost a month after the marriage of Philip Yorke and Elizabeth Cust in Northaw parish church on July 2nd.[29] Fears about his failure to honour his promises, and about the

Mrs Elizabeth Yorke (née Cust) by Francis Cotes.
[Erddig – The National Trust]

existence of conspiracies to influence him, proved to be groundless. However 'profligate' he had been, he still had his house in Park Lane to leave to his sister Dorothy Yorke, and the manor of Newnham, together with £4,000 Bank Stock, to leave to his nephew who was named as sole executor. The will, dated June 19th, 1770[30] also left all his plate, china, pictures, furniture and household goods to Dorothy Yorke, together with all his long Annuities and Dividends, from which she would have £400 a year interest. All this, together with the house in Park Lane, would revert to Philip Yorke when she died (which was not until 1787).

Thus the year 1770 saw a marked upsurge in the Yorke fortunes, a welcome conclusion to a prolonged and diligent effort. John Cust proved to be as magnanimous as James Hutton. By the marriage settlement, dated June 29th, 1770,[31] Elizabeth Cust's portion was fixed at £10,000, and her jointure, should she survive her husband, at £600 a year, laid as a rent charge on the Erthig estate. The jointure, even by the end of the seventeenth century was usually fixed at 10 per cent of the dowry, since when it had tended to escalate.[32] By this standard, Elizabeth Cust's jointure was quite modest, a reflection perhaps of a feeling that an alliance with the Yorkes of Erthig, with their illustrious connections, might be worth a little financial sacrifice.[33] Philip Yorke's marriage settlement incorporated the main feature of the 'strict' settlement, namely the nomination of a number of trustees to preserve 'contingent remainders'. They were leading members of the Hardwicke and Cust families, representing the interests of the bride and groom: Lord Hardwicke and John Lawry, a first cousin to Philip Yorke, and Sir Brownlow Cust, the bride's brother, together with three of her uncles, Richard, Francis and Peregrine Cust. The trustees' task was "to secure in family settlements a provision for the future children of an intended marriage ..."[34] In practice this meant that they had to ensure the smooth transfer of the property from son to grandson, and prevent the son, through greed or extravagance, from destroying the grandson's interest. Philip Yorke, in reality, was but a life-tenant, charged with the duty of preserving the family inheritance and passing it on to future generations.[35]

The terms of the settlement were very precise on how the succession was to be managed. Briefly, when Philip Yorke died his property was to pass to his eldest son, then to that son's male heirs. If the eldest son had no male offspring, then the estate would be transmitted to Philip Yorke's second or subsequent sons and their male descendants. In the words of the settlement itself, "the Remainder was to the first and other sons of Philip Yorke and Elizabeth Cust, and heirs male of such first and other sons issuing severally and successively."

Detailed financial arrangements were also made for the children of the marriage (other than the eldest) from the bride's provision. In addition to her £10,000 portion Elizabeth Cust was to receive a further £10,000 in two instalments of £5,000 each, and the settlement indicated precisely how this money was to be raised from the Cust lands. It would provide her with an annuity of £100 a year, the remainder of the interest from the capital going to her husband. In the event of his wife's death, Philip Yorke would receive the whole interest. The capital was to be kept in trust for his younger children, and to be paid in equal portions to the sons when they were twenty-one, and to the daughters when they were eighteen or on their wedding day. Very sensibly, the actual amount which each child was to receive was not specified in the settlement, since the extent of the commitment could not possibly have been known.[36]

Strict though the controls imposed by the marriage settlement were, the landowner was usually allowed a limited degree of freedom in the management of his estate. Thus Philip Yorke was given permission to lease property for terms of twenty-one years or three lives, except on the Erthig demesne land.[37] He could also, with the assent of the trustees, sell land and with the proceeds buy new property contiguous to, or intermingled with, his existing estate. For a landowner with ambitions to be an 'improver' these were vital concessions. Pending such purchases, the trustees could invest the money in government securities or parliamentary funds.

Some portions of a landowner's property could be excluded from his marriage settlement, particularly if they did not form a part of the main core of his estate. Thus Philip Yorke's new acquisition of Newnham Manor bequeathed to him by James Hutton, who died after the conclusion of the marriage settlement, gave him the freedom, if he so wished, to use the resources of this estate to relieve the burdens on his 'settled' property at Erthig.[38]

After 1770 then, Philip Yorke had reached a position from which he could accelerate and expand his efforts to 'improve' his Erthig estate. In addition to his wife's 'fortune', he acquired a number of other not inconsiderable sums which, as we shall see, he proceeded to spend liberally in the following years. It seems that Elizabeth abetted him in this; letters of hers before their marriage refer to furniture that she was ordering in London and changes in the use and decoration of rooms in Erthig. At the same time she was aware that these, and the handing over of the house to a new mistress, might cause pain to her future mother-in-law and was anxious to minimise that.[39]

Her portrait, commissioned from Cotes, which still hangs at Erthig, shows her as an attractive and graceful young woman – a view confirmed by Nimrod. He did not himself remember her but he wrote that "she was always spoken of as most elegant and beautiful both in person and in mind...."[40] Her letters also suggest that she enjoyed a full social life, and in one indeed she teased Philip Yorke for being "such an unfashionable creature" because he had sent her "a sad account of Bath."[41]

The impression is confirmed by the fact that during their marriage they spent a great deal of time either in London or on visits to the country houses of their relatives. Indeed, six of their seven children were born in the capital.[42]

A gentleman's wife was expected to play an active role in estate and household affairs,[43] and the letters which Elizabeth wrote soon after her marriage in 1770 deal with many practical matters concerning furnishings for her new home, her husband's attire and the farm and dairy at Erthig. These letters reveal a sound common-sense very similar to that of Philip Yorke. Those to John Caesar, for instance, were full of remarks like the following,

> In the first place I wish my dairy to produce more plentifully The quantity of butter does not sound much for 8 cows. I wish there may be a good reason, but I rather fear some of my cows are going off. I did not hear when the last cow came in what became of the calf. I would have you put down the price of the butter when it is potted in the same manner as when it is sold as it must all be charged to the dairy account....[44]

The Yorkes had to confront grief during these years when their fourth child, Philip, died at the age of two. There is no record of the cause, but his father was always very conscious of dangers to the health of his children, and his account books included two payments to Dr. Haygarth of Chester for innoculating four of them against smallpox which killed and disfigured rich and poor, old and young in their thousands. Philip Yorke, himself perhaps a victim of the disease during his schooldays at Wanstead[45] and ever ready to espouse new advances in this and, as we shall see, other areas, had his children innoculated at a time when the procedure was both expensive and risky.[46] His accounts refer to,

> June 6th, 1774 Innoculating Fee (2 children) £31/10/-
> June 26th, 1779 Fee to Dr. Haygarth Attending my two little boys in Innoculation £16/16/-.[47]

The 1770s were to end tragically for Philip Yorke when Elizabeth, who like so many other young married women of her class had to endure the "pernicious martyrdom" of frequent child-bearing,[48] died giving birth to a daughter who survived her. In his tribute to her, Philip Yorke recounted how,

> On the Sunday fortnight preceding her death, she was brought to bed of a Daughter, between one and two months before her expected time, and the Fever which followed upon delivery (in itself very dangerous and critical) left us in a few days little hopes of her recovery... [49]

His account book recorded the cost of trying to save her life.

> January 17th, 1779 To Mr. Orret, man midwife, my dear wife's last illness 1 Jry (Journey) £5/5/January 31st, Dr. Haygarth's fees Ditto Jrys £26/5/-; Ditto Mr. Lloyd Surgeon £21/-/- . [50]

He wrote movingly of her many sterling qualities:

> There was a wonderful sweetness in her manners, in her Countenance and Disposition which engaged, and that, very soon, all persons of all ranks; and if any Comfort can be derived to my deplorable condition, and that, from the very sources of Grief itself, she will be extensively as really lamented. With great chearfulness of Temper, the effect of genuine Innocence, she had a steady and unremitting attention to every humane Duty, was sincere and exact in her

devotions, most diligent in the superintendance and instruction of her Children, and active and accurate in everything which related to her Family business. [51]

The shock of her death did not in any way deflect Philip Yorke's attention from the practical details of the funeral arrangements. His "orders for John Caesar, concerning the Funeral of Mrs. Yorke" were precise and detailed, stressing that everything should "...be conducted in the most decent but private and affecting manner possible". The tone of his opening remarks to his steward was not unlike that which he adopted on more normal occasions.

> Mr. Yorke understood from good Authority, that John Jones the Plumber did not deal fairly concerning the 'Leaden Coffin' that he made for the late Miss. Yorke. [52] This action was passed over by Mr. Yorke as it was too delicate an affair to stir in; but it is not forgotten; and it becomes of more necessity for Caesar to look very sharply into all such things, as his Master cannot in this melancholy case help himself at the time or complain afterwards. Mr. Yorke depends on Caesar's Assurance and Fidelity; of which he has never had any reason to distrust; and hopes it will be exerted in his Master's present very afflicted and distressed situation.[53]

The death of Elizabeth left Philip Yorke with six young children, the eldest of whom was only eight, to care for. Always vigilant in matters of health, his own and other people's,[54] he kept a watchful eye on the children's welfare. On March 9th, 1779, for instance, he wrote to John Caesar,

> I beg that you will say to Betty Thomas that I would have no strangers admitted into the Nursery, so much do we dread the small pox and other infectious diseases. She will particularly remember and I know she will exact in our wishes what Mrs Reynardson said in regard to the matter if any Ladies of the Neighbourhood come they certainly cannot be refused seeing the children, and we must trust to their discretion not to bring improper children with them; during the Fair the Garden is the best exercising place for the children and during any time of great Resort to the woods and walks without.[55]

When his children went for three weeks to Parkgate on the Wirral in the late summer of 1781, he gave very strict instructions to his steward about arrangements for their stay. He was particularly worried about his youngest child, the two year old Dorothy:

> ... if the small pox is not in the place, of which you will on your previous visit enquire, I think the seabreeze and change of air will be of great service to her...

In the same letter, he directed that Betty Thomas, who was in charge of the children, should "take my son John to Dr. Haygarth and take his opinion about his eyes" as they passed through Chester on the way to Parkgate.[56] Philip Yorke was obviously very worried about his son, since he wrote to John Caesar on September 28th, 1781,

> I hear with much concern that my son John's Eyes are not in the state of Improvement that we had reason to hope and expect: You do not tell me whether

Dr. Haygarth saw him at Chester, on his return, or during his stay at Parkgate; you will send the Enclosed pr.post to the Doctor; in which I desire that if he has not already seen the Child, he will take an opportunity of doing so soon, and use an Issue, or some strenuous Medicine with him, as the disease is obstinate. You need not Fee the Dr. should he come over to Erthig, as I will do it on my return.[57]

The Doctor responded to Philip Yorke's request, since later in the same year the latter's accounts referred to "December 26th, 1781 Dr. Haygarth, 2 visits John's Eyes £6/6/- ".[58]

The children were not spared the discomforts of travel to and from family residences, schools and seaside places even at a very early age. The transport of the three year old Dorothy from Erthig to Grantham in June 1782 is a good example of the meticulous care which Philip Yorke took over the welfare of his children on such journeys.

> As soon as Mr. Crew has determined the time of my Daughter Dorothy's setting out for Grantham, you must consider the most proper means of getting her there; the one-horse chair must take her and the elder Betty Thomas, and they must be attended by Green; could not Rocket draw the Chair to Grantham, by the way of Derby, and Nottingham, in four days; (I think the whole distance being about 116 miles), and might not (under such easy Journeys, or they might be made still easier if necessary), Green ride by the side of Rocket with a Rein, on Simon's horse; Green must leave the Chair and Harness at Grantham, which I long since gave to Mrs. Cust with the Horses and return to Erthig, leaving Betty the child and Chaise.[59]

After his wife died, Philip Yorke's sister-in-law, Anne, who was married to Jacob Reynardson of Holywell in Lincolnshire, took charge of his daughters. His accounts record payments to her, presumably for their clothing and keep, over the period 1779-1794, which amounted to a total of £776. The continuation of the payments long after he had re-married in 1782 suggests that Mrs. Reynardson was still responsible, in part at least, for the children's welfare. From March 1780 onwards the two elder girls, aged seven and nine years, attended what appears to have been an academy in London run by a Mrs. Moore.[60] Unfortunately, no details about it are available, and therefore it is impossible to know whether it was one of the more enlightened institutions of its kind which taught its pupils something more than the usual polite accomplishments. To judge from Philip Yorke's expenditure which, of course, need not necessarily be an accurate guide to the school's academic standards, he would appear to have treated his daughters no less generously and responsibly than his sons in the matter of their education. Between 1780 and 1789 he paid Mrs. Moore a total of £904. [61] As a result of their "London education", according to Nimrod, the Yorke girls were looked up to as examples of polite behaviour to which other young ladies in the neighbourhood of Erthig sought to aspire. Philip Yorke spared no expense to give his sons a good education. Before they went away to school, both John and Brownlow were taught at home by Mr. Morris the Curate of Wrexham, who gave his first lessons on May 27th, 1782. He was paid 50 guineas a year for eight hours' teaching a week, spaced out over four afternoons.[63] Simon, who by that time was in school at Cheam, had a great deal of money spent on his school and university education, around £1,300 in fact, as befitted the heir to Erthig. The combined cost of the education of Brownlow and Piers, who both went to Ruthin school and then to Eton, came to around £700.[64]

A number of letters written by Simon to his father and step-mother when he was thirteen cover a variety of subjects, ranging from requests for money and certain items of clothing, to promotion at school, the dangers of coach travel, the parliamentary election at Grantham and various developments at Erthig. The friendly, mature tone of his letters to his father indicates the kind of relationship which existed between them. On May 10th, 1784, for example, he wrote,

> I have been very regularly to Fencing, since I came from Belton, where I had a very pleasant Holiday with my Uncle and Aunt Brownlow. Pray give my Duty to my Mama and tell her I will promise to write to her soon.... Give my love to my Brothers and Sisters and all my Friends. And shall be very glad to meet my sisters in the country. I greatly approve of planting the gravel Pit, as also the Twenty Tribes in the old Billiard-Room.[65]

On November 23rd, he wrote to tell Philip Yorke that school was breaking up for the holidays on December 8th, and that they could return to Erthig on the 13th. At the same time he worried that "I am afraid we cannot avoid the dark nights which are very dangerous over these heaths, as I am afraid there will be no moon about that time."[66] The same kind of relaxed approach was also apparent in his letter earlier in November to his step-mother, in which he complained about lack of money and somewhat cannily asks her to intercede with his father about a new pair of boots.

> I should be glad of some money as it is all gone and I had rather have some than to run into debt for that takes more of it away after the holydays (sic).... Tell my Papa that my boots are gone so little that I shall want another pair at the Holydays and will take care to have them to fit me and not have them as my others were last year.[67]

The apparently close relationship existing between Simon and his father was to mature in later years,when it would seem that Philip Yorke was able to enlist his heir's co-operation not only in running his estate[68] but also in his genealogical research.[69]

Philip Yorke was to face further grief in later life for, apart from his eldest son, Simon, all the children of his first marriage were to die young. Philip died at the age of two, as we have seen, John at the age of sixteen, when he was at Rugby school, Ethelred and Elizabeth at twenty-four and twenty-one respectively, and Brownlow at twenty-six, although he had lived long enough to become rector of Downham on the Isle of Ely. There is no record in the Erthig papers of the date of Dorothy's death, though another source states that she died of smallpox.[70] None of Philip Yorke's daughters married (which, incidentally, saved him the expense of dowries).

In 1782 he was to marry as his second wife Diana Meyrick, a widow from Dyffryn Aled near Llansannan.[71] He was to have six more children by her, the second of his "two hatches",[72] as he called them with characteristic wry humour. This time he was more fortunate, as five of them survived to mature years. Throughout both marriages he appears to have attended as conscientiously to his family duties as he did to his obligations as landowner, MP, JP, and as a Captain of Militia.

CHAPTER 3: Landlord and Steward

There was widespread concern in the eighteenth century about the haphazard and inadequate provision for preparing young gentlemen to deal with the practicalities of estate management. John Sheridan, in a discussion with James Boswell, said,

> There is one rank for which there is no plan of education, and that is country gentlemen. Surely, this is of great importance, that the landed interest should be well instructed.[1]

Earlier in the century, Daniel Defoe had condemned the ignorance of many of the gentry and aristocracy and, referring more specifically to their role as landowners, had berated them for believing "... that it is below them also to audit their own accounts, let their own lands, manage their own revenues, or, in short, to look after their estates."[2] Nimrod's portrait of Philip Yorke as an unworldly scholar whose friends doubted whether "...he ever troubled himself to enquire even how his income was disbursed,"[3] would suggest a landowner of the type Defoe deplored.

Nothing could be further from the truth. While his formal education might not have had much relevance to his role as country squire, his family background and close acquaintanceship with other members of the same class would have given him some indication of the problems he was likely to face. He had two estates to manage, Erthig and Newnham, many miles apart, and his difficulties were exacerbated by his frequent absences in London (usually from January/February until April/May), in one of the Cust or Hardwicke homes at Belton, Wrest, Wimpole or Sunninghill, or, from 1778 to 1782, in various army camps located around the country.[4] This did not mean, however, that he was one of those Welsh squires "... interested only in their rents and the exercise of their sporting rights."[5] As we shall see, his estates, particularly Erthig, were never far from his thoughts and, like other prudent members of his class, he kept careful accounts and memoranda of his personal and estate activities.[6] As all other landowners did who were away a great deal, Philip Yorke had to rely on others, particularly his steward as the man on the spot, to deal with the multifarious tasks involved in organising his estate. The steward's role became especially important in the later years of the eighteenth century as the rate and scale of agrarian change increased. He was responsible for maintaining the estate as a viable financial and economic unit. His main duties, therefore, were to collect the tenants' rents, enforce the covenants in leases, ensure that farm

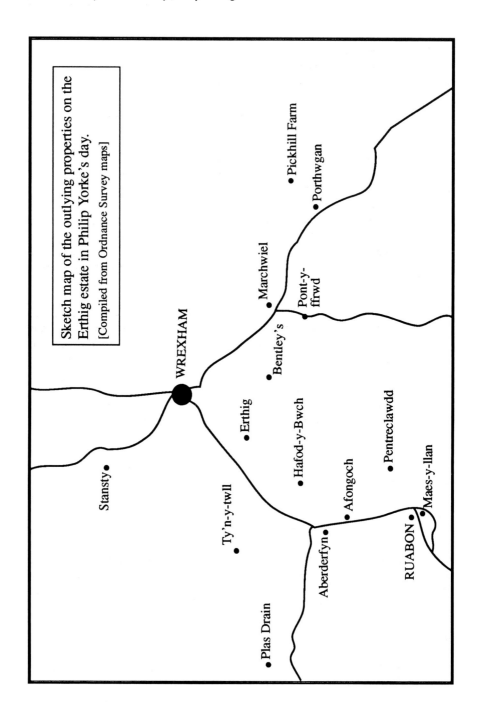

Sketch map of the outlying properties on the Erthig estate in Philip Yorke's day.
[Compiled from Ordnance Survey maps]

buildings were kept in good repair, supervise the labour force and control all items of expenditure.

The library at Erthig contains today, as it did in Philip Yorke's time, a book bearing the title *The Duty and Office of a Land Steward ... to which is added an Appendix shewing the Way to Plenty proposed to the farmers*, by John Laurence.[7] This was just one of a number of manuals on the functions of the estate steward or agent written during the eighteenth century, showing the importance attached to the office and to estate management generally. John Laurence stated that he had written his book because of "The misfortunes and losses that have befallen several of the Nobility and Gentry throughout the Kingdom, on account of the Ignorance and Knavery of bad Stewards".[8]

Many stewards had a reputation for rapaciousness and dishonesty, and a lack of sympathy with the difficulties experienced by the tenants and labourers on their masters'estates.[9] They enjoyed considerable power, as John Laurence wrote, "...What a Trust a Steward has repos'd in him; and how much it is in his power to Improve, or make worse, his lord's Estate." All the more reason, therefore, why the landowner should choose a man of "Honesty and Understanding" as his steward.[10]

Philip Yorke's steward, during his first few years as squire of Erthig, was inherited from his father. In Simon Yorke's time the position had been in the hands of John Caesar. Philip Yorke employed the services of both John and, for a much longer period, his son (also called John but known to Dorothy Yorke as Jacky).[11] This succession, son following father, was not unusual and helped to ensure continuity of administration.[12]

Stewards came from a variety of backgrounds. In Glamorgan, for instance, some were the younger sons of minor gentry or small freeholders, while others had had a legal training and pursued careers as attorneys.[13] John Laurence warned landowners against employing attorneys as stewards because they had too many irons in the fire and could not be relied upon to give their wholehearted and honest attention to their employers' interests.[14] The Caesars, however, appear to have been merely tenants on the Erthig estate. There is nothing in the Erthig papers to explain why or when the family arrived in the Wrexham area or to indicate the social and educational background of the two stewards. They were sufficiently literate, however, to produce accounts and write regular reports to their employer. The fact that Philip Yorke utilised the services of John Vernon, a gentleman from Oswestry, and Thomas Hayman, a Wrexham solicitor, when matters such as negotiating property deals, assessing the value of timber, or drawing up leases required attention, suggests that the Caesars were not qualified to handle certain specialised tasks. On one occasion, after instructing the young and inexperienced Jacky Caesar to consult John Vernon on various matters, Philip Yorke added,

"I know you are not above profiting from men of Experience when an opportunity offers of advising with them. I therefore Entertain great hopes that you will be in time an able man."[15] Apart from any other deficiencies, Jacky

Caesar's youth, as well as his inexperience,[16] also made the squire reluctant to entrust him with the sole responsibility for dealing with major issues. In any case, Philip Yorke, as we shall see, kept a close watch on the performance of whomsoever held the office.

John Caesar and his wife Margaret are shown in the 1756 rental as being the tenants of a farm called Pentremelin, to which had been added some more land, increasing the size of the holding to seventy acres, at a rent of £31 a year.[17] This was a fair-sized farm by Erthig standards. On January 14th, 1769, John Caesar complained to Philip Yorke that he had broken a promise to allow him to have Bryngolau in exchange for Pentremelin. He had, he said, "... procured Cattle and Horses sufficient to stock that land, and if you will let that land from me you will be the ruin of me and my family, as I must sell my Cattle to my great disadvantage."[18] Philip Yorke's reply is not available, but a further letter from John Caesar suggests that the former was not pleased.[19] John Caesar, however, had his way and in the 1769 rental he appeared as the tenant of Bryngolau, a farm of 54 acres at a rent of £21 a year.[20] It is not clear why he wanted a smaller holding. It is true that his health was poor at the time,[21] but thereafter the holding increased, presumably worked by the family. The reference to buying animals specifically for Bryngolau might suggest that the land was more suitable for pasture and could support more stock than Pentremelin. The average rent per acre was also slightly higher and was to rise considerably as the size of Caesar's holding increased, which, since there was no sharp rise in rents at Erthig generally over this period, appears to indicate increasing prosperity for the Caesars. In 1771 John Caesar acquired more land, augmenting his farm to 88 acres at a rent of £62/2/- a year. Thereafter the acreage tended to fluctuate, until in 1780 it reached a peak of 98 acres at a rent of £72 a year. After John Caesar's death in 1783, his widow Margaret continued as the tenant until her own death in 1788, and the farm was eventually relet to Thomas Caesar.[22] The improvement in John Caesar's fortunes, involving as it did an increasing workload on his own farm, would not have pleased John Laurence who viewed such activity as a distraction, preventing stewards from giving their wholehearted attention to their masters' affairs.[23] Some stewards did indeed do very well for themselves.[24]

From 1767 to 1770, while Philip Yorke was away from Erthig for long periods in London or Grantham pursuing his courtship of Elizabeth Cust, his mother, Dorothy, acted as his deputy. He was kept informed about affairs on his estate by a stream of letters from several close friends, but particularly from his mother and John Caesar.

In the three years before his marriage in 1770, Philip Yorke's main efforts, as we shall see, were concentrated on rebuilding the unprofitable King's Mill and draining the low-lying French Mill meadows. Dorothy Yorke's letters kept her son abreast of work in progress in those and other areas. On May 6th, 1768, for example, she reported,

"I am just come off duty from a ride from the King's mill. Eleven hands at

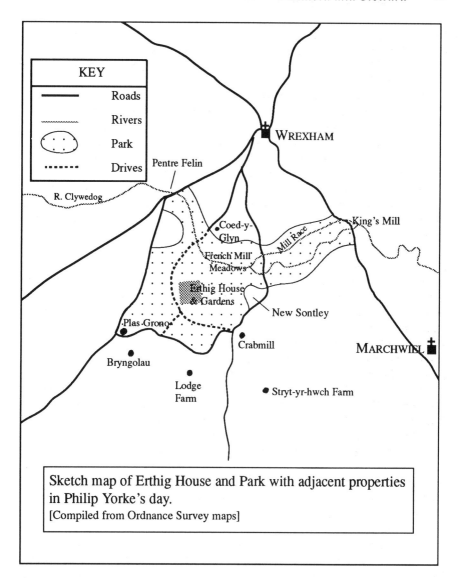

Sketch map of Erthig House and Park with adjacent properties in Philip Yorke's day.
[Compiled from Ordnance Survey maps]

work, 4 of them bricklayers..."[25] On July 20th, 1769 she wrote,

> John Caesar tells me all the slates of your mill was brought last Friday 23 carters dined in your Servants hall near 50 men with Carters and I endeavoured to please them with plum pudden and beef sufficient, with your strong beer and ale, most went away in decent time to those who stay'd till ten ...[26]

The difficulties of deputising for her absent son at Erthig were exacerbated by John Caesar's failing health. In May, 1769, she was reporting that he

"... keeps to his bed till 4 in the afternoon, for the last ten days has not taken an ounce of solid food, trembling and quite forgetful of any subject he hears so an hour before. The tenants & other people are continually calling on him about business & he do's not know a word as soon as they turn their back what they have been saying to him."[27] A month later he seemed "better in health, little in memory,"[28] and some time later she concluded that "Caesar is but a silly old man I think and not to be always minded."[29]

Because of his father's incapacity, Jacky took over his duties. Dorothy Yorke had mixed feelings about his performance; on the one hand she wrote "he is a very careful Lad and for one so very young transacts very well ...", but on the other, felt that he lacked the authority to direct the workers, and advised her son not to "... give the boy any salary whilst he is his father's deputy."[30] Later in the summer while John Caesar was taking the waters at Flint,[31] Dorothy wrote:

"... I have now all my discourses with the lad who for his age and experience is very cleaver and diligent ..." [32] By September she thought that John Caesar's health had improved but that he "chuses his son should officiate at Erthig for him and I believe it is as well."[33]

Philip Yorke evidently did not heed his mother's advice, for an entry in an account book for December 23rd, 1770 recorded that he paid John Caesar £47/10/- for the previous year and seven months and Jacky £5.[34] Neither does he appear to have followed John Laurence's advice to landowners "... to allow their stewards a handsome Salary, that they may be able, without new-invented Perquisites, to live with Reputation and Credit."[35] Bearing in mind that John Caesar's substantial holding might have been a source of some profit to him, his salary of £30 a year was still very modest when compared with those of between £40 and £100 paid to stewards in other parts of Wales.[36] As late as 1780 Jacky Caesar, who by then had succeeded his father as steward, was still being paid only £30 a year.[37]

The surviving correspondence between squire and steward up to 1787 reveals a partnership forged to deal with the multitude of problems of administering an estate, problems which were exacerbated by Philip Yorke's absences, particularly in the 1770s, and the number of changes he had simultaneously set in motion in his early period as squire of Erthig. The sheer volume of letters addressed over the years to his steward from locations as varied as London, Bath or an army camp in Cockermouth, attest to his constant concern for his estate.

His attitude to the Caesars on a personal level was that of the patrician but benevolent landlord; on a professional level he demanded a high degree of efficiency and integrity, and he was prepared to bully, cajole or flatter to achieve his objective. His letters reveal a perpetual, nervous anxiety about his affairs at Erthig. It cannot have been easy for the young Jacky Caesar to take over his father's role without due experience and to assert his authority over the tenants and labourers. He must surely, on occasion, have resented his master's badgering and criticism, and considered that being a steward was a thankless

Mrs Diana Yorke (née Wynn), by Joseph Allen.
[Erddig – The National Trust]

task. Equally, however, Philip Yorke must have been exasperated when his fledgling steward did not pay sufficient attention to his instructions or answer the questions with which he peppered his letters.

On November 1st, 1770, Philip Yorke wrote to him,

> My time is so much employed, that I am necessarily obliged to press my Ideas and orders into a little Room. Be you carefully attentive and obedient to them...You are apt to neglect what I say to you, and I think it is, because you omit to put in writing the things I say to you cursorily, and *when I am walking*. You have omitted in the Rentall you sent me up, to add the outgoings of the Erthig Estate, and the taxes which remain on me. Send a Paper of them as soon as may be – You may have from Jenny of the Mill your mother's sister, the knowledge of what taxes were paid by me, and your duty to me, and advantage to yourself is equally concerned, that I am not made a Dupe to Parish-officers and Tax-Gatherers...Be in all things most diligent, and supply as becomes a Faithful Steward, in carefulness, and a proper spirit of directing, my Absence – In that case, you will have me always yr Friend and Wellwisher.[38]

On another occasion he complained,

> You do not read my letters accurately. In them you will find some questions you never answered; one Relating to the number of Hours the workmen continued in the day in this letter – Answr for the future my letters, article by article.[39]

Philip Yorke kept an eagle eye on the accounts which his steward had to submit on a regular basis. His account book contained an entry for May 23rd., 1771, headed "Revised Caesar's Account from the 1st.of January 1770; Went over the Vouchers with Birch," followed by "Notes taken, for Observations to Caesar, thereupon ..."[40] These notes reveal a meticulous attention to detail, as the following example will show.

> Thos. Crew's bill no. 29; 0..1s..6d pr. day, chargd for a man's day's work; why so much – what 12 shill poor levy, Rec.d by Crew, means...Taxes must be kept in a book distinct. To revert to Bennion's Bill no. 33 p. 19. I never gave an absolute order to pay for the muck which Edwd Davies had from Rd Thomas. I hope Caesar understood Huxley's great Bill £50.18.11 no. 41, p. 20 – at my liesure, to refer to, and Revise this Bill – why pay 6 shill Tythe for Gresford, all I should have thought accd for in £12. 0. 0, pd yearly to Mr. Newcome...Caesar must examine the labourer's Bill very carefully. no. 77 p. 25. He will find one Pound mistake to my loss...The Bills misplaced must be set right, when Caesar goes again over them...

He had also impressed upon Jacky Caesar how dependent he was upon him.

> In my own necessary Absence, I must depend on your Sagacity and close observation, and if any duplicity of Conduct is attempted, I am certain you will think it right and highly proper to communicate it to me; But all this between ourselves. I only tell you my Fears; and you will inform me, whether or not, they be justly formed. For Evils must not grow upon us; if they do, they will bring mischief in the End ...[41]

His final sentence was to prove prophetic.

Philip Yorke was prepared, however, to praise as well as to censure. "I have no reason to doubt either of your ability or Industry; but I have ever to have new and constant examples of it ...", he wrote on November 1st, 1770.[42] In the following year, he expressed similar sentiments and added some 'fatherly' advice: "You will in my absence continue to exert your best care, and Industry in my affairs. I am well pleased with your going on, and have no doubt to find you from diligence, daily improving in every necessary Knowledge. This is the very time of your life, which will best serve you, if you give Encouragement to your Understanding, and I am happy to find you not throwing the opportunity away."[43] Again, some years later, Philip Yorke declared himself "...well satisfied with the Progress you are making in my several orders; and the Exactness with which you observe them is very agreeable to me, which I would have always minutely attended to, except, where, thro' my absence from the spot, they may be incompatible with the design ..."[44]

A respect which had grown over the years for Jacky Caesar's abilities probably accounted for the apparent relaxation of the vigilance exercised in the early 1770s over the steward's accounts.[45] It would be true to say, in fact, that as Jacky Caesar became more mature and competent, Philip Yorke's letters grew less critical in tone. On occasion, he adopted a conspiratorial air, as when he wanted his steward to consult John Vernon about an offer he intended to make to Mrs. More for the purchase of Little Erthig.[46]

This matter must be conducted with great privacy, and whatever enquiries you will find it necessary to make, I think, should rise at some distance. John Hughes might smell out, and apprize Mrs. More of my Scheme, or at least that something was intended; & I would not have her have the least suspicion of my design previous to my offer... [47]

Philip Yorke was always suspicious of his workmen and there are several disparaging references to them in his letters. On April 19th, 1770, he wrote: "I am ever jealous of my workmen. I must insist on your asserting that authority which is necessary to restrain any licentiousness in them, and to make them do their duty towards me."[48] Two years later he delivered one of his frequent homilies: "I have no doubt you will always make up to compensate the absence of the Principal, by the diligence and Authority of the Agent; for mankind are ever to be corrected rather by a distant, and resolute behaviour, than by Intimacy, and too much mildness, and easy nature."[49] Having regard, it might be thought, for Jacky Caesar's comparative youth and inexperience, and the doubts expressed earlier by his mother about the steward's exercise of authority, Philip Yorke continued to impress upon him the need for firmness. He explained what he meant by "resolute behaviour".

I trust you will keep a strict watch upon the labourers, especially the Expensive ones, that they answer the whip, and do their duty to me, and to themselves.[50]

I must have people answer the whip, and I cannot spend my money to no end and purpose.[51]

Perhaps Philip Yorke's most infuriating pronouncement was the following in his letter of May 2nd, 1775:

> The Sentence following (which is the first matter I have occasion to take notice of, in your last letter). That *my Presence* will make things more regular – and satisfactory to us – has so ambiguous a turn, that when I endeavour to entangle it, it should seem to intimate, that in my absence there are certain improprieties or irregularities at Erthig, which you do not hold yourself competent to judge of, and correct, and therefore they must be suffered to increase till that time I shall be on the spot, to correct them myself. If it be so, to what distraction must my affairs run in those absences which may now become increasingly long. If this was your reasoning, supposing you applied a precise and direct meaning to the words above, I must beseech you to understand, that it is in the moment of my absence, that you are of the greatest consequence to me, and you can only be so, by feeling the same power to correct abuses as myself; and I must insist always having to exert it.[52]

The need for economy was stressed again and again. In January 1776, for instance, he objected strongly to paying wages to the workmen employed in levelling the French mill meadows during the frosty weather:

> If they cannot do me justice during this frost, I beg Carmody may stand still till the weather opens, for I really am not able to keep the Idle poor, whether they become so thr' Inclination, or Accident. I satisfie myself that you will overrule Carmody or Worrall if you see things linger or money surrendered, and in this I trust, you will see with my eyes, and feel as I would myself in the same Circumstances.[53]

On occasion, Philip Yorke declared his intention to evoke the ultimate sanction. Hearing, for instance, that his Pickhill tenants were very slow in carrying out repairs to the bank of the river flowing through their land, he warned them that "I will certainly reenter as I have the Powr to do thru' a defect in the lease."[54] However, in those areas where written verification is possible, there is no evidence that the high-handed tone of the foregoing pronouncements was ever matched by the appropriate action. The rent rolls show, for instance, that threats to evict tenants, like those at Pickhill, were never carried out.[55] Philip Yorke, it would seem, was a landlord whose bark was considerably worse than his bite. Far from being an ogre, he was considered to be, above all, a benevolent man. Nimrod wrote, "Then his extreme good-nature was apparent in every thing, and in nothing more than his treatment of his domestic servants, where, it may be said, the master was lost in the kindness of the man."[56] Samuel Strong referred to his "most benevolent disposition. His hospitality, friendliness, and charity made the ample fortune he inherited a common benefit ..."[57]

There is evidence also in Philip Yorke's letters to his steward to reinforce these sentiments. On January 4th, 1772, he wrote,

I am very willing and always desirous that my (constant) workmen should derive from me, every comfort, and reasonable advantage, and I am happy to fallow for every year (whilst it is to be found) a Part of my Feilds, for the Planting of Potatoes to supply them in the Winter, but I must insist, that when such Peice of Ground is checked out, they be strictly cautioned to abstain from cutting or Pruning such young trees, as may grow there on, and this Restriction is the more necessary (and may be a General one), as the land appointed for Potatoes, is ever such as requires Cleaning (with trees and Bushes).[58]

In the same month he referred to his previous visit to Erthig, when the Dairy maid had impressed him:

I would not have her without her Reward, and you will give her half a Crown as a mark of my Approbation – When the Tenants Teams are carrying the Stone, the Servants who drive the Teams, should I think, be treated with some bread and cheese, and small Beer; let them have such Refreshment with due economy & moderation; and you will take out what Cheese is necessary for that purpose, and acquaint me what is used therein.

He made it clear that this magnanimity tempered by economy would eventually be followed by "a more generous treat."[59]

There were instances also of kindness to individuals. He was worried about the health of Daniel the Lodgeman, whom he was willing to spare for a week to take the waters at Flint;[60] and he was concerned about the death of "poor Davies. I had a value for that man, and I believe he deserv'd it."[61]

The Caesars, too, elicited his sympathy. On June 22nd, 1775, he wrote to Jacky Caesar:

I hear with concern of the hurt you have Received on your Collar Bone; am glad however to find that it is not broken, and in these busy times you are able moderately to move about. I am afraid you are rather impetuous in your motions, and at this season of the year and at your season of life, you must carefully avoid by violent and hearty exercise, putting your blood into a ferment ...[62]

In another letter to Jacky Caesar he wrote, "I am much concerned to hear that your Father suffers so much from that inveterate distemper, the Rheumatism..." [63] He had recently expressed his concern through a generous act:

As fruit is a wholesome and cooling thing, I would wish your Father to have some, and yr wife when they like it, and Miss Betty Ratcliffe and her mother at Borras.[64]

Another glimpse of Philip Yorke's consideration for those who served him was revealed in the arrangements made in 1777 for Jacky Caesar's visit to London. The purpose of the visit was to discuss certain documents. In his letter of April 18th, 1777, Philip Yorke set out the arrangements for the management of Erthig during his steward's absence, and then concluded,

I suppose you will come up by the Fly; we will take care of you whilst you are here, and I think you may get a week to see the London wonders, of which perhaps, you may be tired much sooner.[65]

In view of the thoughtfulness he had shown to Jacky Caesar, Philip Yorke came to feel betrayed by the whole family. He was to have cause to regret his parsimony over the steward's salary, because in 1787 he discovered that Jacky had defrauded him of £632/4/10. As he wrote to John Jones, Jacky Caesar's successor as steward, "The impropriety and Injustice of the whole family concerned in not making this known to me before need not be commented on."[66] It is somewhat surprising, therefore, to find the squire accepting a share of the blame. In his letter of January 5th, 1787, dismissing Jacky Caesar, he wrote, "Perhaps on the whole your salary was not too much, but the manner of raising it, had a very bad aspect."[67] He also accepted responsibility for failing to exercise a sufficiently close surveillance over Jacky Caesar's accounts in recent years. He wrote to John Jones, "The last Cash Book tells a sad tale, and I take much shame to myself for suffering Caesar to keep his totals these last year's so long out of sight under pretence that the details of the Workmen (which appeared alway's as one large annual sum in the acct.) were not fairly written and ready."[68] These sentiments, uttered in such trying circumstances, say a good deal about Philip Yorke's tolerance and magnanimity. However, shocked and hurt though he undoubtedly was by his steward's disloyalty, he was too much of a pragmatist to allow his feelings to deflect him from the main business of running his estate. His detailed instructions to John Jones reflect this hard-headed side of his nature.

In the Box that Mrs. Salisbury will drop with the Key at Your House, you will find my two duplicates of the Erthig Acct. Books, also all the Vouchers filed in year's, since 1767 the time of my Father's death, to the present; You will also find there all the Rentall's from the same, to the present time. These and the Books will give you at the first Blush, the State of the Arrears, and I must desire you to write peremptorily to such Tenants as are in that situation …So soon as you can get over to Erthig, you will please to give the enclosed Paper to Caesar, and he will make over his Room and business to you, and I hope according to my orders will make you acquainted with all unfinished accounts, so that they may now be brought to a final adjustment.

Lastly, he instructed John Jones to make an inventory of his stock on the farm and grain in the granary. [69]

Philip Yorke did not believe Jacky Caesar's excuse that he was not aware of any wrongdoing on his part, and his disappointment was all the greater because he had come to entertain a high opinion of his steward's abilities. "…but all this is not like a Man of business, which he was in a very good degree…" [70]

One other facet of Philip Yorke's character was revealed by the Jacky Caesar crisis, if we are to believe Nimrod. Much as he abhorred his steward's dishonest conduct, he still found a vein of humour in the situation. According to Nimrod, Jacky Caesar absconded to America with £800. When told of this, Philip Yorke was said to have observed that his steward was determined to be *aut Caesar aut nullus* (Caesar or nothing)."[71] There is no further evidence to corroborate Nimrod's story, and his figure does not tally with Philip Yorke's, but, as we shall see, this flash of humour was not untypical.

CHAPTER 4: Lease Agreements

Philip Yorke's interest in land utilisation extended beyond his own boundaries to Wales as a whole, and he joined his voice to the chorus of those who were striving, by word and deed, to promote the exploitation of its natural resources.[1] The appendix to his *Tracts of Powys*, published in 1795, included an article written, he stated, some years earlier, on the subject of the Crown lands in Wales. These were destined to be the subject of bitter conflict between Welsh landowners and the Crown in the nineteenth century.[2] Philip Yorke, along with others,[3] urged the sale of the lands so that they could be utilised to greater advantage. He felt that in North Wales generally, and in the lordship of Bromfield and Yale in particular, the existence of so much unreclaimed waste and common land was hindering the progress of agricultural improvement. With regard to the terrain, he said...

> ... much of it is cold, savage and unprofitable; *Mons undique, et undique coelum.–* The upper country improvements are checked from the causes just given, and the mountain waste, at present, starves a third again of what it breeds; it fattens none; large extents of plantation would probably be soon made if it was once appropriated; hence in time wood would clothe and warm the mountain, and bring habitation and culture into it ...[4]

Not surprisingly, Philip Yorke's interest in more productive land use in the wider sphere went hand in hand with his efforts to effect 'improvements' to his estate at Erthig. His name has appeared more than once in accounts of agricultural improvements in eighteenth century Wales,[5] as an example of a 'spirited proprietor' who boldly proclaimed that "Every Feild will be kept to the Culture I shall dictate."[6] To be strictly accurate, he was actually referring on this occasion , not to his estate as a whole, but rather to his demesne land which he intended to let for one year so that he could concentrate all his resources on the task of draining his meadows.[7] His ultimate aim, in common with that of other landowners who carried out 'improvements', was to make a larger profit. In the words of one historian, "Indeed, when landlords spoke of 'improvement', it was usually an 'improved rental' they had in mind".[8] Philip Yorke's main income, like that of other landowners, came from rents. Of primary importance, therefore, were the measures adopted to impose his 'improvements' on his tenants.

Most agricultural experts maintained that the long lease was a major instrument of progressive farming.[9] Nathaniel Kent, for instance, emphasised that "Leases are the first, the greatest and most rational encouragement that can be given to agriculture."[10] John Laurence, as did other writers, condemned any form of rack-renting, and advocated an agreement for fifteen or twenty-one years, "taking care to insert proper covenants."[11] The terms of leases varied considerably in Wales during the eighteenth century, but the most usual type was one for a duration of three lives. In Pembrokeshire, for instance, such leases predominated until the end of the century,[12] while in Glamorgan those for three lives gradually gave way to leases for terms of years, usually twenty-one, or annual agreements.[13] Walter Davies (Gwallter Mechain), reporting his investigations made in the late 1790s and early 1800s in his *A General View of the Agriculture and Domestic Economy of North Wales*, asserted that he had found a variety of leases, some agreements for twenty-one years, but most for terms of lives in Anglesey, Caernarfonshire and Merionethshire, while "in the other counties, leases are entirely out of repute; not only by self-interested men, but by the most liberal, who have the good of their tenants, and of the public, at heart."[14] In Cheshire, the English county bordering on Denbighshire, a wide variety of leases existed in the late eighteenth century, most for lives, but also a considerable number for terms of years. Though many were converted to tenancies at will, leases for lives were still being concluded in the early years of the nineteenth century.[15]

There was considerable discussion about the relative merits and drawbacks of the different types of leases.[16] Advocates of long leases claimed that they gave tenants security of tenure and a foreknowledge of rents for a substantial period which encouraged expenditure on improved methods and allowed them to exploit any improvements they might have made. Their opponents maintained that short-term leases increased the landlord's control over such matters as the level of rent and his tenants' political opinions and also facilitated his efforts to effect improvements on his estate.[17]

Only four leases concluded by Simon Yorke, all after 1750, have survived, and of these two are for twenty-one years, one for twenty-eight years and one for two lives. In only two cases is it clear that the tenants surrendered old contracts in return for new ones from Philip Yorke when he took over the estate from his father in 1767. However, because so few leases remain, it cannot be assumed that no others existed. It is hard to believe that Simon Yorke would have had written agreements with some of his tenants and not with others. The Erthig archives contain several gaps and this could very well be one of them.

Philip Yorke, when he became squire of Erthig, wasted no time in concluding lease agreements with many of his tenants. Thomas Hayman, his solicitor, wrote to him in 1769 urging him to ensure that his marriage settlement should include "... a Power of Leasing not only for 21 years but also for 3 lives, wch upon some occasion you may want ..."[18] His marriage settlement, as we have seen, did indeed grant him this power. Many of the agreements had in fact been concluded before the settlement was drawn up in 1770. During the previous three years, Philip Yorke had set in motion a number of 'improvements' to his estate, such as levelling the French mill meadows and rebuilding the King's mill. Presumably, as part of his general strategy he took advantage of the period before his land was 'settled' to rewrite his lease agreements so as to incorporate a number of husbandry covenants in them. Though the evidence is scanty, it seems reasonable to assume that Philip Yorke's agreements were renewals of earlier ones, especially since the names of the tenants in the rent rolls were virtually the same after 1767 as before.[19] At the very least, therefore, continuity of tenure was maintained save in the case of new farms which were created by combining a number of smaller properties.

Of the leases concluded by Philip Yorke thirteen were for twenty-one years, seven for fourteen years, three for one year, one for ninety-nine years, one for eighteen years, one for twelve years, two for three lives, one for two lives, and two for one life. The 'articles of agreement' attached to the leases (but not the lease agreements themselves) allowed the tenant in some cases to terminate his agreement after a shorter period.[20] The one-year agreements, though few in number, were concluded after 1779, and reflected a general trend towards short-term leases which gathered pace at Erthig and elsewhere in North Wales in the closing years of the eighteenth and the early years of the nineteenth century.[21]

On the very slender evidence of Simon Yorke's four surviving leases, it would appear that the agreements concluded by his son, in terms of their duration, were cast in the same mould. Where Philip Yorke parted company with his father, and apparently with most other landowners, was in the inclusion of husbandry clauses in his agreements. As far as England was concerned it would appear that such clauses were not very common at this time, and leases containing covenants of a definitely progressive nature less so.[22] Referring to the situation in Wales, D.W. Howell has concluded that, up to the end of the eighteenth century, Welsh leases placed almost no constraints on cropping, with the result that "tenants exhausted the soil, and impoverished themselves by taking from five to seven or eight crops in succession from the same land." To prevent this, landowners in the early nineteenth century introduced clauses into their leases restricting the tenants to a particular rotation of crops.[23]

A number of enlightened landowners in different parts of Wales were, however, practising progressive methods in the cultivation of their estates in the eighteenth century.[24] For instance, Edward Wynne of Bodewryd in Anglesey,[25] Richard Pennant at Penrhyn and the Asshetons of Faenol in Caernarvonshire,[26] Arthur Blayney of Gregynog in Montgomeryshire,[27] and even Thomas Johnes on his inaccessible estate of Hafod in the mountains of Cardiganshire,[28] all promoted progressive crop rotations, amongst other improvements on their land.

One wonders, therefore, whether there might not have been some bias in the comment of a contemporary observer, J. Cradock, that "the remoter they are from the English counties, the less there is of the spirit of industry and improvement among the inhabitants."[29] Despite the efforts of a small number of enlightened landowners, however, David Thomas, on the basis of information provided by the Board of Agriculture Reports, 1794-1796 and 1810-1814, and other contemporary documents, has concluded that,

Apart from the gentlemen farmers there seemed throughout the country a general prejudice against anything which was new or different from the traditional method. While all farmers acknowledged the advantages of improved systems, few practised them.[30]

This is the regional background against which Philip Yorke's lease agreements have to be viewed. As for the local scene, though no exhaustive examination of the surviving records of neighbouring estates has been undertaken, the sample of lease agreements issued by Wynnstay, Plas Power and Chirk Castle which has been studied did not contain any stipulations about crop rotations or matters of husbandry in general. It would appear, therefore, that Philip Yorke might have been ahead of his time, in north-east Wales at least, in including detailed covenants governing farming practice in Erthig leases from 1767 onwards. What then prompted Philip Yorke's actions? No doubt, his reading of works by writers like John Laurence upon whose suggestions the terms of his leases were closely modelled.[31] Discussions with like-minded landowners,such as his friend Arthur Blaney,[32] were also likely to have had an influence, and it is perhaps significant that Belton House[33] and Newnham manor,[34] with which he had such close family connections, were situated in agriculturally advanced areas. Furthermore, what little evidence there is suggests that his father, Simon, was also keen to practise good husbandry on his estate. Philip Yorke's own experience as clerk to the Wrexham market in 1771 should also, perhaps, not be discounted.[35]

With some slight variations in lay-out and minor differences arising from the peculiar nature of individual properties, all contracts were drafted along similar lines by Thomas Hayman.[36] Each lease was accompanied by what were termed 'Articles of Agreement' –many of which have survived– giving a summary of the main clauses of the lease and including other relevant information relating to it.

The early clauses were the usual ones dealing with the rent, specifying when it was to be paid (twice yearly, on March 25th, and September 29th, in all but one case), and allowing forty days' grace, at the end of which the landowner could repossess his property if he chose to do so. They also preserved his right to permit hunting over the tenanted land. Other clauses forbade the sub-letting of the tenant's holding,[37] and safe-guarded the landowner's rights over mineral deposits and timber on his land. They ordered the tenant to grind his corn at the landowner's mill and made him responsible for all taxes raised on the property. The tenant was also responsible, at his own expense, for keeping all the buildings and gates, fences, stiles, hedges and drains in good repair. In return, Philip Yorke covenanted to have them all 'in tenantable repair' when the tenant first took over the property, and allowed him 'rough timber' when later upkeep was required. "All the hay, straw, fodder, muck, dung, compost and manure" were to be used for the benefit of the tenant's land and none of it was to be sold. Special provisions were made for the last year of the lease to ensure that the property was left in good order. These were very important in a lease granted for a number of years since, when the date of termination drew nearer, the land might otherwise be exploited and so seriously harmed. Thus Philip Yorke could sow and harvest a crop of winter corn on the tenant's land if the latter chose not to do so. Clover was to be sown in the last Spring before the end of the term and the crop handed over to the landowner on the November 1st following. He could also plough the winter corn stubble at any time after that date. All 'muck' had to be left on the premises when the tenant vacated the property.

The following clauses most specifically represent Philip Yorke's commitment to progressive farming methods. The tenant was not to plough more than a third (some leases gave the precise number of acres)[38] of his land in any one year, under a penalty of £5 for every acre above the stipulated amount. No more than three successive crops of corn or grain were to be sown on any field; at the end of this period such land was to be sown with clover seed, at the rate of fifteen pounds of seed per acre, and not cultivated again for three years. This follows very closely the advice given by John Laurence.[39] None of this land was to be mown except the first crop of clover, and no clover was to be cut for seeds to sell. The tenant was to spread a stipulated number of tons or cart-loads of lime ('the *sine qua non* of the lease', according to Walter Davies)[40] on his land each year at 5s. 6d. a load, and bring the receipts from the lime man to Philip Yorke when he paid his rent. The tenant, however, would not have to lime any acres which he had marled in any one year. A certain number of acres were designated as a summer fallow each year, new ditches were to be made to protect the winter corn, hedges were to be pleached and quicksets planted in the gaps under a penalty of 3s. 0d per rood for any neglected areas. Furthermore, the tenant was forbidden to sow any hemp or flax.

The six course rotation was basic to every lease, but some modification was permitted in one or two cases. Thomas Crew's agreement of October 26th, 1767, for instance, allowed him "... not to till any Field above three years, except he make a summer Fallow of an oat stubble. He may then till for four years. At the End of every third year or fourth (if Summer fallowed as above) to be clover'd of seed ..."[41] No explanation is available as to why Thomas Crew was singled out for this concession. A clue may lie in John Caesar's report of 1772 that his lands were "in a good state of husbandry",[42] which might suggest that he was also a good farmer five years earlier. A similar concession was made for Timothy Owens in his lease of October 26th, 1767, for he was also adjudged to have kept his land in good order.[43]

The lease for New Sontley was not concluded until 1779, eleven or twelve years after the majority of the leases were issued.[44] Its terms vary slightly from those of others on the estate. The contract, while adhering to the six course rotation, stipulated that "... the lands now in tillage, from which there have been two successive crops taken, shall in like manner be laid down in pasture next Lent seedness; and those from which one crop only has been taken to be laid down the following Lent seedness..." The other difference lay in the number and severity of the fines to be levied for non-compliance with the terms of the contract. Thus, a strikingly heavy fine of £100 would be imposed for not leaving muck or dung on the premises when the term of the lease was up; a £2 fine for every acre of the fifteen acres which the tenant failed to Summer fallow; a £60 fine for not spreading sixty tons of lime on the land, or a fine of £10 an acre for ignoring the stipulation forbidding the ploughing of certain fields.[45]

Why New Sontley was singled out for this special treatment is not easy to explain. Perhaps because it had formed part of Philip Yorke's home farm from 1772 to 1779, before it was let to Thomas and Charles Bowen,[46] he felt that the highest standards of husbandry had to be sustained. Possibly also, the Bowens were wealthy enough to pay such fines. It is, perhaps, significant that by far the heaviest fines would be imposed for neglecting the stipulations for improving the nature of the soil itself, rather than for infringements of those concerning cultivation. Unfortunate experiences with tenants in earlier years could also have led him to tighten the clauses and increase the penalties.

Agreements similar to those of Philip Yorke had, of course, been concluded in areas such as East Anglia since the 1720s. They enjoined the tenant to follow a four or six-course rotation.[47] Such agreements remained much the same until the 1790s,[48] though the famous four-course 'Norfolk' rotation was apparently little used in the eighteenth century. Even in its homeland of north-west Norfolk this system could be followed on only the best soils on the Holkham estates. In Hertfordshire and Lincolnshire, two other agriculturally advanced areas, a five or six-course of cropping was more usual.[49]

Philip Yorke, like other eighteenth century landowners, appreciated the value of clover to restore fertility to the soil after successive grain crops.[50] Clover was being cultivated in certain areas, such as Glamorgan for instance, before the end of the seventeenth century.[51] There is also a rare reference to it at Erthig in a letter from Richard Jones the Steward to John Meller, the squire at that time, on May 17th, 1721: "... the field by the house is sowed with barley and Clover Seed ..."[52]

The Crop Returns for 1801 reveal that even by that date turnips occupied only 5 per cent of the total arable acreage of eastern Wales.[53] Turnips were not a major crop in the Wrexham area,[54] since they were not suited to its heavy, clayey soils. Not surprisingly, therefore, they were not included in the Erthig crop rotation, and not mentioned in the leases nor in the home farm accounts. Some must have been grown, however, since there is an occasional reference to them in the correspondence. On July 17th, 1778, for instance, Philip Yorke wrote to John Caesar, "I think the very fine showers will bring on the Turnips", and on August 14th, "If your Turnips failed much, I take for granted that you would sow the ground again. The second sowings, which have been necessary, turn out well I see as I pass on."[55]

He was careful to see that the terms of any lease did not interfere with his own schemes and interests. One of his major projects in the early years concerned the King's mill.[56] The holding leased to John Stearndale, for example, was bounded by lands belonging to the King's mill and the agreement contained a clause concerning the right of Philip Yorke to "... finish the Cut or Mill Race going through part of John Stearndale's land (for better conveying of water to the King's mills) ..." while an addendum ordered John Stearndale to make good all the waterworks upon the river adjoining the premises, "except the waterworks belonging to the Gwerny and the materials in that part of the river where the Course of it was altered in about 1767."[57]

However, tenants who had to accomodate changes which were in the landlord's interest were to be fairly treated. Philip Yorke, like other landowners of his day, was anxious to eliminate any gaps in his estate land by exchanging some of it for property which was more suitably located. This was the case with Porthwgan, one of the tenements leased to Edward Fabian in November, 1767. The articles of agreement stated:

> The landlord to have a Power (whenever he shall have an opportunity) to change what part of this Tenement shall be convenient, with Mr. Cunliff, or anybody else whose Land interferes. Tenant to have a deduction or Increase of his Rent in proportion to the Quantity and Quality of the land so exchanged, more or less.[58]

Daniel Owens, who leased Pentremelin in 1769 (after John Caesar, the steward, moved to Bryngolau), also had to agree to similar stipulations. A note appended to his contract stated that Philip Yorke was "... at liberty to sell or Exchange any parts of the demised premises during the said term giving Daniel Owens...other convenient lands of equal value instead of them, making a proportionable abatement in the Rent taken from him..."[59] When William Edwards, tanner, of Wrexham, in 1770 leased two pieces of land which formed part of the French mill tenement he had to agree "... to keep up the Causeway that dams the water to the French mill, provided it is not prejudicial to the King's Mills."[60] Coedyglyn, as its name implies, was a heavily wooded area, and Mrs. Jones, who leased the property in 1767, had to allow "... Mr. Yorke to plant Trees at the top of the wood in Cae Pen Y Coed, Cae Coed and Cae Porth at his Discretion, allowing Mrs. Jones for the ground so taken in proportion to what she pays."[61]

One important reason for granting leases was that responsibility for the care of farm buildings and other property fell on the tenant.[62] This did not mean that Philip Yorke was completely absolved from having to contribute himself to the cost of repairs. The estate account books, articles of agreement, and an interesting note book covering the years 1772-1773 provide evidence that he took his duties in this area very seriously.[63] In January, 1771 he had written some notes on what had to be observed and done at Erthig during his many absences. John Caesar was to execute his orders or provide him with reasons for not doing so. To this end he furnished his steward with a "Book of Particular

Instructions",[64] the style of which in places tends to be lively and colourful. On January 21st, 1772, for instance, he gave orders that Crew's house should be painted in March, "... as, I think it will be a great Preservative against the Beating Winds, and Rain from the West...at the same time the Timber which lies upon the Wall-work of the Pigstye to be painted Red, which I take to be the strongest Colour and Best Preservative".[65]

On November 18th, 1772, Philip Yorke stated that the tenant of Stryt yr Hwch had converted a building near the house into a malt kiln at his own expense. "... I have permitted the alteration, but hold myself no ways Engaged to Assist or mix in the Expense! However as it may be an advantage to the Farm hereafter, I have made him a present of one Tree for Sparrs, one for Knogging or making Partitions, and Old Boards, which may well answer the Flooring Part."[66] Thomas Davies, however, was to be allowed £5 towards repairing his malt kiln "... if the sd Thomas expends so much fairly in that work."[67] When Plas Gronw was leased to Thomas Apperley (the father of 'Nimrod') in 1774, a considerable amount of work was obviously needed to put the buildings in 'tenantable repair' and the new tenant was allowed £54 "for the inside Repairs, Mr. Yorke doing the Outside. Locks, Keys and Bolts to be kept by Mr. Apperley." Mr. Apperley was also allowed to have sawn posts and rails to make a new drain below the orchard and for a breach in the hedge of the field called Bryn y Pysin. In his usual careful fashion, Philip Yorke insisted that all the new locks and bolts were to be left by his tenant when his lease was up, and that he was also to provide him with an inventory of what lay in the house and on the farm.[68] Repairs were also needed at Pickhill and Philip Yorke agreed that, "The Whole House (was) to be silled where necessary and Timber to be allowed by the landlord for that Purpose. Much thatching wanted to be done by the Tenant Mr. Jones ..."[69]

Problems arose inevitably from the squire's frequent absences from Erthig. On one occasion John Caesar had to enquire whether he had given his consent for Thomas Crew to have a room made over his 'Cow house' to keep his cheese and corn.[70] Again, in 1775, Philip Yorke wrote to his steward,

Altho' it was not within my power to describe the particular and precise Repairs at the Crabmill (not being apprized of the immediate necessity before I last left the Country) yet I can trust, you would direct them with all possible care and oeconomy, and not suffer the Tenant's Sollicitation, or the ill and partial advice of Workmen (should it be attempted) to lead you into more Expence, than the occasion absolutely required.[71]

Philip Yorke had a dread of fire, and time and again he warned his steward of its dangers and stressed the need for great care. The following extract from a letter to John Caesar dated November 1st, 1770, provides a good example of his feelings on the subject and is worth quoting at length.

I hope in our absence you will have all, a general care and attention to every-thing, but above all to be most careful of Fire; I think when you have occasion to

Write by Candle-light it would be safer, and better you should have a Fire, and table in the Steward's parlour. In your own closet the light is too much mingled with Papers, and must not be left even for a moment. And now I am on this Subject, it occurs to me a mistake I observed in the new building at Fabian's. In the Chamber over the new Kitchen, a Fire-place is made, and the Beams placed immediately over the Hearth-Stone – I spoke to H. Stephen to alter it, as those were done at Plasgronw. You will *see* it *is* done, and in no case, in any future building, let the same mistake occur again.[72]

Though his anxiety may seem excessive, it is clear that he had had experience of the damage fire could do, for in 1772 this had occasioned the rebuilding of Thomas Prichard's buttery and dairy.[73]

Unfortunately, Philip Yorke's notes on building work at his tenants' farms cover one year only but the estate account books reveal that such work inevitably went on over a much longer period and at no little expense, as the following examples covering the years 1770 to 1785 will show.

Table 1: Building work on Erthig estate farms, 1770-1785

Tenant	Years	Cost
Edward Fabian	1770-1772	£157/18/9[74] (including thatching)
Thomas Crew	1770-1774	£159/11/2[75]
D. Jones	1771-1773	£95/5/2[76]
Daniel Owens	1772-1774	£23/9/0[77]
Thomas Prichard	1772-1774	£12/17/8[78]
Timothy Owen	1772-1773	£5[79]
M. Jones	1781-1785	£117[80]
John Edwards	1782-1783	£ 43[81]
John Caesar	1784	£14[82]
Thomas Apperley	1784	£ 27[83]
W. Rowlands	1784-1785	£43/15/- [84]
New Sontley	1773-1777	£296/4/9[1/2][85]

These figures indicate that, at least for his first fifteen years at Erthig, Philip Yorke spent quite considerable sums on building work in fulfilment of his obligations under his leases.

What efforts did he make to enforce the covenants relating to the cultivation of his land? Walter Davies concluded, as a result of his investigations in the latter years of the eighteenth century that, as a rule, where leases with specific stipulations had been granted, no improvements resulted.[86] Moreover, as has already been seen, twentieth century studies tend to support this view. Even on the estate of one of the pioneers of advanced agricultural techniques, Coke of Holkham in Norfolk, it would seem that lease provisions were often breached and a wide variety of cropping practices was adopted.[87]

Philip Yorke's meticulous attention to detail is evident not only in the general content of the leases, but also in the special provisions made to meet the particular situation of certain tenants. It would appear, too, that he was well aware that a degree of vigilance and enforcement was necessary on his own part, and especially on that of his steward, to ensure that his tenants adhered to the terms of their leases. John Laurence, who had insisted that tenants should "perform their Covenants",[88] had also stressed that "... a Steward should ride over the whole Estate at least once a Month, in order to view both the land and stock of the Tenants carefully and distinctly, taking memorandums of the same from time to time ..."[89]

A record of 'memorandums' made by John Caesar, under orders from Philip Yorke, has survived.[90] It covers only a short period but the information it supplies about the efforts made to enforce the terms of the leases can be supplemented from the letters of squire and steward over a longer span. As we have seen, Philip Yorke himself was by no means a passive spectator, or an absentee landowner, giving his steward a free rein. He had his own ideas based on information supplied to him in the letters of the Caesars or some other of his friends and agents, or formed by him during his visits to Erthig. Thus on January 2nd, 1772, he wrote to John Caesar,

> I had meant the Muck Hill (collected by Caecochion this last Decr.) should have been spread on the Big meadow, in Febr'y or March next; but I have altered my sentiments in that matter, and would for the Reasons following Postpone it till the middle of August next. My objections to the former use, are that as sharp and Drying Winds may be expected naturally, in March, and Febr'y, the muck will thereby be dried up, and the Essence Exhausted, and the Sun at that time of the Year being High, and reigning long, will much assist these, the Inconveniences of the Season, and instead of Fertility, the muck may be even made to produce Barenness, and excessive drought. On ye Contrary, in Augt. the sun is declining, the Rains to be expected, and the manure will retain its moistness, and be washed into the ground, while it is soft and in a proper state to absorb and Receive it.[91]

John Caesar's own notes of his observations reveal a wide range of tenant-performance. They vary from Thomas Crew whose lands were in a good condition, "... he observing all the Covenants of his lease", and Edward Fabian who "... so nearly observes the Covenants of his lease that his Tenement much improves ..." to Daniel Owens, who,

> ... has lately been extremely slovenly and backward this year in not carrying lime and making a fallow sufficient according to the Covenant of his lease and even neglected to sow Wr. Corn what little is made. He is now carrying some soil upon his lands, but that seems to be laid on injudiciously. In short his whole Management is that of an inactive and bad Farmer and he requires to be closely watched and forced to perform what his lease contains, or otherwise he may not be able (in all Probability) to pay his Rent and the Landlord must take up the Premises in worse Condition than they were when he Sett them.[92]

In 1772, Thomas Prichard had "not carried the Quantity of Lime this year according to his agreement, nor sufficiently ditched his lands." In 1773 he failed to sow any clover; in 1774 his land was reported to be "in but indifferent management".[93] David Jones of Plas Drain was, "… very much short in Carriage of his lime this year which he says is occasioned by his too much work abt. the new Building; but promises to make that good the next year…Promises to make a Summer fallow of thirty measures seedness the next year and to fallow a large Field for leys for Barley and lime it well."[94]

There was no mention of any penalties being imposed in these instances. But this was not always the case. The report on Daniel Owens for 1773 and 1774 stated that he "neglects to sow clover and upon the whole, no Better than in 1772."[95] In the articles of agreement of his lease, there is an entry for 1774 which stated the penalties meted out to him for "Nonperformance of Covenants", namely, £15 for not sowing clover seed, and £20 for not summer fallowing.[96]

These fines indicate an intention of enforcing the covenants. However, there is no record that the fines were ever paid, and a perusal of the estate rentals shows that, twenty years later, Daniel Owens was still farming his 51 acres for which his rent was still £32 a year![97]

Another problem tenant was Richard Davies of the Crabmill, who appeared unable or unwilling to drain an area of marshy ground on his land. His lease, dated October 24th, 1767, stated that Philip Yorke allowed him £5 to drain the meadows in the following year, "and Mr. Davies to keep at the draining work so made in repair during his term."[98] By 1772, Richard Davies had taken no action in the matter,[99] and John Caesar's report for 1774 stated that he "still neglects to drain and probably always will …"[100] It is interesting that Richard Davies' general performance was described as "tolerably fair",[101] apart from this one failure. This might suggest that, like so many other tenants, particularly in Wales, he lacked the necessary capital to carry out such improvements. In cases of this kind landowners frequently helped out a needy tenant, recovering the money by means of an increase in the rent.[102] Although such help was rather slow in coming, in this particular instance that is what Philip Yorke finally did.

> Mr. Yorke proposes to sufficiently drain at his own Expense all the low lands in Richd. Davies's Holding, called the Bogs containing 28 Acres or thereabouts, before Michas 1775, Richard Davies paying him from Lady Day 1776 an additional Rent, after the Rate of £10 p. cent pr. Ann: for the money expended in such work for so long as he holds the Tenement.[103]

There is no record of this additional rent having been paid however. It is clear that Philip Yorke's approach to his tenants was flexible; some he expected to pay the cost of marling or draining themselves, others he helped. In 1772, Samuel Evans was reported as "draining the meadow lands in an effectual manner" presumably at his own expense, but his landlord was willing to help him to fund the building of a new milk buttery and corn chamber.[104] Again in

1774, Caesar stated that Samuel Evans "has done a good deal of draining and well."[105] At Plas Drain, on the other hand, the lease allowed the tenant £10 for draining and erecting quick fences around the fields near the house.[106]

It was Philip Yorke's custom also to make concessions to tenants to enable them to improve their land; for instance, they were allowed £3 a year for the first three years of their lease, for the purchase of lime or some other appropriate substance. Thus Timothy Owens received £3 for three years for manure,[107] and Daniel Owens, the problem tenant, had a similar amount for marling his land.[108] Here, too, there were variations according, presumably ,to the particular circumstances of individual tenants. To Edward Fabian, who had to spread thirty loads of lime on his holding at 5/6 a load, a total of £8/5/-, his landlord's contribution was less than half the cost.[109] Thomas Crew, on the other hand, was allowed only £2 a year for three years for lime, but since one of the tenements he was leasing had previously been rented by someone else, he was allowed £17/11/- for the "purchase of his predecessor's muck."[110] The concessions, it seems, were effective in one case at least, since in 1772 it was reported that Timothy Owens had "...carried lime, summer fallowed according to the Covenants of his lease or nearly so, and is now clearing a field for fallowing next year."[111]

There were two interesting reports of tenants, both women, whose performance showed improvement, the one on her previous practice, the other on that of her predecessor. In 1769, Widow Davenport was reported as being the greatest debtor amongst Philip Yorke's tenants, who was hoping, however, to sell her cheese to pay the rent she owed.[112] In 1771 he warned John Caesar " to keep a sharp eye on the Widow Davenport ..."[113] but by 1772 his steward was reporting that "Her lands are in fair Husbandry, except that she has not made quite so much Summer Fallow as she ought to have done, but that is a little excusable, she having carried lime sufficient for her arable lands this year and uses the Dung for her grass." In 1773 she had "carried too little lime", but by the following year everything was "all fair". [114]

In 1774 John Caesar reported that Timothy Owens had assigned his farm to his sister "who observes the Covenants in the lease very well, and makes much better Husbandry than her Brother did."[115] This statement is striking in view of the fact that in the previous year, as noted above, Timothy Owens himself had had a favourable report.

Two important changes occurred after Philip Yorke died in 1804. As the existing leases came up for renewal, his son Simon relet the farms on a yearly tenure and raised the rents.[116] This was in line with a general movement towards yearly agreements, brought about largely because landowners were becoming increasingly wary of granting long-lease agreements during a period of rapid price rises. By 1810, yearly tenures were the norm in Denbighshire.[117] Simon Yorke was also, no doubt, influenced by his father's extreme reluctance to raise the rents of his properties over a period of thirty-six years.[118] Might he also, like other landowners, have considered that long-term leases tended to produce tenants who, their positions secured by their contracts, tended to neglect their land?

Moreover, the specific husbandry clauses of his father's day were omitted from the new agreements which merely stated that the tenant "shall and will at all times use and manage the said demesne lands in a fair and husbandlike manner according to the usual course of good husbandry."[119] While it is clear that Philip Yorke had attempted to enforce the precise covenants of his leases in his earlier years at Erthig, there is no similar evidence for the later period. Indeed, at no time is there information showing how closely the majority of the tenants actually adhered to the six-course rotation which their contracts enjoined. Perhaps, therefore, Simon Yorke decided that the husbandry clauses were unenforceable. In any case, a yearly agreement rendered the tenant more vulnerable and, it was now commonly believed, would be more likely to make him intensify his efforts to cultivate his land successfully.

The fact that certain aspects of his policy were discontinued by his son in the changed circumstances of the early nineteenth century should not cause us to underestimate Philip Yorke's efforts in this sphere. A great deal of care had obviously gone into drafting his agreements, which were designed both to protect his interests and to promote the more enlightened farming techniques of his day. In theory, at least, he appeared to have been more advanced than other landowners in his neighbourhood and to have battled to ensure that theory was translated into practice. If he did not always succeed and did not always exact penalties for infringements, it is clear that he was not alone in this. As we have seen, in the best regulated circles of 'improving' landowners, lease covenants were often disregarded and landlords did not always practise what they preached. However, a review of the farms on the Erthig estate, carried out for Simon Yorke in 1806, which commented favourably on the condition of the land and buildings of most of them, would appear to testify to his father's determined efforts to leave him with a legacy of well-organised, thriving properties.[120]

Chapter 5: Rent Collection

In general, rents on estates in England and Wales rose steadily in the first half of the eighteenth century, more sharply after 1760, and quite spectacularly after 1793 during the French and Napoleonic Wars.[1] In some areas, such as south-west Wales for example, they doubled between 1760 and 1780; in Caernarfonshire they rose by over 50% between 1750 and 1790, while on Erthig's near-neighbour, Wynnstay, they rose by 37% between 1775 and 1780 alone.[2] Such increases, however, did not occur everywhere and, since the figures are averages, they conceal considerable variation. Examined in this general context, the gross rental value of the Erthig estate appeared to increase very gradually during Simon Yorke's time from £1,067 in 1736,[3] £1,169 in 1744,[4] £1,178 in 1756,[5] to £1,210 in 1764.[6] This represents an advance of over 13% between 1736 and 1764, while in the same period the size of the estate rose from around 1,657 to 1,801 acres, an increase of 9%.

In the first four years of Philip Yorke's ownership he issued new leases to a number of his tenants, as we have seen, and acquired additional land, so that by 1771 the gross rental value stood at £1,383 (an increase of 14%) and the acreage at 1,958 (an 8% increase).[7]

The picture is complicated by the fact that rent rises did not apply to every property on the estate and that the rate of increase varied considerably between one farm and another. The rent of Pentreclawdd, for example, a farm of 259 acres, the largest on the estate, retained its 1764 valuation of £150, as did the rents of Stansty (£50) and John Ebrill's holding (£9).[8] A number of others, however, rose by substantial percentages, as Table 2 shows:

In addition to increasing rents on existing farms, Philip Yorke also created

Table 2: A sample of rent increases on the Erthig estate, 1764-1771 [9]

PROPERTY	1764 RENT	1771 RENT	% INCREASE
Cae Eithin	£ 7	£15	114
Crabmill	£55	£68	24
J. Henry's holding	£40	£50	25
Maesyllan	£39	£68	74
E. Bennion's holding	£ 4	£ 5	25
Stryt yr Hwch	£60	£70	17
Aberderfyn	£55	£74	35
Pickhill	£69	£79	14
Plas Drain	£34	£74	118

larger holdings by amalgamating several smaller ones. John Laurence, who supported such a development, also warned,

> To alter Farms, and to turn several little ones into great ones is a work of Difficulty and Time; for it would cause too great an Odium to turn poor Families into the wide world, by uniting Farms all at once, in order to make an Advance of Rents; Tis much more reasonable and popular to be content to stay till such Farms fall into hand by Death, before the Tenant is either rais'd or turn'd out.[10]

Unfortunately, a gap in the rental accounts between 1764 and 1768 makes it difficult to state precisely how these enlargements were obtained. Having regard for Philip Yorke's general attitude towards his tenants it would have been surprising if there had been any summary evictions. A number of these amalgamated holdings are referred to in an ambiguous fashion. For instance, "William Yeud acquired the late Wright's 148 acres and P. Ellis's late 12 acres" reads as though Wright were dead but that Ellis was the previous tenant of the land concerned.[11] It is difficult, however, to be certain that this represents an intentional distinction and not merely inaccurate wording. In any case, the amalgamation may have followed Philip Yorke's acquisition of more land before 1772.

The policy of combining properties did not originate with him; he, as an 'improver', bent on creating more viable economic units, merely continued the practice on a much more comprehensive scale. The 1715 survey of Erthig showed how, for example, Samuel Davies had added the 27 acres of Tŷ yn y Twll to his original property of 4 acres, and how Benjamin Ridgeway doubled the size of his 53 acre holding with the addition of Bryngolau.[12] By 1764, the King's and French mills, Weston's holding and Cae Dibbin had all been combined, as had Aberderfyn, Bryn'r Owen and Felin Sych.[13]

Philip Yorke himself began to lease newly consolidated holdings almost immediately after inheriting the estate in 1767. A number of these represented quite considerable expansion, suggesting that some, at least, of his tenants had both the resources and the desire to undertake farming on a larger scale. In 1768,

Table 3: A comparison of farm acreages on the Erthig estate, 1736-1795[14]

YEARS	1736	1756	1764	1771	1783	1795
No. of properties	40	35	30	30	35	32
Acres.						
0-20	18	13	8	8	6	6
21-50	10	6	6	8	12	8
51-100	5	9	8	7	9	9
101-150	5	6	7	4	4	5
151-200	1	-	-	2	2	1
201-250	-	-	-	-	-	1
251-300	1	1	1	1	2	2

for instance, Thomas Crew extended his holding from 20 acres to 100, by adding two more properties of 75 and 5 acres respectively.[15] Moreover, the steward, John Caesar, while he did not increase his acreage so strikingly, consolidated a patchwork of small tenancies in 1771 to extend his original farm of 54 acres (Bryngolau) to 88 acres, by the addition of part of the Lodge tenement (15 acres), a number of crofts (6 acres) and part of the Erthig demesne (13 acres).[16] By 1771, seven such amalgamations had been made, involving substantial increases in the size of the holdings of the particular tenants concerned.

Although the number of properties does vary over the years shown so that Table 3 does not present a strictly accurate comparison, nevertheless the overall pattern is clear. There was a distinct fall in the number of small holdings of 20 acres or less, especially after 1756. Conversely, the number of properties of between 51 and 100 acres had increased considerably by that date, a level which was maintained with only minor fluctuations until 1795. The largest farms show a marked increase. In 1736 there were two farms with more than 150 acres, in 1756 and 1764 there was only one, but by 1771 there were three, and in 1783 and 1795 four, three of them by the latter date being over 200 acres.

These changes, which were in line with trends elsewhere in England and Wales, served to create more viable units on which to pursue more progressive farming and so increase their value. It is all the more surprising then that, after the initial increases, when new leases were issued between 1767 and 1771, no rents were raised, except those of new tenants, until Philip Yorke's death in 1804. This led his heir, Simon, to append the following note to a document comparing the Erthig rentals of 1795 and 1804:

> N.B. the above Estates (except the Farms mentioned were to be raised to New Tenants) have not been advanced since the year 1768; –a considerable addition may therefore be expected in the Rental according to the value of Estates in the neighbourhood.[17]

At first glance this assertion would appear to be a wild exaggeration since the gross rental value in 1771 was £1,383 and in 1803 £2,280,[18] an increase of 64%. However, around £600 of that increase was derived from rents for the rebuilt King's mill leased in 1772,[19] for New Sontley leased in 1779 and for his other purchases,[20] while another £128 came from the farms mentioned by Simon Yorke as having been let to new tenants. There was an overall increase of 18% in the acreage of the Erthig estate from 1,958 in 1771 to 2,327 in 1803.[21]

Faced with financial difficulties in the period following his father's death,[22] Simon Yorke proceeded to make a considerable addition to the Erthig rents. Between 1804 and 1807 they rose by 30% from £2,432 to £3,170.[23] Therefore, substantial increases in rents at Erthig were made a decade at least after they had occurred on most other estates.

What explanation can be offered for Philip Yorke's seemingly negative policy on rents? Others took advantage of the economic climate to bolster their finances in the latter years of the century, while he, so eager in other respects to improve his fortune, apparently did not. This cannot be ascribed to the terms of the leases he concluded in his first four years as squire, because most would have come up for renewal and upward rent adjustments would then have been possible.

From the very outset, however, he had found that even to collect the existing rents was no easy task. John Laurence had written "... the least part of the Business of a Steward is to collect the Rents, and he may as effectively wrong his Lord for want of proper and regular surveys, as for a neglect in gathering his Rents."[24] John Caesar, however, devoted a great deal of his time to collecting the rents.

Money must have been in short supply before and after Philip Yorke's marriage in 1770. Hence the necessity for the rents, the main source of his income, to be paid on time. His mother's £600 jointure, paid quarterly, was a pressing responsibility, particularly in the early years. Dorothy Yorke was clearly aware of the strain this placed on the estate's finances since, on November 1st., 1768, on her way to Bath, she wrote to her son,

"... as to money affairs have enough to set out with, that you need not hurry your payment now, and when I am at Bath I will let you know when I want some. I think I could stay very well till your tenants pay you at Xmas or longer if I could have that is owing to me from the Gentlemen at Bristol."[25] On December 17th, she again expressed her concern: "You make me uneasy,you give yourself so much trouble about me, be sure to send me but £200 whilst here." (i.e. in Bath)[26] To discharge her duties as her son's deputy at Erthig during his absence, Dorothy needed a supply of ready cash to cope with the day-to-day expenses of running the estate, and there is a note of urgency in her letter of June 25th, 1769.

You will think I vary vastly in my want of money. I shall now really be very glad of what you can spare, I am constantly obliged to advance sums of money to the Caesars where there is much more call for it, than they can or do receive, they beg that you will trust them with a sum that will last – they will take equal pains to get in your arrears ...[27]

The Caesars were indeed the recipients of many admonitions on the prompt collection of rents. The nature of the steward's responsibilities, particularly his role as rent collector, made him unpopular with the tenants. He was placed in the invidious position of having to compromise between the demands of the landlord and the reluctance or inability of the tenants to meet their obligations. The problem was exacerbated in John and Jacky Caesar's case by the frequent absences of Philip Yorke from Erthig. On May 17th, 1770, Philip Yorke wrote to complain: "I am not pleased you so soon want money, as it argues great backwardness in my tenants' rents, which I shall never submit to . ..."[28] The steward found himself under constant pressure to insist on the punctual payment of rents and, on occasion, was moved to explain the tenants' difficulties in discharging their duties. On January 2nd, 1769, he wrote,

I do expect that the greatest part of your tenants will this week finish paying the first half year's rent for 1768. John Lewis and John Jones of the Coach (that took part of Coedyglyn meadows) went last week into some Welsh fairs a great way off, and are not expected home till tomorrow Tuesday, therefore must wait for their rents till they return. Randle Davenport is in a bad state of health and says that he will sell his cheese and a deal of corn as soon as possible in order that he may pay your rent. Richd Thomas will sell his cattle in order to pay his rent as soon as they are marketable. I shall send a list this week of what your tenants have paid me since 26th, Dec. last ...[29]

The situation did not improve over the following months and on September 3rd, John Caesar informed Philip Yorke that "only Few Tenants can pay the half year's rent before the latter end of next month as they don't Receive but little money from their Corn and Cheese before that time."[30] On another occasion he expressed a wish that many tenants would sell their cattle in the forthcoming Wrexham fair in order to pay their rent.[31]

Philip Yorke's replies, however, show that he was adamant that his tenants should not accumulate arrears of rent. He could not afford to permit them to do so. The day-to-day costs of running the estate, which included, as we have seen, the rebuilding and repair of farm buildings, not to mention Philip Yorke's more grandiose schemes, with their heavy demands on labour and materials, were met primarily from rents. Hence the note of urgency in his instructions to his steward. On April 6th, 1771 he wrote to John Caesar,

I shall never permit them to delay their Payments till midsummer –as it will bring my Erthig affairs into considerable distress, for no money are you to expect from me. This being the case, they must pay by instalments, and those must be brisk, and repeated; how otherwise are you to discharge the Daily demands upon you, and the Bills I left with you ...[32]

The great majority of leases stipulated that rents should be paid twice yearly, on Lady's Day and at Michaelmas, allowing forty days' grace before the

Table 4: Number of instalments by which some tenants on the Erthig estate paid their rents between 1771 and 1780.[33]

Tenant	Annual Rent	1771	1772	1773	1774	1775	1776	1777	1778	1779	1780
T. Crew	£60	5	6	3	5	4	4	6	4	2	5
E. Fabian	£73	6	4	4	6	4	6	4	6	5	4
R. Davies	£68	8	5	5	3	4	5	6	7	4	1
D. Owens	£32	7	5	6	4	4	1	6	3	6	7
T. Owens	£37	-	4	3	2	5	2	2	3	5	-
W. Yeud	£70/10/-	-	4	4	3	4	2	4	5	6	5
M. Jones	£150	-	6	6	2	5	5	2	5	4	5
D. Jones	£80	-	7	6	4	5	2	2	2	2	2

landowner could repossess his property. This respite gave tenants an opportunity to sell their stock and produce in the fairs and markets when prices were most favourable. A large number of tenants, dependent on the sale of their produce for the money to pay the rent, could only pay by instalments. Table 4 shows the wide variations in the number of instalments by which some of the tenants paid their rents. These varied in individual cases from one year to the next. There was little to choose between 'good' tenants like Thomas Crew and Edward Fabian, and 'unsatisfactory' ones like Richard Davies and Daniel Owens,[34] nor between those with large and more modest holdings.

The problem of arrears was by no means unique to Erthig, however. In his *General View of the Agriculture and Domestic Economy of North Wales*, Walter Davies concluded,

> Rents are always paid in money, on two half-yearly payments, but, in several instances, the first payment is not made until the second has become due, and so on, the tenant being at every payment, half a year in arrear.[35]

So it was at Erthig, but the situation was made even worse because, despite Philip Yorke's constant rebukes, many tenants were a great deal more than six months in arrears. Table 5 shows that the problem became more serious during the period 1771 to 1781, when the proportion of tenants who were over a year behind in their rents more than doubled.

As early as 1774-75 Philip Yorke's plight was such that he was forced to sell some timber,[36] but that clearly did not raise sufficient capital, for an advertisement appeared in the *Shrewsbury Chronicle* of November 12th, 1774 for the sale in one lot "of All the materials in the body of that capital well built messuage, Sontley House ... consisting of a large Quantity of Lead, Bricks, Stone, Slates, Timber, Flooring Boards Dantzic Oak, Wainscot, Sash Frames, Sashes, Glass, &c all in good Preservation ..." Though there is no map which clearly identifies the building, it appears to be an older house on the Sontley estate which had become redundant when New Sontley was built.[37] Ever mindful of his own interests, Philip Yorke was careful to add: "N.B. The Purchaser will be liable to certain Conditions, as will be stated upon View of the Premises." The nature of these conditions was made clear in a letter to his steward on December 27th, after the building materials had been bought by a Mr. Lockitt for 500 guineas.[38] It seems the old house was likely to be demolished

Table 5: A comparison of arrears of rent on the Erthig estate, 1771-1781.[39]

Year	Number of Properties	6 months in arrears	7-12 months in arrears	More than 12months in arrears
1771	30	20	4	6
1776	31	18	2	11
1781	30	9	7	14

but Philip Yorke was concerned to salvage anything of value first. His attention to detail, his anxiety to foresee every eventuality, combined with his determination to abide scrupulously by the terms of the agreement with the purchaser, are so typical of him that the letter is worth quoting in full.

The Kitchen Grate, late Laundry; & unless it be already Removed, it shall be left with him. All other Boilers or Coppers Cisterns or such things, you must instantly remove to Erthig, and I trust you will not use delay in a matter like this which requires dispatch, for the instant they begin to demolish every thing of mine will be overwhelmed. It just occurs to me, there is a Boiler in the Scullery, that ought to be left, an ancient one belonging to Mr. Roberts, and which I think you & I thought should be left with the House; every Vessel, Sacks, Sash frames for Erthig etc. that lye in the House at present for Security, must be instantly Removed, for Lockitt will soon fill it with Purchasers of small Articles, and Persons to measure; But by the Articles you observe that he cannot Pull down a Brick, or Remove any thing whatsoever, till the 500 Guineas be Paid into yr. Hands, & then the destruction of the dwelling House is altogether optional. You see, he is accountable for all damage, and in throwing down the House I shall make him repair any Mischief he should do to my Offices, or Corn Ricks, as well as the Gate at Sontley. Lockitt will let us know how much Ground he may want for his Materials, and to the Part appointed him, he must steadily adhere. He asked me for a small Dutch Oven in the Kitchen, but I told him that it was most probable I should make use of that at Erthig, but in case hereafter I should not, I would give it him: I desire you will file, this as well as my other Letters, for it tends to Preserve with Exactness the Conversation which Passes on these Subjects, whilst the circumstances are fresh, which otherwise are often misrepresented thro' the want of some Written Note at the time. You understand that I do not mean to Remove anything from Sontley House, that it was not predetermined, & necessarily implied, before I made a Bargain with this Man.

A letter to his steward, dated January 7th, 1775, however, shows that his financial situation was still parlous:

I am sorry to Receive a list of Bills, which I cannot Enable you at this time to Discharge. The Persons concerned who have had a taste of my Exactness to Expence, may rest assured that they shall be paid with the first Convenience. As soon as Lockitt comes with the money for Sontley, they shall be instantly paid; in the mean time, they must satisfie themselves with the security their money is in. I will Endeavour to send you some Bills to answer the weekly demands ...[40]

There is a note of desperation in Philip Yorke's instructions to Jacky Caesar who had the unenviable task of trying to pacify his creditors. In addition to instructing his steward to try to fob them off, Philip Yorke told him,"if in absolute distress", to approach Tom Lloyd who "I daresay will give you money for your Bill on me."[41] In 1776 he bewailed his "exhausted finances",[42] and in 1777 such was the scale of his financial crisis that he talked of postponing any new projects in and around Erthig because "I shall have no money for new Expences or Extraordinary Excess."[43] His resources were obviously stretched to the limit when, in May 1777, he raised a mortgage on recent purchases, New Sontley and a property in Marchwiel.[44] The money which he borrowed was actually half of his wife's £10,000 dowry.[45] £1,000 of the loan was used to pay half of his expenses in the Helston election of 1775,[46] but there is no record of how the remainder was spent. The loan was not repaid during Philip Yorke's lifetime.[47] In 1778 he had not even the money for the return to Erthig from Maryport[48] and announced, "I have exhausted my Bankers with the Expence of this place, and of travelling, and therefore shall be glad you could send me so much as fifty pounds of the Micha's Receipts, to bear me safe home ..."[49]

There was to be no immediate alleviation of his obvious financial distress however. Indeed, the "sharp but short-lived price fall"[50] at the start of the 1780s only served to exacerbate his problems. Writing to John Caesar on August 4th, 1780 from Southsea Camp, he showed that his absence from Erthig on military manoeuvres had not erased financial concerns from his mind and that he was even considering legal action against one defaulter.

> The state of arrears is a very serious matter indeed; I have actually no money to send you, and therefore those tenants who are largely in debt, must understand, that they must advance from time to time what is wanted at Erthig from these arrears; and unless they make a decent payment at Michaelmas, I shall be distressed every where; You must direct Mr. Hayman to write to Davies of Crabmill, and if that does not succeed, he must proceed to Extremities with him; It cannot be otherwise.[51]

Whether matters ever went as far as this is not clear but a year later he was lamenting:

> ... when the Times are so truly distressful that little or no money is to be had, or expected from tenants (In the collection, however, of what is to be had, I trust you are most diligent, and will now make an early and certain Remittance to Mr. Birch), it certainly is not the moment to press alteration...

He noted also that,

> ... in the state of my Arrears, my Quarterly Payments at Micha's will put me in a sad hobble, and my Newnham Tenants (however well they pay, do not do so, till near or quite Xmas).[52]

In another letter, of which only an undated fragment has survived, he expressed the hope that a quick sale of ewes and lambs would help him to make ends meet.[53] If his home farm had been a really profitable enterprise as he had hoped it might be,[54] it is quite possible that the sale of stock and produce on a regular basis, and not as an emergency measure, would have helped to offset his financial difficulties and reduced his dependence on rents. He chided John Caesar, "You have sunk my Purse at Erthig so low, that you must now be content to make up ground gradually. I have no money for large muckhills of bone or dung ... (indecipherable) ... I am very much chagrined with the Marchwiel Tenants, and by the next Post I will send you a Circular letter which

Table 6: Arrears of rent on the Erthig estate, 1783-1797 [55]	
YEAR	ARREARS
1783	£1002
1784	£ 768
1785	£ 778
1786	£ 327
1787	£ 216
1788	£ 260
(A gap in the records)	
1795	£ 222
1796	£ 188
1797	£ 221

you will write out, and send to the defaulters and which I shall certainly follow with all Execution."[56] Unfortunately, no record remains to tell us whether or not this action was taken.

Philip Yorke did not follow the example of some landlords who tried to help those tenants who were genuinely unable to pay their rents on time, by rent reductions or, at least, temporary abatements.[57] Three reasons can be suggested for his failure to do so. Firstly, he probably thought that the rents were low enough in any case; secondly, from the tone of some of his remarks, he appeared to doubt the sincerity of some of his tenants' excuses, and thirdly, he simply could not afford to offer rebates. The average annual rental of the Erthig estate in 1780s and 1790s was around £2,000, but, as Table 6 shows, the arrears were certainly very high in the early 1780s, after which they declined sharply.

In the absence of any statement by squire or steward about the decrease in arrears, one can only suppose that the improvement in prices for agricultural products in the later 1780s, reinforced by the food shortages of the war years after 1793,[58] made it easier for tenants to pay the rents, especially as at Erthig they had failed to keep pace with inflation.

The paucity of letters to Jacky Caesar after 1781, and to his successor after 1787, however, leaves us in some doubt about the depth of Philip Yorke's concern with rents at this period. Although, after Jacky Caesar's defection in 1787, his successor John Jones was instructed "to write peremptorily" to the tenants who were in arrears with their rent,[59] it could be argued that Philip Yorke might have had less reason to worry about such matters by this time. In 1782 he married Diana Meyrick and through her became the life-tenant of her estates at Dyffryn Aled and her property in Yorkshire. These acquisitions, together with Newnham, could be utilised to relieve financial pressure on Erthig.[60] Furthermore, his expenditure on 'improvements' to the house and park at Erthig had been reduced by the second half of the 1780s, when, in any case, the arrears were diminishing.

These reasons do not, however, explain fully either Philip Yorke's failure to raise his tenants' rents or his apparent reluctance to rid himself of inadequate tenants. Like other landowners, he was aware that tenants with sufficient capital to stock a farm were difficult to find, and was therefore reluctant to disturb existing occupiers even when they had huge arrears of rent to pay. Tenants were rarely evicted except for misbehaviour. Too great an insistence on prompt payment of rent, and subsequent evictions, could result in the landowner being left with a number of unprofitable, untenanted properties on his hands; "... to distrain for arrears would merely ruin the tenant and almost invariably leave the farm vacant."[61] In the words of Samuel Johnson, "... if a landlord drives away his tenants he may not get others."[62] In 1781, when his fortunes were at a very low ebb, Philip Yorke had written to Jacky Caesar, "I am sorry to have more land coming upon my hands. I am already plagued with a great deal at Newnham which is at present a dead Expence to me, without any yet Returns. It must be understood that Bailey's land is to be let."[63]

Despite his fears, however, the evidence of the Erthig accounts would appear to vindicate Philip Yorke's policy of low rents. It shows that, with the exception of Bryngolau after Widow Caesar's death in 1788, he had no vacant farm on his hands until 1795.[64] Only during the years 1795 to 1804 did Philip Yorke have any property "in his own occupation" over a protracted period, and even that did not amount to very much.[65] Unfortunately, the Erthig papers do not throw any light on the reason for this state of affairs during a relatively favourable period for farmers.

CHAPTER 6: The Home Farm

Philip Yorke's efforts to increase the profits of his estate began very soon after he had taken over the reins at Erthig in 1767. By the following year he had launched two projects, one to drain the low-lying French mill meadows and the other to rebuild the King's mill. A third, to enlarge his demesne and create a substantial home farm, took shape after 1772.

The French mill meadows were subject to periodic flooding from the river Clywedog which snaked its way in a series of great loops through them, with the result that the value of the land was declining. The problem was described by his friend and neighbour, Thomas Birch, who wrote to inform him that workmen were going to dig two cuts in the Coed-y-Glyn meadows,

> ... these cuts are absolutely necessary for much of the heart of the meadows is gone and more going every flood ... Oldfield offered £26 per ann. for the meadows and it was to be hoped that when the cuts had been completed they would be worth £40 a year ... and all for an expense in comparison trifling.[1]

Philip Yorke's scheme rationalised the area; the valley floor was levelled, slopes modified, or, where necessary, created, to divert surface water into a series of ditches, and thus avoid erosion on the one hand and flooding on the other. Further 'cuts' eliminated the meanders and established a new course for the river on the south side of the valley.

The task of draining the meadows was closely bound up with his decision to rebuild the King's mill and make it a going concern. Central to the whole enterprise was the need to divert the course of the destructive Clywedog and create a new leet to power the mill. Philip Yorke was obviously very excited about the project. On September 24th, 1768, he wrote to Brownlow Cust that he had decided to let his demesne for one year "... that I may throw my whole Weight, my total complement of Teams and Workmen immediately on the Meadows." He hoped, he said, that the fifty-four acres of land concerned would be worth 50 shillings an acre by the following Spring, a total of £135 instead of the £36 which he was currently receiving for it.[2]

Although John Vernon was obviously in charge of the whole operation, a great deal of responsibility fell on John Caesar who played a leading role in its organisation and planning. The latter, it seems, thought that a scheme for creating the new mill race from the diverted Clywedog costing an estimated £1,000 too expensive, and produced another plan himself which would have reduced the cost to around £350.

> Mr. Caesar thinks that this whole scheme can be completed for about three Hundred Pounds at most, and for fifty more the old Rivers can be filled up by

sloping the banks of the present Streams, which will make all that land worth 30s. an acre at least, and the Mill worth £50 a year at least also.[3]

A number of reports from John Caesar during 1769 kept Philip Yorke up-to-date with progress on the activities concerning meadows, river and mill. On January 3rd, he wrote of "Turning the river and making Bulwarks in Coedyglyn meadow (where you sowed Barley and Clover) in order to prevent that good land from being forcibly (?) wash'd away ..."[4] On January 29th he complained that he would have to hire teams to fallow wheat stubbles and sow barley and clover because the Erthig teams were otherwise engaged in carrying timber to the King's mill.[5] Then on March 5th he reported, "Some of the Labourers are hedging around the French mill meadows, & others turning the River and making Bulwarks in order to turn it to the new Course, and when the whole is Completed you will have your meadows on one side of the river quite from the wood house to the King's mill which will be two miles in length."[6] With their value thus enhanced by these measures, part of the meadows became attached to the King's mill and part to the enlarged Erthig demesne after 1772.

The French mill meadows were destined, however, to make further demands on Philip Yorke's purse during the following years. In spite of the improvement, the nature of the terrain and the surface system of drainage meant that almost yearly maintenance was required. Philip Yorke's letters during the 1770s made frequent and anxious references to the continuing danger of floods[7] and, between 1772 and 1775, he employed the services of William Emes, the landscape designer,[8] to carry out a further levelling project at a cost of just over £1,100.[9]

Much the same outlay[10] was required for the rebuilding of the King's mill during 1768 and 1769. The expenditure seemed likely to be fully justified, however. The rapid increase in population and the growth in demand for wheaten bread after the middle of the century led to a general expansion in milling capacity throughout England and Wales. Increased productivity could be achieved by demolishing out-of-date premises and replacing them with larger, more efficient mills.[11]

The King's mill had already been improved in 1717 and 1718 by John Meller,[12] and there is no evidence that Philip Yorke's reconstruction involved any technological advances. It had long had two overshot wheels, the type preferred by experts,[13] each operating a pair of millstones. These were French burr stones from an area around La Ferté-sous-Jouarre, of a type which had been imported since the seventeenth century.[14] An entry in an account book for July 6th, 1769, shows that Philip Yorke paid £35 for a pair of these French stones which produced fine quality wheat flour of the type so much in demand.[15]

John Caesar's letters kept his master fully informed about the work in progress. One of the main problems was to maintain a reasonable balance between the competing demands on the limited resources of mill and estate. As the steward explained on January 29th, 1769, "... Andrew Williams employs 2 pair of sawyers and eight men of his own constantly at work which occasions a good deal of money to you every week, the more hands he employs the sooner the new mills will turn out profit."[16]

In May, John Caesar was reporting that the Erthig teams were finding it difficult to cope with the demands of the masons at the mill for lime and stones, "and most of your labourers beside strangers are employ'd there ..." He added, "I go there every day to see that the masons have material to their hands ..."[17] The stone came from a local quarry[18] and was conveyed by horse and cart to the mill. Timber came from the estate itself and, in his letter of September 30th, John Caesar discussed this and other aspects of the work:

> We have fell sixteen of the fir trees in the nursery & have saw'd the greatest part of them into Boards which we hope will be enough for the floorings. Hugh Hughes the Slater is Continually slating the mill, and after he has finished that work, Andrew Wilkins will immediately set up three pair of stones. The labourers are employ'd in Cutting Brushwood for the waterwork,and and the Team is Constantly employ'd in Carrying timber to the mill.[19]

Once the reconstruction of the mill was completed, Philip Yorke's next task was to make it profitable, which it had patently not been in the recent past. On April 23rd, 1770, he purchased the Crown title to the King's mill for a payment of £595/10/-, which also included the extinguishment of Crown interests in the tolls of Wrexham fairs and markets, and in Glyn Park,[20] which ensured that all profits of mill and markets would be Erthig's. On April 28th, 1770, he wrote to his steward,

> The Mills I must beg you now most closely to give your time and diligence into, from your great industry you may be able to collect the real intrinsic value of the obligatory business none of which you must suffer to escape you . Let your Mill books be distinct and carefully correct and close. The late Miller acted a dirty part, they have totally and entirely forfeited all connection with me and see they may be instantly dismissed so that the lands and everything else they held under me may be ready to be delivered over to any new tenant I shall approve ...[21]

Not surprisingly, he had advertised for a new tenant for the mill in September 1769, well before it was completed.[22] In the following year, effecting one of his rare exchanges of properties, this time with Philip Puleston, he acquired possession of the Puleston mill which lay upstream on the Clywedog, together with the mill house,[23] and converted them into a farmhouse and outbuildings. These, together with about forty acres of land, were added to the King's mill to form a farm unit. By doing so, he removed an impediment since, in the previous century, the Puleston mill had impaired the efficient working of the King's mill by causing it to have an insufficient flow of water.[24] These changes made the King's mill a more attractive proposition for a prospective tenant.

From the middle of the century it had become fairly common practice for millers to raise stock as a secondary occupation, to assure themselves an additional income and a source of food for the family.[25] Furthermore, a competent, experienced millwright was required to operate the reconstructed mill efficiently. In 1772 the mill and farm were let to a practising miller from Mold, John Lowe, whose lease was for fourteen years at a rent of £240 a year. This figure, with slight variations remained fixed until 1807, when Simon Yorke raised the rent, along with that of several other properties, to £360.[26] In 1786, after the death of her husband, Margaret Lowe was designated as the lessee of the mill.[27] These sums represented considerable gains when compared to the £10 a year which the mill brought in before its reconstruction.[28] The terms of the lease, as far as the farm was concerned, were the same as those of the other agreements drawn up for Philip Yorke, but there were additions in respect of the mill itself. John Lowe was to keep the mill machinery, water-course and mill-race in good repair, to treat all his customers fairly, charging the "ancient, lawful tolls," and to report to Philip Yorke those inhabitants of Wrexham Regis and Stansty Issa who did not perform suit of mill.[29] The age-old problem of enforcing suit at the King's mill on the inhabitants of Wrexham and Stansty Issa had been exacerbated in the early 1770s by the growth of a number of malt and horse mills in the Wrexham area which were taking business away from the King's mill.[30] On February 6th., 1769 John Caesar had reported that "very few Wrexham Innkeepers send their malt to the King's mill."[31]

Philip Yorke's answer to this problem was to send a letter, drafted by his solicitor, Thomas Hayman, to the defaulters and "pirating mill owners," threatening them with legal action unless they agreed to certain terms. Among these were stipulations that those concerned should grind all their corn and grain at the King's mill, and that owners of malt mills should suppress them or enter into a £100 penalty bond "not to grind Malt or other Corn or Grain for any of the inhabitants of Wrexham Regis or Stansty, nor for their own Consumption, unless by Agreement with the Miller of the King's Mill."[32]

While the alterations to the meadows and the mill were still going on, Philip Yorke had embarked on a programme of land purchase to enhance his estate. Like other ambitious landowners he appreciated that the ownership of land was the key to social and political as well as economic and financial success. His marriage settlement in 1770, as we have seen, had allowed him, under certain conditions and with the assent of the trustees, to buy and sell land.[33]

His first significant purchase came in 1771, when he bought Bryn y Grôg, the estate of John Jones, a Wrexham grocer, for £1,625. In 1772 he made by far his largest single purchase, New Sontley, for £7,879, from David Roberts. Philip Yorke's acquisition of New Sontley was particularly significant. It had a sizable,[34] perhaps recently renovated house[35] and an impressive range of outbuildings which included a coach house, brew house and stables.[36] The property was conveniently located less than a mile from Erthig, while the two estates were contiguous over a considerable distance. Thus the addition of 146 acres of Sontley land allowed Philip Yorke to extend and round off his existing 159 acre Erthig demesne. The new bloc of 305 acres was assessed at a nominal rental value of £285. Some slight temporary adjustments of land increased the total acreage to a peak of 363, with a rental value of £320 in 1778, whence it reduced to 339 acres assessed at £309 in 1779.[37] During the period 1772-79, these acres constituted a greatly enhanced home farm. In those years, too, Philip Yorke improved the farm buildings at New Sontley; general repairs and a new dairy house cost £137/4/9^1/2 in 1773-1774, while in 1776-1777 he built a hay bay and cart house for £112, and a new barn for corn for £43.[38] Entries in his account book reveal how Philip Yorke financed these purchases. In 1772 he,

> Called in and received Principal mortgage money of Mr. Westphalen £4,000.
> N.B. This money was disposed of in purchasing Jones' Estate in Marchwiel; and part of it went towards the Purchase of Sontley.

Another entry shows that in July 1773 he sold £5, 000 of Old South Sea Stock for £4,234/9/6 and £3,500 of New South Sea annuities for £2,948/15/-. This money financed the purchase of New Sontley and "the caseing of Erthig".[39] It is indicative of Philip Yorke's urgent need for money to pay for his new properties that both sales of stock were made at a loss.

The sources of the money for these investments are obscure. It did not come from the sale or exchange of land referred to in his marriage settlement, nor from his wife's £10,000 portion which had been invested elsewhere at 4 per cent. interest.[40] H. J. Habbakuk maintained that portions were usually spent, by the families receiving them, on the purchase of land.[41] However, the Yorke family, in this instance at least, was one of those which did not utilise the portion in this manner.[42] The £4,000 could have been the money bequeathed to Philip Yorke by James Hutton,[43] which he had subsequently loaned out on mortgage. The source of the two sums of £5,000, which had been invested in South Sea Stock, is a mystery. Philip Yorke had also acquired more stock which he had proceeded to sell at a loss. Between May and September 1770 he sold £4,250 worth of South Sea Annuities for £3,528, using the money, not to pay for any new property, but to meet the cost of legacies and current expenses for such items as clothes, travel and housekeeping.[44] A letter to John Caesar, dated July 1st, 1772, showed that Philip Yorke felt that he had had a bargain in his purchase of New Sontley. He had acquired, in addition, six oxen, and offered David Roberts £30 for a large crop of hay. However, neither these 'extras' nor the estate itself would come into his possession until Christmas. In the meantime, he sought his steward's advice: "John, collect yr thoughts together, and see if you can start anything that I may propose to Mr. Roberts, and may have a future view to my advantage ..." John Caesar advised him to pay no more than £24 for the hay, and "also the Brick that lye upon the premises..."[45]

A good example of Philip Yorke's anxiety and wariness, and his suspicion of workmen, was his instruction to John Caesar to keep a close eye on his new estate until he came to take possession of it at Christmas 1772 ,

> ...I am sure he (i.e. David Roberts) will prevent all lopping of Trees, but his men are not so well to be trusted; Walk over the Estate of Sontley when you have got this, and if you see any workman lopping or damaging any Tree, tell Him, you

may venture to say, it is against Mr. Roberts orders, and desire to withold till he hears further from his master – But all of this if it is necessary to be done, must be done delicately – I hope it is only extreme caution in me.[46]

These two purchases did not assuage Philip Yorke's desire for more land, however. In 1777 he made two further acquisitions to round off his estate: the property of Maurice Wilkinson Pugh in Marchwiel for £1,200 and Hafod-y-Bwch from Hugh Bowen for £1,300.[47] It was suggested to him by John Vernon that the latter was a very worthwhile purchase, "being so contiguous to your lands."[48] The negotiations for the property were in the hands of John Vernon, who viewed it on behalf of Philip Yorke and bought it for him by "private contract". To pay the £2,500 for the two purchases, Philip Yorke borrowed £2,400 from Matthew Yatman, an apothecary of the parish of Saint Mary Pancras in Middlesex.[49]

Meanwhile, he had embarked on his third project for the estate. In November 1772, two months after his purchase of New Sontley and a month before he was due to take possession of it, Philip Yorke had declared his intention to take up farming on a substantial scale on his own account. In view of his earlier enterprises, it would be fair to suggest that this one had been lurking at the back of his mind for some considerable time. The declaration itself, which reflects his anxiety and hesitation concerning the venture, and his usual shameless habit of manipulating his steward's feelings, is worth quoting in its entirety.

It is not that I think the trade of farming unprofitable in itself, (perhaps it is otherwise in the Present times, and with the Advantages a Gentleman has before Him) but, that it becomes so through want of Attention, Judgment, & Oeconomy in the Management; and as I must of necessity be myself often absent, and even at home engaged, I confess I am often deterred from undertaking it. However having a Confidence in the Industry, Honesty, & increasing Judgment of my Agent, I am willing to make a Tryal, and to hold in my Hands a large Quantity of Land for different Uses = Pasture, Arable, & Meadow, as each hath an alliance with the other, & conspires to one general Profit. I shall notwithstanding never rest satisfied without a very Close, and regular Account of Profit and Loss, that I may Know to retire in time, and not Blunder on to my great disadvantage. Much will certainly depend on good Judgment in buying in & Selling-out. Much will be Consumed on the Premises, and therein I am guarded from any great Loss in the latter Article, if Plenty leadeth not to Prodigality, and Profusion. Workmen are a great Expence and will eat up the Profits if not strictly watched. In short in my particular Situation the Success, or Ruin will infinitely depend on my Agent. I trust it will be his Pride, as well as Duty, not to say Advantage to comprehend the business before Him & to exert his utmost Abilities in the Conduct of it; nor must he look on it as a light and common undertaking. These I allow, are general Principles, however they are leading ones, and the Work will fail unless they are duly attended to.[50]

Philip Yorke's declared intention was, therefore, to promote a profitable enterprise. Generally speaking, since landowners in England and Wales were, first and foremost, rentiers and were not wholly dependent on the profits of direct farming, they were not renowned as agricultural producers. The home farm existed primarily to provide for the domestic needs of the landowner and his family, and to produce fodder for his animals, so that only the surplus stock and crops were sold.[51] Did Philip Yorke's home farm fit this description? As he hinted in his declaration, the time, with prices for agricultural produce rising, was propitious for an enterprising and potentially successful farmer.

The farm records cover only the years 1772-83 and are not entirely complete even for those. Fortunately, however, they include the period from 1772-79, when the home farm reached its maximum extent, with the acquisition of New Sontley and its addition to the Erthig demesne to form a working unit of between 310 and 363 acres.

Naturally there were fluctuations in the quantities of grain this produced. Weather conditions must have affected the output and, from time to time, the ratio between the three major crops altered, presumably in response to the demands of the estate and also,possibly, to market prices.

As Table 7 shows, wheat was usually the smallest of the three crops but its

Table 7 Production of grain on the Erthig estate, 1772-1783 (in measures) [52]				
YEAR	WHEAT	BARLEY	OATS	TOTAL
1772	283	444^1/2	*	-
1773	162^1/2	392^1/2	934^1/2	1489^1/2
1774	308^1/2	416	611^1/2	1336
1775	419	979	831^1/2	2229^1/2
1776	572^1/2	524^1/2	1206	2303
1777	927	870^1/2	1012^1/2	2810
1778	609	683^1/2	1120	2412^1/2
1779	560^1/2	1505	1451	3516^1/2
1780	339	569^1/2	304	1212^1/2
1781	*	1035	195^1/2	-
1782	*	*	273^1/2	-
1783	*	*	177^1/2	-
* Not recorded				

production appears to rise very sharply in these years, by nearly ninety per cent in 1774, showing at its peak in 1777 an increase of more than four hundred per cent over its 1773 figure, before it declined drastically.

Unfortunately, the true significance of these figures is obscured since they also include those for unspecified amounts of mung corn and rye. The recorded output of barley and oats follows a similar overall pattern, though the increase is less regular and does not reach its highest point until the bumper year of 1779 when barley shows a rise of three hundred per cent and oats of fifty-five per cent over their 1773 figures. The acreage devoted to arable may well have been increased in these years, since the total grain production in 1779 is over sixty-

Table 8: Consumption of grain on the Erthig estate, 1772-1783 (In measures)[53]				
YEAR	WHEAT	BARLEY	OATS	TOTAL
1772	215$^1/_2$	444$^1/_2$	*	
1773	125	392$^1/_2$	1251	1768$^1/_2$
1774	228$^1/_2$	416	1661	2305$^1/_2$
1775	219	428$^1/_2$	2002	2649$^1/_2$
1776	572$^1/_2$	442$^1/_2$	1847	2862
1777	459	568$^1/_2$	1482	2509$^1/_2$
1778	116$^1/_2$	437$^1/_2$	1739$^1/_2$	2293$^1/_2$
1779	172	709$^1/_2$	1451	2332$^1/_2$
1780	40$^1/_2$	202$^1/_2$	711$^1/_2$	954$^1/_2$
1781	*	289$^1/_2$	814$^1/_2$	
1782	*	*	957	
1783	*	*	674$^1/_2$	
* Not recorded				

six per cent higher than in 1773. If not, Philip Yorke's methods must have achieved a striking improvement in yield

The grain was produced mainly for consumption on the estate. Wheat was ground into three grades of flour, namely fine, second and third flours or, as they were termed in the Erthig records, fine, bolted and batch. Fine flour was preferred for making both bread and cakes, while the second and third flours, though they could be used for bread, were usually mixed with the finer variety for that purpose.[54] Small amounts of wheat were also ground for use in the farm house and some was kept for seed. Barley was used mainly for feeding fowls, pigs and dogs.

Any wheat and barley, surplus to the needs of Erthig, was sold, however, and the rise in output from 1775 onwards is high enough to suggest that these might have been grown specifically as cash crops from that date. Certainly their saleable value was substantial, ranging from £171 in 1775 to £294/19/- in 1779. In view of the desperate shortage of money which Philip Yorke revealed in his letters to his steward during these years such sums must have been very welcome. This is possibly the reason for the sale of such large percentages of wheat from 1778 to 1780, and of barley in 1780 and 1781. Nevertheless, it is difficult to account for the fact that no wheat and only 82 measures of barley were sold in 1776, realising a mere £16/8/-, even though the yield in both was quite heavy.

Though the quantity of oats in store was normally several times that of either wheat or barley, none was ever sold. In fact, save for one year, oats from the home farm were regularly supplemented by substantial purchases from tenants. Oats served a number of different purposes; primarily they were a fodder crop for a great many horses (coach, saddle, cart and militia company horses) and dogs, as well as much of the farm stock, cows, oxen and fowls. In addition, a substantial amount went to provide for the needs of the farm house

Table 9: Sales of grain at Erthig, 1772-1781[55]

YEAR	WHEAT			BARLEY			
	Measures sold	% sold	Value at 7/- per measure	Measures sold	% sold	Value at 4/-per measure	Total Value
1772	68	24	£23/16/-	-	-		£ 23/16/-
1773	37¹/₂	23	£13/2/-	-	-		£ 13/ 2/-
1774	80	26	£28/-/-	-	-		£ 28/-/-
1775	200	48	£70/-/-	550¹/₂	56	£101/-/-	£171/-/-
1776	-	-		82	16	£16/8/-	£16/8/-
1777	467¹/₂	50	£163/12/-	302	35	£60/8/-	£224/-/-
1778	492¹/₂	81	£172/7/-	246	36	£49/4/-	£221/11/-
1779	388¹/₂	69	£135/19/-	795¹/₂	53	£159/-/-	£294/19/-
1780	298¹/₂	88	£104/9/-	367	64	£73/8/-	£177/17/-
1781	*	*		745	72	£149/-/-	£149/-/-

* Not recorded

and some, of course, was reserved for seed. As a result, in six out of the eleven years for which figures are available, tenants supplied over half the oats required and when, after 1779, the total quantity was radically reduced, the proportion of the tenants' contribution rose to 70 per cent. or over, in three out of the four years recorded.

The stock records are even more fragmentary than those for crops. From the few available, however, some impression can be gained of animal husbandry at Erthig in the 1770s. In those five years, for which records exist, the total value of the stock rose steadily, as Table 11 shows. Unfortunately, in only two of these years was the stock categorised. In 1773 the cattle comprised 16 milking cows (in the summer, presumably), 5 three-year -old heifers, 3 yearlings, 1 bull calf, 2 other calves, 3 pairs of working oxen and 1 pair of three -year-old oxen. There were 3 cart-horses and 3 colts, 4 pigs and a flock of 30 wethers. The pattern was much the same in the following year.

Table 10: Percentage of annual consumption of oats purchased from tenants at Erthig, 1773-1783 (in measures) [56]

Year	Amount in granary	Amount supplied by tenants	Percentage
1773	1251	316¹/₂	25
1774	1661	1049¹/₂	63
1775	2002¹/₂	1171	58
1776	1847	640¹/₂	35
1777	1482	469¹/₂	32
1778	1739¹/₂	619¹/₂	35
1779	1451	None	-
1780	711¹/₂	407¹/₂	57
1781	957	683¹/₂	70
1783	674¹/₂	497	74

Table 11: Total value of stock on the home farm at Erthig, 1773-1777 [57]

YEAR	VALUE
1773	£301/12/-
1774	£477/15/-
1775	£613/6/-
1776	£688/9/2
1777	£863/12/-

Table 12: Value of animals slaughtered for meat at Erthig, 1773-1779 [58]

Type	1773	1774	1777	1778	1779
Cattle	£11/13/2	£2/16/6	£41/1/10	£10/18/9	£6/5/6
Sheep	£16/16/5^{1}/2	£22/17/9^{1}/2	£25/1/11^{1}/2	£16/9/9^{1}/2	£11/16/6^{1}/2
Pigs	£16/10/10^{1}/2	£10/13/8	£17/12/9^{1}/2	£27/8/11^{1}/2	£8/19/5

Table 13: Value of butter made and sold at Erthig, 1773-1774 [59]

Year	lbs.of butter made	Value	lbs.of butter sold	Value	% sold
1773	877	£27/1/4	187^{1}/2	£5/17/6	21
1774	947	£29/16/4^{1}/2	80	£2/15/-	8.5
1775	947^{1}/2	£30/1/3	236	£7/0/3^{1}/2	25
1776	1,066^{1}/2	£32/19/2^{1}/2	159	£5/5/11	15
1777	1,296	£39/0/8^{1}/2	*	£9/18/0^{1}/2	approx.25 (to judge by price)

* Not recorded

Table 14: Cheese made at Erthig, 1775-1778 [60]

Year	Best(Value)	Skim (Value)
1775	£21/15/-	£4/13/1^{1}/2
1776	£37/10/-	£5/8/9
1777	£26/19/11	£4/19/-
1778	£50/4/3	£4/0/7

A number of animals were sold but these were usually described as 'old' and, in any case,were replaced by others. The main purpose of stock-raising was to supply meat for Erthig, but the farm records provide only the value of the animals slaughtered and not the number or, in most cases, the weight of individual beasts. Such prices as are given seem to have been almost identical for beef and mutton (none are recorded for pork) and, at between 3d. and 4d. per pound, indicate that enormous quantities of meat were consumed,though there was great variation from year to year.

The milking herd fluctuated in number according to the season. In the period between June and the beginning of October it usually included fifteen to twenty cows, but only four to eight during the winter months.[61] The accounts, admittedly scrappy, do not record that many of these surplus cows were sold or slaughtered in the autumn, though the latter would be the usual practice. The alternative would be to winter them elsewhere but there is no indication of this either, and it does not seem a likely practice for a farm in Erthig's situation. The output of the herd was used, either as milk or cream, by the squire and his household, or as skimmed milk for the labourers. In addition, butter was made and, in summer, potted for winter use. The butter records give the quantities used in Erthig Hall itself and in the farm house, both the amount potted and that which was sold.

Some of the milk was used to make two grades of cheese, namely 'best' and 'skim'. As Table 14 shows, the value of the former grade far outweighed the latter but, since only the worth was recorded and skim cheese would obviously be cheaper, it is impossible to determine the proportion of the total production which fell into each category. It is not clear, either, whether any of the cheese was actually sold or its value merely computed for the farm records.

As far as horses are concerned the picture is complicated by the presence in the stables of additional animals for limited periods. In 1773, for instance, the temporary additions (with the cost of their keep) included,

	£ . s . d
June Philip Yorke's horse for 3 weeks	. 12. 0
October Gentlemen's 2 horses for 3 weeks	1. 4. 0
Militia Company's horses -5 for 10 weeks	10. 0. 2
Coach horses; Philip Yorke's horse	6. 0. 0
December Philip Yorke's horse for 9 weeks &	5. 8. 0
2 Company horses for 9 weeks 4 Gentlemen's horses for 5 weeks	4. 0. 0
	27. 4. 0
(The account also listed): 15 horses for 52 weeks	156. 0. 2
8 oxen employed in the meadows for 6 months at £5 a month	30. 0. 0
	Total 240. 8. 2 [62]

John Caesar also drew up a list of "Unprofitable and Waggon Horses Kept on the Farm" in 1774:

		. s. d
March	Hay for Gentlemen's 2 horses for 3 weeks	1. 4. 0
October	8 oxen in meadows for 4 months and 1 week	21. 5. 0
November	Hay for 5 Gentlemen's horses for 23 weeks	23. 0. 0
	2 Coach Horses for 24 weeks	9. 12. 0
December	Philip Yorke's horse for 29 weeks	5. 16. 0
	12 Cart horses for 52 weeks	124. 16. 0
	4 Saddle horses for 52 weeks	41. 12. 0
		227. 5. 0[63]

Horses therefore represented to the estate a considerable expense. It is interesting to note that in these years, 1773 and 1774, sales of farm produce were negligible, whereas, later in the decade, sales of grain would have risen to a point where they would have off-set such an expenditure on horses. After 1779, however, when the farm shrank to its original size, a number of horses were likely to have become redundant and the sharp drop in the consumption of oats seems to confirm this, though the crop, of course, provided fodder for other animals too.

How far did Philip Yorke himself practice what he preached in the husbandry clauses of his tenants' leases? The evidence on which to base a verdict is thin and confined to one year, 1773, the first full year of the enlarged farm. All one can safely conclude is that some at least of the current good farming practices were observed, as the farming calendar for that year shows.

Erthig Farming Calendar for May - December, 1773[64]

MONTH	ACTIVITIES
May	Teams carrying lime, sowing barley.
June/July	Ploughing and fallowing Turnip ground. Ploughing and spreading lime on Summer Fallow. Carrying hay and clover.
August	Mowing oats, reaping wheat.
September	Carrying wheat, corn, liming, ploughing Summer Fallow.
October	Sowing wheat in summer fallow.
November/December	Ploughing, spreading lime, ploughing for barley.

There is little evidence of attempts to improve the quality of stock during the 1770s and early 1780s. As far as cattle are concerned, there are several references to Scotch heifers being bought, sold[65], or killed[66]; otherwise Philip Yorke seemed to own a random mixture of animals drawn from a surprisingly wide range of locations, though this could represent an attempt to improve the stock by introducing other strains. The only comprehensive list available dates from 1785 when the home farm enterprise had passed its peak.

Large Newnham Cow, Oswestry Red Cow, Old Daudle, Young Daudle, Erthig Old Red Cow, Small Newnham heifer, Oswestry Pide Cow, Newnham Black Cow, old Alderney Cow from Newnham, heifer from Newcastle, 10 yearlings from Leek, 1 Bull from Staffordshire.[67]

The number of cows from Newnham is yet another illustration of Philip

Table 15: Erthig Home Farm accounts, 1773-1779		
YEAR	CASH RECEIVED	CASH PAID
1773	£79/4/2	£392/13/5[68]
1777	£511/11/4	£695/1/1[69]
1778	£594/4/2	£503/17/10[70]
1779	£632/0/6	£545/9/0[71]

Yorke's readiness to utilise the resources of one of his outlying properties for the benefit of his main estate at Erthig. To the same end, the occasional load of wheat, oats or barley would make the perilous journey from Dyffryn Aled to Erthig.[72] In the 1790s Dyffryn Aled was to supply a base for Philip Yorke's experiment to improve the breed of sheep.[73]

Did he succeed in his declared intention of promoting a profitable enterprise? Again, on the available evidence, it is difficult to reach a firm conclusion. The figures in Table 15, perhaps, tell their own story.

At best, therefore, it would seem that Philip Yorke's home farm project began shakily and then barely succeeded in paying its way by the late 70s.

In view of the fact that landowners generally preferred to rent out their lands rather than to tie up their capital in running a home farm,[74] it is, perhaps, a mark of Philip Yorke's venturesome spirit that he should have chosen to retain such a large demesne from 1772 to 1779, especially since his profit margins, for the most part, were so small and hardly to be compared with his income from rents. As we have seen, however, his zeal was invariably tempered with caution and, as he had stated to John Caesar in 1772, he would have to judge from the accounts the exact degree of profit and loss "so I may know to retire in time and not Blunder on to my great disadvantage".[75] By 1779 he must have decided that his profits were too low to justify his continuing to pay the labour and other costs of maintaining such a substantial home farm since he let New Sontley and its demesne to Charles and Thomas Bowen, a total of 201 acres for £245 a year, to which were added another 96 acres of Crabmill land in 1781, all for an annual rent of £313. Thus his Erthig demesne reverted to 144 acres.[76]

The winding-down process affected, it seems, all areas of the farm. Production and consumption of all three crops declined radically in 1780, though barley recovered in 1781. The demand for oats fell to about half that of the previous year, suggesting a reduction in stock. This was certainly true of the milking herd. In 1775 the number of cows in the winter varied between four and six, and rose to sixteen in the summer. By the following year there were between four and six in the summer, and by 1780 only two or three in the winter. All this meant that less labour would be needed and Table 16 illustrates this decline.

Philip Yorke's decision to retire in time has to be viewed in the context of his precarious financial situation. Unlike his neighbours, the Wilkinson, Wynne, Myddleton and Grosvenor families, he made no serious attempt to bolster his

Table 16: Cost of labour at Erthig, 1773-1782	
YEAR	COST OF LABOUR
1773	£124/18/2
1775	£115/4/8
1776	£126/13/10
1779	£98/2/8
1780	£61/16/1
1781	£26/7/4
1782	£26/18/11$\frac{1}{2}$[77]

finances by exploiting the mineral resources of his estate. He chose, rather, to follow the example set by his predecessors at Erthig whose participation in industrial activity had been minimal.[78] Both Philip Yorke and his father probably lacked the capital to make the necessary investment in a large scale enterprise. There are two references in the records to some slight interest and involvement in mining, but these occur towards the end of his life.[79] He was also involved in a legal dispute over royalties from a lead mine in Flintshire but there is no record of the outcome of this litigation.[80] The few surviving records also suggest that Philip Yorke was not very concerned with the transport developments of his day. In 1793 he applied for a £1,000 subscription in the Ellesmere canal but his account book shows only one payment of £50 in 1795.[81] His name appears as a trustee of only one turnpike trust.[82]

It would seem reasonable to conclude, therefore, that Philip Yorke's main interest, like that of many others of his class, lay in the realm of farming and it says much for his enthusiasm that his experiences did not stifle the venturesome side of his nature and prevent him, years later, from participating as an 'experimental' farmer in a scheme to improve the breeding of sheep in different parts of England and Wales.

CHAPTER 7: Peripheral Properties

1770 had been a good year for Philip Yorke as far as his own and his family's fortunes were concerned; he had inherited Newnham manor and married Elizabeth Cust. 1782 was destined to be another favourable year when he married his second wife Diana Meyrick and so acquired a life interest in Dyffryn Aled, her estate in Llansannan, situated some forty miles from Erthig.

James Hutton had bequeathed Newnham manor, together with the smaller estate of Radwell in Hertfordshire, to his nephew, and his house in Park Lane to his sister Dorothy. [1] The house would revert to Philip Yorke on her death, which occurred in 1787. The Newnham estate, however, was encumbered with a number of legacies to various individuals.[2] The surviving material will not support a detailed analysis of the financial situation of the Newnham estate. This included three farms (two of them over 300 acres) and twelve cottages, while Radwell had two farms (each over 240 acres) and two cottages.[3] However, from the records that do remain, we learn that the gross rental for 1779 was £1,064,[4] while a document of 1804 gave the figure for 1795 as around £1,000 which had, due to the efforts of a Mr. Crowther from Yorkshire, increased by the latest date to £1,355/10/-.[5] The only documents dating from Philip Yorke's time gave the acreages as 865 for Newnham and 331 for Radwell, a total of 1,196.[6] There was a tendency among landowners who had acquired, through inheritance or marriage, a property remote from the historic core of the family estate, to look upon it as peripheral and subordinate. In the initial stages, particularly, of his ownership of Newnham, Philip Yorke appeared to regard it as a treasure house from which to enrich his property at Erthig. On April 6th, 1771 he wrote to John Caesar,

> As I have let my Newnham farms, I hope you will be ready within a month to receive a waggon and six horses. If you can recolect anything from Newnham farm which may be of use to Erthig, and will not be very heavy Conveyance, you will remind me of it in your next.[7]

On May 11th, he told his steward to expect a team from Newnham:

> There are many things of value and consequence contained; and you will of course be very careful in unloading and in placing them in proper places in the House - yr mistress has written long orders in Relation to that Business - Pray see that no Boxes be cast aside and lost but lay them all carefully by ... .[8]

Not surprisingly, an observer at Newnham reported to John Caesar,

> ... I think you would hardly know Newnham, now the Cupola is taken down,

and the house stript of its furniture, tho' here there is still plenty of good things, surely Erthig is very full at present?[9]

The transfer of material possessions from Newnham to Erthig included more than valuable furnishings and *objets d'art*. A number of cows made the long journey and, in 1775, Philip Yorke informed John Caesar that he had got rid of his team of horses, except for a number which were disabled and those which he had sent to Erthig because he had no use for them at the time. He had considered selling his stock and had actually sold his hay, but had kept his corn which, he said, would soon require horses to harvest. Accordingly, he instructed John Caesar to send to Newnham by August 12th, five horses, namely two horses belonging to his mother, and Old Lion, Kicking Gilberd and Ball, accompanied by a man and a boy. He could not spare any of his own Erthig workers, so the man and the boy would have to be especially chosen for the assignment. "… Cannot you pick out a man and a Boy (both talking English) within your Knowledge and sufficiency, and not immediately at present in our service … ." When the horses returned to Erthig in September they would be employed to carry "a large load of Goods" back from Newnham. Philip Yorke also planned to "… send down from Newnham Chains and Pullies very well contrived for the drawing and raising large Pieces of of Timber, and which will be of better and more frequent use with us, than in Hertfordshire …."[10]

Philip Yorke kept the same close surveillance over the activities of his steward at Newnham, William Simkins, as he did over John Caesar. His notebook contained a heading for April 21st, 1775, "Memorandums in Passing the Yearly Newnham Accts. of the Year 1774". He noted, for example:

> For 1775, Mastr. Payne and Mastr. Phillipps to agree with them to sow seed the last yr of their term with their corn. Pay them for the seed and trouble - Mastr. Phillipps, Dove house considd.
>
> For July 26th, 1775, To Mrs. Phillipps … To write tenderly that I hope for the time to come she will be more attentive to her lease … hedges cleared; to avoid cross-cropping according to particulars which I shall not at present observe in Hopes of amendment.

Similar entries were made for later years – "Agree with Cowper, who comes to the Golden Lion St. John Street wheat delivered to Wrexham waggon", he wrote in 1776. In 1778, he reminded himself "To write to Mr. French that if Barziller's [?] pump will not do, Sim [i.e. Simkins] may have that from the dairy". [?][11]

One lease appears to have survived from Philip Yorke's time; it is an agreement signed on July 13th, 1771, with Zachariah Moule, for a farm at Newnham for a term of nine years at £360 a year.[12] Its clauses resemble very closely those of Philip Yorke's Erthig leases, except that the tenant was permitted to grow crops for two successive years rather than three as in the Erthig agreements. Failure to comply with this ruling would result in an addition of £10 to the rent. Apart from this stipulation, the husbandry covenant

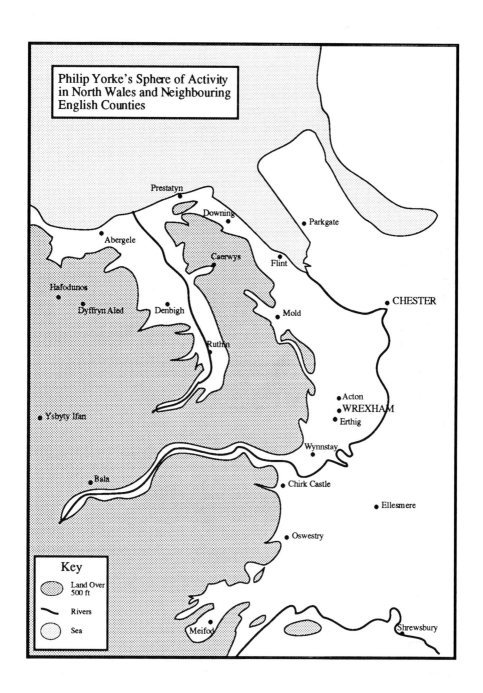

Philip Yorke's Sphere of Activity
in North Wales and Neighbouring
English Counties

Prestatyn

Downing

Parkgate

Abergele

Caerwys

Flint

Hafodunos

CHESTER

Dyffryn Aled

Denbigh

Mold

Ruthin

Acton

WREXHAM

Ysbyty Ifan

Erthig

Wynnstay

Bala

Chirk Castle

Ellesmere

Oswestry

Key

Land Over
500 ft

Rivers

Sea

Meifod

Shrewsbury

in the lease was, oddly enough, much vaguer than the equivalent clauses in Erthig leases. In an agriculturally progressive county like Hertfordshire one would expect a rotation of two year blocks, of the kind advocated in East Anglia, but there is no information in contemporary Newnham papers which shows how closely this was followed in practice. When Zachariah Moule's lease came up for renewal, Philip Yorke reminded himself,

> ... Must send notice to Moule of quitting before Xmas 1779, if I mean he should go out at Michas. 1780 when his lease expires. At all events must write at end of 1779 to give me an acct. of the £30 to be expended the last 3 years on good Manure and that I expect all the Manure he has on his yards may be there (?) before 1780 ...[13]

When, thirteen years later, a new lease had to be drawn up with Elizabeth Moule, Zachariah's widow, it is clear that Philip Yorke was trying to exercise the same care as he gave to his affairs nearer home when, with his own hand, he drew up an agreement for Mrs. Moule to sign:

> I agree with my landlord Philip Yorke Esqr to conduct the farm I hold under him at Newnham according to the rules and conditions of the lease formerly granted to my husband, Mr. Zachariah Moule ... and paying for the same the rent of four hundred pounds a year to commence from Michaelmas 1793 Mr. Yorke allowing me to cut and dispose of the wood of more hedges than are allowed by that lease on condition that I protect with proper fences for three years the said hedges so to be cut, the quantity of such extraordinary cutting shall previous to such cutting be set out by the said Philip Yorke or his Agent for the time being.[14]

To judge from the alleged behaviour of certain individuals at Newnham, Philip Yorke's vigilance was thoroughly justified. Since the evidence is limited in scope and in time (relating mainly to the period 1784-87), it is difficult to gauge whether the attitudes described were typical of the majority of the tenants. Nevertheless, William Simkins, the agent, presented a depressing view when he wrote on July 7th, 1784 to Philip Yorke,

> If Moule, or any of the tenants should write to you again about Repairs or plough Timber, I wish you to be Carefull how you answer them, for they are scheming to get you with measures that you will very much suffer by, and I am sure if you give way on any of these points you will find in time they will fritter away your Estate more than you may think for just at first.[15]

William Simkins himself was not too happy with his lot. He complained at length that Philip Yorke had reduced his wages by £30 a year in 1771 and had failed to keep his promise to reward him for his labours in running Radwell Grange farm before it was let to a new tenant, "... for I cannot work for nothing now for my comings in will not maintain my Family ..."[16] He complained further in September that,

> I have managed the Farm since it fell into your hands to the best of my judgement & I am sure that's as sound & as able as any man's in the

Neighbourhood to manage any Farm. Though I have been so unfortunate to give up the Farm I had yet hope for another Chance for the sake of my Children.[17]

Philip Yorke's reaction to these grievances is not recorded, but in the 1804 Newnham Rental William Simkins was listed as renting a farm for £60 a year. [18]

John Sampson, a substantial tenant paying £265 a year for his farm in 1804,[19] caused a great deal of consternation. The rent of a poor family, the Lawmans, dwelling in a cottage on Philip Yorke's estate, had been paid by the parish until John Sampson's arrival on the scene. As an overseer he had refused to pay the Lawmans' rent and instead had offered to certify the family's removal to another parish. When William Simkins, following Philip Yorke's instructions, brought the matter to the notice of a local Justice of the Peace,

> ... he told me they had nothing to do in such a case. Mr.Yorke should a been more carefull how he took such a Tenant in as Mr. Sampson ... The Gentleman Treated me very civil & look over his Law Books to see if he could get at Sampson but he said he thought that they could not & seemd surprised that a Tenant dare act in such a manner to his Landlord. I am sure Sampson is a Compleat bad man.[20]

Fortunately, two of the other more prosperous tenants volunteered to pay the rent of a family who "Can't earn enough to get a belly full of bread only."[21] One of these, a Mr. Payne, complained to William Simkins that John Sampson was "destroying the sward Baulks & stocking up the Bushes in the great out Field," and cutting down willow trees before they had died. When the steward remonstrated with him "he only damnd. me." William Simkins asked Philip Yorke to deal with the matter on his next visit to the estate. He also asked him not to mention Mr. Payne's information if he wrote to John Sampson, "for very likely Sampson may abuse him sometime at market about it."[22]

In addition to the truculent Sampson there were problems with a Mr. Froggatt who "has not used you well in many little things," cutting and burning his hedges, and selling his year's supply of dung to another tenant.[23]

The perpetual advowson and right of presentation to the living of Newnham was vested in the owner of the manor[24] and one of Philip Yorke's greatest problems was the Vicar, John Festing, who suffered bouts of insanity which forced him to spend periods in hospital.[25] The surviving correspondence was addressed to Simon Yorke in 1805, but a number of comments show that his father had had to endure the vicar's erratic behaviour. On October 3rd., 1805, for instance, Simon Yorke, writing about him to the Bishop of London, remarked,

> The situation of this unfortunate man certainly claims great compassion, but I was sorry to observe in him a very malignant mind towards my late father. [26]

The main burden of the vicar's complaint was that, as the head of a family of six children "and likely to have more", his yearly stipend should be raised from £65 to £100, and the vicar's traditional rights to common pasture for two cows and to a piece of land on which to keep a horse should be restored. He needed the horse to service the two curacies he was compelled to hold in order to make ends meet, and the cows to provide milk for his large family.[27]

> Milk has been an uncommon scarce thing in our House. This I think is very hard; & your Tenants would rather throw it to their Hogs, than let us have it. The Cottages have had milk all along. Surely I think Sir, you can in Justice insist upon it, that they let my Family have what they want.

He asked for an increase in his income, which he claimed Philip Yorke had promised him, and said that his plight "is poor Encouragement for a Clergyman & one that has had an expensive Education."[28] On October 2nd, 1805 he wrote to Simon Yorke again claiming that he had been verbally abused by William Simkins:

> He called me a dirty shit, & a dirty Bitch ... This is the Treatment we have received repeatedly from that man, and his Family. I will give you an Idea of the Man just before your Father died. I heard him say that your Father would go to Hell, and be damned for turning him out of his House, and not provide him with another ...[29]

If these are not simply the delusions of mental illness, they suggest that William Simkins continued to harbour resentment against his employer in spite of the long relationship between them. The tone of his remarks in his letters to Philip Yorke are perhaps symptomatic of the decline of traditional habits of deference to the upper classes which, it has been suggested, occurred in the later years of the eighteenth century.[30] These individual cases, and perhaps others too, would have been a continuing source of anxiety, especially in view of the distance between Erthig and Newnham. Whatever the problems, however, the 1804 survey of the Newnham and Radwell estates reported that "All the Farms are in excellent cultivation & the Buildings too."[31]

It is interesting to compare Philip Yorke's handling of Newnham and Radwell with that of Dyffryn Aled and the lands in Yorkshire and the south of England which he acquired by his marriage to Diana Meyrick in 1782. Prior to that, his financial situation, after a decade and more of heavy expenditure, was, as we have seen, very unsound.

Diana, whom he married in Llansannan in 1782, was the daughter of Piers and Margaret Wynn, a family descended from Marchudd ap Cynan, chief of one of the Noble Tribes of Wales.[32] From her father she had inherited Dyffryn Aled, the family seat in the uplands of west Denbighshire, and from her first husband, Owen Ridgeway Meyrick,[33] to whom she was married from 1771 until his death in 1773, an estate in south Yorkshire and some land in Devon, Dorset and Wiltshire.[34] She was, in fact, a considerable heiress and once again fortune appeared to have smiled on Philip Yorke, as he explained to the Earl of Hardwicke on September 29th, 1782.

> As your Lordship hath always most kindly distinguished me by your regards, and attention, I persuade myself to think that any Event which essentially serves

Dyffryn Aled by Moses Griffith. [Erddig – The National Trust]

my Fortunes and gives me the fairest prospects of Happiness, will not be uninteresting to you; and I therefore take the liberty of informing your Lordship of my marriage last Thursday to a lady of most respectable Character and Property in this County, of the name of Meyrick; and one, that in her Person, and manners, is moreover peculiarly agreeable to me.[35]

In so far as one can rely on her portrait which is to be seen at Erthig, her face was attractive but, according to Nimrod, she did not possess an elegant figure. He also commented on her "extreme plainness of attire".[36] As to her character, she had an "extremely benevolent disposition," but unfortunately "the good nature of this lady bordered upon weakness." Nimrod also accused her of indolence, superstition and false humility. At the same time, however, his description of an evening spent at Erthig in the company of Philip and Diana Yorke emphasised the easy-going, amiable relationship between the two. "At the end of a long discussion of some theological theme, Philip Yorke said, 'Well, Di, you certainly have much sense; but, I am sorry to say, still more of nonsense'. A good-humoured smile from his amiable partner was the usual result of these harmless rebukes, never intended to provoke ought but a smile."[37]

On a more mundane level, the alliance had its advantages. The figures quoted in the marriage settlement of September 25th, 1782 showed that Dyffryn Aled produced a gross yearly income of £1,405/14/1 and the Yorkshire estate £785/12/1.[38] A surviving rental book shows that for 1790 and 1791 the figures for Dyffryn Aled remained much the same at £1,468 and £1,451 respectively, minus arrears of £185 and £168.[39]

The 1782 marriage settlement presented an opportunity for Philip Yorke to settle his affairs anew and to put the inheritance on a secure footing. In particular, it would enable him to establish the relationship of Newnham (not included in his 1770 marriage settlement) *vis-a-vis* Erthig. Having stated that Newnham was to be settled on Philip Yorke for life, the settlement arranged for the Trustees to raise certain sums of money charged to the estate for any offspring of the marriage.[40] Thus burdened with such heavy encumbrances, it was obvious that Newnham's role as defined in the settlement was to serve the interests of Erthig, and when Simon Yorke became squire in 1804 this process was to be carried a step further.

Meanwhile, his wife's properties would appear at first sight to have constituted valuable assets to Philip Yorke at a time when his financial situation was causing concern. But there were problems. The major drawback of marrying an heiress was that there was no guarantee that her properties would become a permanent addition to her husband's estate, and her lands were indeed settled on him for life only; thereafter, the succession reverted to any children of this, his second marriage.[41] Other, more immediate, difficulties were the direct result of his wife's extravagant lifestyle during her widowhood. A series of letters written to her between 1777 and 1780 by her friend and agent William Lally[42] reveal the precarious nature of her finances, and at the same time reinforce Nimrod's impressions. William Lally's estimate of her debts varied from year to year, but he left her in no doubt about her overall financial position.

The root cause of her problems was the splendid mansion she was having built for herself at Dyffryn Aled on a wooded hillside above the old house. The architect of the main block was Joseph Turner (also involved in the alterations at Erthig),[43] and the interiors and flanking pavilions were by John Woolfe, co-author of the later volumes of *Vitruvius Britannicus*.[44] Thomas Pennant recorded that the day the workmen finished building, the entire facing of Portland stone, thirty tons of which had been shipped from Bristol to Conway and conveyed overland to Llansannan, fell off and had to be replaced at great expense.[45] On October 31st, 1777, William Lally wrote "…I had no conception till I saw it what a place you had built…" Later in the same letter he added.

> I dont suppose you co^d live at Dyffryn Aled with your present number of servants & finishing & furnishing but a small part of the house under £1,000 or £1,100 a year & if you finished it all it wod. cost you double your Income to live in it … . I wish to God I had seen it & known what it was & what was doing at ye farmyard before you began ye wings. I much fear that if you dont stop soon you will sadly repent it. I wish you wod consider whether the wings and part of ye body had not best rest as they are for ye present.[46]

Mr. Lally's pleas appear to have fallen on deaf ears. On April 30th, 1778 he wrote,

... my heart aches whenever I think of your immense house ... pardon my anxiety my dear Madam wch prompts me to say that if you think of finishing and furnishing more than 2 rooms & a few bedrooms, £4000 a year wod. not be enough to maintain your establishment. I wish to God you wod. leave all the rest as it is; for many thousands wod not complete it, & to what end shod you furnish rooms, to be locked up, your debt is at present so considerable that any increase would distress you exceedingly.

He went on to calculate that with her annual interest payment of £693 on her debt of £14,400 and an annuity of £100 a year, with a maximum possible income of £1,300 from her Yorkshire estates and, he estimated, £1,200 from her Dyffryn Aled estate (minus £217 for repairs), her "certain income" would be approximately £1,600 a year.[47] The marriage settlement two years later put her debts at £15,323 and, as we have seen, her income from Dyffryn Aled at £1,405/14/1 and from her Yorkshire estates at £785/12/1.[48] Despite the discrepancies,there is no doubting the extent of her indebtedness. William Lally, continuing to give wise, 'fatherly' advice, suggested a number of possible solutions, encompassing a more frugal life-style with fewer excursions around the country, fewer servants and workmen, and the keeping of careful accounts, as this desperate letter urged:

Pray calculate your Expence for the last year as soon as you get home & see whether 'tis not greater than yr Income exclusive of building & get Mr. Gosling to help you. I know you can do it very accurately, ... if you have not done it yet, I beg you will begin it the day you get home for if you dont keep an accot (by doing wch alone you can see yr Expence) you will be ruined before you know it, pray read this last side every Sunday, when you say your prayers till you have begun the accot ... .

Other suggestions included selling her corn and cattle to meet current expenses, rather than borrowing more, and letting out the bulk of her demesne cheaply. Finally, seemingly in utter despair, he wrote,

I wish to God, you cod get a husband of £40 or £50,000 in his pocket to set you rich ... [49]

Perhaps this desire coloured his descriptions of her in two letters to Philip Yorke shortly before their marriage. The first on March 19th, 1782, described Diana Meyrick in the most glowing terms.

I am sorry to hear, that tho' the widow looks very handsome, she looks very shy... she is a most excellent and amiable Creature & had no fault in a wife but being too fond of her husband, a very unfashionable failing ... if you can win her you will gain a treasure.[50]

Three weeks later he declared,

... was I young & single with a million a year & a Dukedom I know not a woman whose alliance I shod more Covet ... there is no woman I more sincerely love, without being in love ...

However, it seems that his desperate anxiety for the match was tempered by a desire to be fair to Philip Yorke, for he goes on to warn him that this "inestimable treasure" was likely to be too soft with any children they might have. Even more surprisingly, he warned the prospective bridegroom to give careful attention to the terms of the marriage settlement which he himself was to draw up.[51] Having asked Philip Yorke to let him have certain details about the estate, he then wrote,

> ... give me leave to suggest an Idea for her and your consideration, viz. to consider your Hertfordshire Est. and her Jointure Estates as funds to disincumber your other Estates in the first place & then to provide for younger children and having thereby a prospect of the elder branch of both families having each a clear Estate, for a great house & great Rental with a load of incumbrance is really leading a young man, into the distruction of his fortune, & happiness ... .[52]

These points were enshrined in the marriage settlement which stipulated that Dyffryn Aled should be settled on Philip Yorke for life, with the remainder to his first and other sons by Mrs. Meyrick, then to their daughters; that the encumbrances of the Dyffryn Aled estate were to be borne by her jointure estates in Yorkshire, from which she would also draw £200 a year 'pin money', and that the Hertfordshire estates of Philip Yorke, as we have seen, would be charged with the responsibility for raising portions for any children of the marriage.[53]

Diana Meyrick's distant jointure estates were thus subordinated to the financial interests of Dyffryn Aled just as the Newnham estate was to those of Erthig.

Entries in one of Philip Yorke's notebooks reveal that in the year following his second marriage he was taking an active interest in the Dyffryn Aled estate.

> Tho. Hughes of Hirwen says that there is a tree in dispute between us, and Davies of Llanbedr; to see the same, when we go to Mrs. Greens. Wm Jones of Fryth, Flintshire, has a promise of having some Repairs done. John Davies of Kilken complains that his Barn is out of Repair. I have given notice to Edwd Lloyd of Hengoed to quit his Tenement, unless he makes up his Rent to Michas. 1782 on the 1st of May, 1783. Edwd Jones of Carregfynydd promises to pay his Arrear of that Tenement in a week; and to pay the Mill Rent the day the twelvemonth is up, viz. 5 days before may-day...

He mentioned eight tenants who had promised to pay their arrears, one tenant who was to have a Stone Barn Floor, "... The tenant to carry the stone, and not to cost above 18 or 20 shillings ...", and he also promised to examine the state of the river at Cegor, and "to examine exactly the Smith's Bills."[54]

Dyffryn Aled, like his Hertfordshire estate, was made to serve the needs of Erthig. A significant comment on his financial situation in the early eighties appeared in a letter of October 23rd, 1783 to Brownlow Cust. He informed him that a Mr. Gestlin, Diana Meyrick's second cousin, had left her, quite unexpectedly, £4,000 in Old South Sea Stock and the reversion of seventy pounds Pr. Ann ...a pretty addition in these reducing Times."[55] These "reducing times" caused him, as we have seen, to prune his home farm at Erthig, and he sought to compensate for the loss of produce by raiding Dyffryn Aled as he had previously plundered Newnham. The Erthig accounts show the significance of the contributions it received from there. In 1782 it provided the total supply of wheat (102 measures). In the following two years it accounted for 175 out of 204, and 135 out of 205 measures of barley respectively, while in 1785 the total delivery of oats (141^1/2 measures) was also from Dyffryn Aled.[56]

The combined resources of Dyffryn Aled and Erthig served to support the only truly experimental work in the sphere of farming which can be ascribed to Philip Yorke. Attempts to increase the size of sheep and the length of the wool staple had a long ancestry, but the development of scientific, selective breeding belonged to the eighteenth century. Though the main emphasis, to cater for the needs of the time, was placed on the carcase of the sheep, considerable attention was also given to the quality of the wool. Many argued that fine wool was needed to provide for the weaving industry.[57] Attempts to improve the quality of the fleece were greatly encouraged by the arrival in the 1780s of the Merino sheep, producers of wool of the finest staple in Europe.[58] The idea underlying much of the experimentation pursued by landowners like Philip Yorke was that a British ewe crossed by a Merino ram and her female progeny then mated back to Merino blood for three more generations would produce a British Merino possessing both the fleece quality of the Spanish sheep and the virtues of its British ancestry.[59]

Philip Yorke's involvement in this field came about through his association with Sir Joseph Banks, landowner, botanist, agricultural scientist, President of the Royal Society from 1778-1820 and of the Royal Merino Society from 1811-20, and with Colonel Robert Fulke Greville, equerry and Groom of the Bedchamber to King George III. The two men were the prime movers in the efforts to introduce the merino sheep to Britain and to promote the subsequent experiments in breeding with native flocks.[60] The nature of the association is not clear but, whatever it was, Philip Yorke's name had been put forward by R.F. Greville in August 1784, as someone who was to receive rams from the King's Spanish flock of over 150 sheep in the Little Park at Windsor Castle.[61] George III gave orders that Spanish rams not needed for the use of his experimental flock were to be distributed to landowners who were keen to improve the local breeds.[62] Some North Wales squires, including Philip Yorke, were among the recipients.[63] His claim had originally been put forward by Lord Walsingham, and R.F. Greville had acted as go-between. On August 27th, 1794, Philip Yorke replied to Lord Walsingham's letter from Weymouth and asked him to convey his thanks to the King for the present of the Rams. He went on to say,

> I wish I may be able in any degree to forward His Majesty's gracious and benevolent dispositions to this Principality; a great many sheep are bred on an Estate, I have, among the mountains in the upper part of this County; and as yet

they have had very little choice or delicacy in the article of their Rams, and it is supposed they have failed much on that account ... [64]

Following Sir Joseph Banks' suggestion, Philip Yorke sent a horse and covered cart to Windsor for the two rams, instead of entrusting them to the "Wrexham waggon, which sets out from the Blossoms Inn, Laurence Lane, every Saturday at noon, and arrives the Saturday following at Wrexham".[65] He informed Banks that the rams had reached Erthig safe and well after more than a fortnight's journey.

I wish I knew what the best, to make of them; I have bought a lot of Shropshire Ewes whose wool seems most to assimilate to theirs, and I have also a lot of Mountain sheep to cross with them. I shall keep a strict account of the Event ...[66]

His letter to R.F. Greville dated October 16th, 1794 showed that he had resolved his previous doubts and was now on surer ground. At the same time, his comments on the subject of sheep-rearing are an indication of his efforts to become conversant with its attendant problems.

It is my anxious desire, as far as in me lies, to make his Majesty's very gracious and generous intention towards Wales, of very real efficacy in that Country, and I will spare no pains in my small compass, to that effect. I had thirty maiden Ewes brought down from my flock in the upper Country (as we call the upper hills of Denbighshire) to meet the rams at Erthig, and I had sent for another sett from Shropshire, but what number came I have not yet learnt; however I will fill up this year to the number you mention. They have just put the Tupps to the Ewes in this Country, You give me Sir, great hopes on your own experience of the Welsh Cross; sheep fed as in Spain, on short dry mountains, and such we have, will I apprehend, breed the finest wool; whilst on the contrary, high, rich and artificial grasses will coarsen it; but in some Counties, as in this, fineness, I understand, is not the object. I will attend to the cleaness of the fleece, and endeavour to avoid too much pitch on marking, and I shall wish to keep the flock hereafter in the cold weather on the South, and in the Summer, on the North side of the hills; we have a choice in each situation, and to shew them some tenderness in the Winter. If I should find on my return to Wales, that I could spread the advantage by the prospect of one or two more rams, I will again take the liberty of worrying you.[67]

In 1795 Philip Yorke received six more rams and in 1797 six ewes, thus enabling him to become a ram breeder himself with the pure Spanish stock.[68] It was typical of him that he should have tried to fill in a questionnaire which Joseph Banks had circulated. Doubts about the success of the experiment had obviously crept in, however.

The weight of Carcass in the Spanish Rams will be no very great advantage to the farmers of this country, as there are Rams in this and the adjoining Counties of greater weight than the Spanish, and hardier in their Nature, but there appears in the Spanish a stronger inclination to feed than any sorts we have in this neighbourhood, when kept on inclosed ground. The greatest benefit to be expected from this breed is in the superior fine quality of the wool, altho' at present the people of this country are ignorant of the real value of it, and will give but little more for it than the comn wool, and the quantity being as yet too small to induce a manufacturer of fine cloths to come into the Country to buy it. – It appears evident that the Spanish breed are too tender, and their wool too short to enable them to stand the cold climate of the Welch Mountains, but may answer extremely well on low comns & enclosed lands of Midling quality.[69]

In February, 1799, to provide more information on the results of his Cambro-Spanish sheep experiment, he sent Joseph Banks a piece of broadcloth, seventeen and a half yards long, manufactured in Chester from a mixture of wool from the Welsh mountain and Spanish cross. The manufacturer had complained about the waste; he had expected to make twenty yards from the fifty pounds he had taken. Joseph Banks thought that the waste was due to the fleeces being "ill washd", and said he was pleased to hear that Philip Yorke would have someone from the Delamere forest to superintend his clip in the following year. He offered to renew the Spanish blood in Philip Yorke's breed.[70]

Philip Yorke's friendship with Walter Davies, so fruitful in another context, [71] no doubt helped to earn him an honourable reference in the latter's *Report on the Agriculture of North Wales*. In 1797, while Walter Davies was roaming the country carrying out his investigations for his report, Philip Yorke had made an offer to assist him which, on the surface, appears guarded:

> ... I believe my good Agent Mr. Jones of Coedyglyn knows much more and if you can see him, both on my account and his own, he will shew you every attention. He is a very modest, knowing man, and I could not recommend you to a better in these parts. Had I been myself on the spot, I could have offered you no assistance, but in taking you to others who could ...[72]

However, bearing in mind that Philip Yorke was away from home at the time and that his agent would be likely to give more help with the practical information which Walter Davies was seeking, the squire's offer was more generous than it seems at first glance.

Other landowners in the Wrexham area were also keenly interested in agricultural improvements. In 1796 an Agricultural Society was formed in the town with Sir Watkin Williams Wynn as its president.[73] Philip Yorke played the role of intermediary between Walter Davies and another local landowner, Sir Foster Cunliffe of Acton, who had tried "to ascertain the merits of different breeds of cows such as belonged to me", but who did not consider his findings to be sufficiently important to merit a place in Walter Davies' published report.[74]

Philip Yorke made an interesting comment on the native Welsh mountain sheep:

> ... I have examined my husbandman here respecting the Kempsey wool. It is too well known to him, by the term saith-flew, if I spell it right, and is the character of the wool of these hills. I have often myself thought that the faces of these upland sheep are half goat.[75]

The results of Philip Yorke's excursion into the realm of livestock breeding were included in Walter Davies' report, under the heading *Results of Experiments made by Mr. Yorke at Erthig, in crossing the Welsh, and Shropshire Breeds of sheep with the Spanish.* Tables drawn up for the report compared the weights of the carcase and fleece of the common mountain Welsh breed, whose wool was of very poor quality,[76] cross-bred half-Welsh ewes and half-Spanish rams, whose wool was of considerably better quality, and a cross between three-quarters Spanish ram and a quarter Shropshire ewes. The conclusions of the experiment were that, "A cross between a Spanish ram and small Shropshire ewes, bred in the hills, was very little heavier than the Welsh ewes, but finer woolled," and that " the difference between the three quarters Spanish and a quarter Shropshire, and the half Welsh, half Spanish crosses seems to be only in the quality of the wool, which is nearly as fine as that of the Spanish ram; to this may be added a greater tendency to fatten."[77]

Despite achieving some degree of success, Philip Yorke came to share the growing disillusionment with the Spanish Merino sheep as he realised that they were not sufficiently well suited to the prevailing climate to have any long-term value. Walter Davies retained his early enthusiasm for the Merino breed and thought that a cross combining three quarters of Welsh blood with one quarter Merino would become acclimatised to the high land of North Wales. Philip Yorke, however, shared the view of the majority of sheep breeders in Wales, and reiterated the verdict he had reached nearly two years previously, namely that although Merino crosses would survive under lowland conditions they were unable to withstand the climatic environment of the exposed hills. They were, he said, "… too tender for the country in the mixed state", and would be even less likely to succeed "in a purer one… ." Sadly he declined Sir Joseph Banks' offer of more rams for his flock.[78]

It is true that Philip Yorke's experiment had only a negative outcome so far as upland Wales is concerned. That does not diminish his role as an experimenter, however. Over a period of about five years, he organised on his estates an on-going trial of the viability of this particular type of selective breeding. In spite of his disclaimer in his letter to Walter Davies in 1797, he clearly had a personal involvement in this. Moreover, his acceptance by such men as Joseph Banks and his inclusion in the favoured circle of those who received animals from the royal flock are evidence of his standing among some of the foremost agricultural improvers of his day.

At his death, however, he left to his heir, Simon, the twin burdens of a substantial debt and the need to provide portions for the 'second hatch'. Landowners were always extremely reluctant to sell any part of their estates and only did so when driven to it by the need to pay debts or to meet other financial obligations. If forced to take such a step, it was the peripheral, outlying territory they sold, not the historic core of the estate. An heir who was already the owner of an estate, but one far removed from his inheritance, might well want to sell and spend the money on his patrimonial estate.[79]

This was the situation which confronted Simon Yorke in 1804. His need for money made him consider selling the King's mill and eleven acres of land in 1806.[80] Not surprisingly, since this was part of his main estate, he did not proceed with this plan, and by the following year had changed his mind. John Cragg, a land agent whom he employed, wrote to him on June 26th, 1807:

> If you Sir are really obliged to raise in a short time a large sum of money, are determined not to sell Estates in Wales, and it is certain that the person who now bids £37,000 for Radwell and Newnham be actually Mr. Ready Money. I would were it my own case Sell – I don't like the prospect of the Times. Things are lowering and we have more and more complaints from Tenants.[81]

Simon Yorke did not, in any case, have much choice. The settlement drawn up on the occasion of his marriage in 1807 to Margaret Holland of Teyrdan stipulated that he should sell the Hertfordshire estate, and use the money to pay off a total of £9,000 in mortgages raised by Philip Yorke, and to raise money for the children of Philip and Diana.[82] The sale of Newnham and Radwell was agreed on June 27th, 1807. It was bought by Samuel Mills of Finsbury Place for £37,100[83] The other portion of the Hutton legacy, the house in Park Lane which had become Philip Yorke's after his mother's death in 1787, was leased in 1790 to Frederick Choppin for seven or fourteen years at an annual rent of £140,[84] and sold to Lord Dudley in 1810 for £2,600.[85] No doubt the money from the sale of these two 'subsidiary' properties also retrospectively helped to pay for Little Erthig, bought by Simon Yorke in February 1807 for £6,300,[86] a purchase once contemplated by his father,[87] which would round off his lands on their western boundary.

It seems that these transactions were only the culmination of a policy which had throughout sacrificed the Hutton properties to the interests of Erthig. It is perhaps significant that their sale not only enabled Simon Yorke to start married life without the encumbrance of his father's debts, but permitted him to strengthen his main estate by the purchase of additional land.

CHAPTER 8: House and Park

Anne Grosvenor of Eaton Hall, near Chester, commenting to her brother Richard on changes which had been made to Chirk Castle, not far from Erthig, ascribed them to the habit of "young Gentlemen when ye come to theare Estates to be turnying every thing up side down."[1] Bearing in mind that the upper classes were identified by their family names and country seats, and that the house itself was the outward symbol of the landlord's power and prestige, it is not surprising that each generation of owners felt impelled to modernize and improve it and so leave a permanent memorial to their successors.[2] Philip Yorke was no exception, but whether in the process of making changes to his mansion and grounds he "turned every thing up side down", the following pages will attempt to show.

In the absence of any general statement of principle governing his considerable alterations to the mansion and grounds at Erthig, Philip Yorke's intentions have to be inferred from odd comments and instructions in his letters and, above all, from one letter which he wrote to his brother-in-law, Brownlow Cust, dated May 17th, 1775, on the subject of improvements to Belton House and park. His own alterations at Erthig would have been quite advanced by this date and, therefore, he could speak with some authority on the subject. Beneath the customary veneer of irony which characterised their correspondence, Philip Yorke's words display his usual common sense.

He concluded that "Belton has a goodly appearance and is in excellent repair, and order, within and without ... However, as I ride round it in that sort of Absence, which a dull horse, and an unbusied Mind naturally throws one in, I dream of the Works which the present taste, and a Modern Improver, might raise about you." Philip Yorke then proceeded, in considerable detail, to describe precisely those "Works" which his "Modern Improver", sparing no expense, might construct. His distrust of fashion and pointless extravagence were revealed in his depiction of "... a Brownist mixing the pretence of profitable Improvement with Expensive ornament..." What Belton house lacked, he felt, was elevation, and his detailed proposals for achieving that included, among several other measures, felling a great many trees in various parts of the estate and removing "the Pillars, Ironwork and Gates" from the south side of the house to the Grantham entrance to the park, this last measure inspired, no doubt, by a similar action already taken in his alteration to the west front of Erthig. He signed his letter as "The most unprofitable Improver".[3]

The West Prospect of Erthig from Badeslade's engraving of 1740. [Erddig – The National Trust]

Although these proposals concerned another property, they do, nevertheless, give some indication of his attitude to 'improvements' in general. His suggestions, which have about them the air of studied authority of someone well versed in such matters, reflect the pragmatic approach which governed his actions in other areas. Any changes had to be based on sound economics and beauty had to be combined with utility. Writing to John Caesar on July 22nd, 1775, for instance, about the construction of a dam on the Clywedog, he was most insistent that his steward should ensure that he understood completely the plan proposed by a Mr. Leggatt: "… and you will thoroughly comprehend his meaning and Intentions that all Errors may be Detected in the Theory, and that we may not, at the Hazard of our Judgement and Pocket build up a Heap of absurdity and practice a useless Expense …" and, on the same theme, he decided that a new mill race was unnecessary, "I am very glad to understand that the Old answers every purpose, and that the water will (when the Dam is finished) take its usual course - any alteration to add to Beauty may be made hereafter …"[4] Even in much smaller matters he showed his dislike of useless and expensive ornamentation. The following letter to John Caesar, dated November 1st, 1770, was a good example.

> … I would have you order … Geers for my Four Coach-Horses, who will occasionally draw in the Team – Pray take Pains in ordering 'em, and if there be any improved manner of constructing such things, seek it out. I would have no finery or nonsense (which the Sadler may perhaps think of) in the ornamenting of them, but let the Work only be good, the materials substantial and seasoned, and the whole, useful …[5]

Alterations to the exterior of Erthig were made in two areas. Philip Yorke's modifications to the original house, built by Joshua Edisbury between 1684 and 1687 and extended by John Meller's two wings between 1721 and 1724, were confined to the west front which underwent radical changes. The cupola and balustrade were removed and the open arcades and *oeils-de-boeuf* of Meller's wings were replaced by conventional sashes. The stable block and wrought iron screen which had closed off the terrace were swept away.[6] The effect was to destroy the appearance of a courtyard and to give a clearer view of the west front, thus resulting in the kind of open prospect so admired at the time.[7] As this front was exposed to the prevailing winds from the hills, its weather-beaten russet brick was faced with a stone cladding,[8] while a central pediment was added to the main block. Thus the appearance of that side of the house was completely altered. Philip Yorke's account to the Earl of Hardwicke of his alterations combined modesty and pride, and showed his concern for the utilitarian and aesthetic aspects of the project.

> You flatter me much in your enquiry after my alterations, Improvements, as your lordship is partially pleased to call them. I am this Summer compleating a substantial Repair, which was begun the last. I have cased with a plain coat of stone, of the thickness of six inches, the exposed and worn brickwork of my

House. As the work is well executed, the stone of a good colour, and that I have had able advice and assistance, in some modern Alteration of the Front itself it shows indeed! upon the whole very handsomely.[9]

No less a person than Lord Temple, who, with assistance, had "made his way up our steepest Bank and Chief Point of Prospect" had praised the work.[10] This aspect of his 'improvements' seemed to Philip Yorke of such significance as to deserve a commemorative note in his commonplace book and on the house itself.[11]

It is not clear who precisely provided the advice and assistance referred to in this letter. There is some evidence that the eminent architect James Wyatt might have been involved in a number of the improvements to the exterior and interior of the house. One of Philip Yorke's notebooks contained a list of subjects "to take Mr. Wyatt's opinion upon", which included repairs to the eastern parapet wall, the stairs to the billiard room, and how to lay lead under "the block-stone of the House".[12] James Wyatt could also have been responsible for designing a much more far-reaching alteration to the west front, involving colonnades and pedimented pavilions.[13] These features were rejected in favour of the more austere design to be seen today. In any case, it was more usual for squires like Philip Yorke, who were bent on improving their mansions, to employ the services of provincial architects,[14] and in the event, William Turner of Whitchurch, Joseph Turner of Hawarden and a Mr. Franks were seemingly responsible for the changes to the house.[15]

In the absence of any direct evidence, one can only surmise why Wyatt's plan was rejected. Firstly, there was the matter of cost. Philip Yorke, as we have seen, had problems trying to satisfy the many demands made upon his purse at this period, and James Wyatt's ambitious scheme – though no costing can be found – would surely have been more expensive than the one which was actually adopted. Secondly, another factor might have been the well-known unreliability of James Wyatt himself, a drunkard who accepted more commissions than he could fulfil.[16] Thirdly, Philip Yorke had his own ideas on landscaping and architecture. His choice of style depended on the setting and, in this instance, he may have preferred the simpler scheme of uncluttering the western side of the house. He may well have concluded that the clear-cut classical outline of that front, exposed on its steep escarpment but softened by tall trees, made a more harmonious picture than the elongated central block and flanking wings proposed by James Wyatt. On the other hand, the fact that the stone facing was confined to the west front might suggest either that the utilitarian motive had been given precedence over the aesthetic, or that Philip Yorke simply could not afford to cover the whole house.

The second main area of improvements was located on the south side of the house where a new block, with domestic offices, stableyard and kitchen, was constructed. In Philip Yorke's time the kitchen was not connected to the house. This separation was due not only to the danger of fire, as is usually suggested, but also because it was more fashionable to site such buildings in a separate block connected to the main house, as happened later on at Erthig, by a tunnel or passage-way.[17] It is very probably fair to say that Philip Yorke was happy to follow this fashion because he could see its practical advantages and considered it to be aesthetically more satisfying to have these buildings sited on one side of the house, even though it produced an asymmetrical effect. But that, too, was in line with the current fashion.[18]

Very careful accounts were kept of these alterations, the costs of which were quite substantial. The cost of fronting Erthig house with stone from a local quarry and putting in new sashes, between 1772 and 1774, came to £814, while that of the new domestic offices, stable block and kitchen came to £1,517 for the years 1774-77, and a further £317 between 1781 and 1784.[19]

It was characteristic of Philip Yorke that he exercised a very close personal supervision over the progress of the work, his detailed notes revealing an amazing knowledge of the minutiae of the whole operation. The installation of new sash windows, for instance, was a subject which he must have studied with great care.

> The lower windows at Erthig, must of course be square, & the same width with those of the Hall Story immediately above them – In all the Front window two lifts only; and the upper lift or sash throughout to be fixed. The door of the Hall in one Piece to the upper lift; all Glass but the wooden Wicket: to this door a brass Bolt to the second Bar. Masons must be watched they dont use much lime or Fail thereby in fixing the Joints Close. N: If the Lowr Windows want the Security of Bars note Mr. Lloyd of Tyddyn's Plan whether there might not be under the Great Hall door of the width of the same, an Iron Grate, with Bars as contiguous as may-be, not put parallel, but horizontally; which Grate may receive the Rain beating back from the door, and which may be carried away into the Area on each side by a Groove in the Stone, under this Iron grate."[20]

With his usual keen eye on expense, he queried the valuation placed by William Worrall, the mason in charge, on items such as bricks, window and door frames, and timber, declaring it to be too high, and drew up his own list of what was required, together with what he expected to pay for each item. This list was headed "Prices of Work at Erthig, 1773"[21] and contained entries such as the following:

> Plain work that is Ashler at 4d.pr Foot; the work alone done at 3d. pr.Foot; all moulding work done at 6d pr. Foot …Joiners Work – Dantzick Oak window shutters framed of inch and Quarter stuff 4d pr. Foot…Dowell'd floors of dantzick Oak 16s. pr. square; Deal dtto fivteen shill: pr. square. Nail'd floors of deal 9 shill. pr. square. Oak roofing 6s. pr. square. Deal dtto. five shill: pr. square…[22]

Somewhat unusually, since Philip Yorke generally used his own timber for building work on his estate, William Worrall sent for materials for a new cart-house to Chester and Liverpool, namely "252 'cubical' feet of timber for

West front of Erthig towards the end of the 18th century by Moses Griffith. [Erddig – The National Trust]

flooring, Principals for roof 872 'cubical' feet. Hope to have it at 13 pence halfpenny pr. foot".[23]

Within the house changes took the form of a rearrangement of a number of rooms and their functions. After 1770 it had become fashionable in older houses for the bedrooms to be moved upstairs as the amount of living room on the main floor expanded.[24] Philip Yorke chose to follow the trend and converted the original state bedroom into a dining room. This replaced John Meller's 'eating parlour' which became a drawing room. On the same floor, the partition between the original saloon and withdrawing room was removed, and the two rooms combined to produce a much-enlarged five bay saloon. Changes were also made to the Entrance Hall, so called because , until the nineteenth century, it formed the main entrance to the house. The door which led into the saloon was blocked up and the room was made strictly symmetrical by the addition of a false door in the north wall. Its dark panelling was removed and the room, together with the new drawing room and the new state bedroom, was redecorated.[25]

The same mystery surrounds the question of who precisely was responsible for the various alterations to the interior of the house as it does for changes to its exterior. The designs for new marble fireplaces and chimney-pieces, doors and friezes have traditionally been attributed to James Wyatt. Entries in the Erthig account books for the period refer to the mason John Devall, in whose workshop the new fireplaces were made, and to Joseph Rose and Company, responsible for the friezes. Philip Yorke's account book included, for July 12th, 1772, "Devall's Bill for Cistern £8/15/9,"[26] and he noted that "Mr. Rose the Plaisterer's men came to Erthig on Saturday, the 7th of Aug: 1773, and left on September 18th".[27] It is significant that Devall and Rose were often used by James Wyatt on other projects.[28] The only incontrovertible piece of evidence for James Wyatt's participation in the changes to the interior of Erthig is one and a half sheets of paper (undated), in his own handwriting, relating to alterations to the housekeeper's room.[29]

Two letters from Philip Yorke to John Caesar in the summer of 1772 were concerned with the refurbishing and redecoration of less important rooms and reveal,once again,the squire's personal involvement with the minutiae of these activities. It is not clear to which rooms the letter of June 18th was referring though evidently the second was one of the garrets, and it is perhaps surprising, therefore, that its decoration was receiving such attention from the owner.

> ... I think I fully explained to you, how this door was to be; the lower Part of the Panel – Painted, the upper papered to suit with the rest of the papering and pannelling of the Room – The other two doors will remain you understand, as they are, only Painted a dead White; and you will seek out a Painter of Character, to execute it, by the yard And so you will do, to find a Person who can paper it decently, and this Room must be gone upon immediately, as it must be thoroughly dry, and the Smell gone (if possible) by the time Yr. Mistress gets down, perhaps in the end of July. Miss D. Davies of the Beast Market can tell you the Paper which

is appointed for it, and you will see the exact Quantity which shall be necessary. The Hearth in this Room must be new, and blacked as the Chimney Piece – The Colour of the Paper is red & white – When you have gotten the Painter and Paperer in the House let the Garret Mrs. Reddish lay in, be also papered and Painted; the Colour of the Paint a dead White as to the Skirting Board, and Shutters, but the door of a chocolate Colour – The Paper appointed for this Room will be Green and White. Miss Davies knows it – In this Garret, for Safety, which is the first thing, I believe a new Stone Hearth is wanted. See it well done ...[30]

In his second letter, dated July 2nd, Philip Yorke referred to certain queries which John Caesar had communicated to him: "...Whether the new Pannellings in the Parlour are to be put up & Painted, and whether the Backstairs leading to the Nursery are to be drawn and Plaistered..." Unfortunately, Philip Yorke did not choose to answer the questions on this occasion but proceeded to deliver more instructions. "When the Paper comes for the Garret you will set about it immediately, and attend to its being well and neatly furnished – I expect the Plaistering of the Dairy Room will be rather tedious, but whilst it is drying you will have Employment for yr Plaisterer in other Parts, and in executing other subsisting orders..."[31]

At times, Philip Yorke complained about the rate of progress of the building work. On June 6th, 1772, he wrote to John Caesar that "... the House seemed I thought to linger ...",[32] and on June 18th that "I find all our Neighbours think the House moves on slowly."[33] On July 22nd, he wrote, "The Floor of the little (Kitchen) Room in which Bennion lives need not be floored immediately, for I would have nothing interfere with the progress of the House".[34] Two years later he wrote to Lord Hardwicke, "I am still immersed (being the 3rd. year) in all the dirt of new buildings, and the Ruin of old, but I think with Great Pleasure of having done with Stone and Mortar by the Winter."[35] Even as late as 1780, however, Philip Yorke was complaining to John Caesar about slow progress;

> You are aware how fast the fine season wears away, and in six weeks time, Hugh may be scarce able to stand so high as the chimney work requires, and I shall be very much vexed if the chimneys, and the stone flagging in front of the House is not finally concluded by the time of my Return, probably early in November.[36]

Philip Yorke's detailed scrutiny of the estimates seems to have been worthwhile since, in spite of the length of time spent on the major alterations to the interior, the cost was no more than £397, a minor outlay compared with the £2,648 ultimately expended on the exterior.[37]

If doubt exists as to the real architect of the alterations to the house at Erthig, no such mystery enshrouds the identity of the man responsible for the changes to the grounds. William Emes (1729-1803) has been called a disciple of 'Capability' Brown, though there is no evidence that they ever met. He had an extensive practice as a landscape designer and worked mainly in Staffordshire. It is generally agreed that Brown often provided both the inspiration and practical basis for much of Emes's work.[38] He was responsible for extensive changes to the gardens at Chirk and Powys,[39] and produced plans for the Hardwicke and Cust residences at Belton House and Wimpole.[40]

In addition to his task of levelling the French mill meadows, already referred to,[41] which cost in the region of £1,100 between 1772 and 1775, William Emes was also responsible for 'improvements' of a more strictly aesthetic nature in other areas of the estate. He paid several visits to Erthig over a lengthy period. For instance, he spent three days there in December 1771 and a similar period in November 1777.[42] Philip Yorke wrote to John Caesar that he was due to meet William Emes on February 8th, 1775,[43] and as a tribute to his status, perhaps, ordered his steward to have the Great Wrought Room (probably the State Bedroom) ready for him.[44] Even so, Philip Yorke appears to have regarded him with some misgiving. He had warned John Caesar to "keep a wary eye on Mr. Emes" in February 1772,[45] and on August 19th, 1778 he wrote, "I hope Emes men are by this time, off your back."[46] Anxiety and suspicion, fuelled by absence and financial problems, probably accounted for Philip Yorke's attitude.

William Emes had a reputation for being able to create lakes and cascades,[47] and his ability to design the latter could have been a strong recommendation for his employment by Philip Yorke, because he devised the famous cascade, known somewhat prosaically as the 'cup and saucer', along the course of the Black brook. This is a particularly interesting example of the eighteenth century designer's skill in creating a picturesque feature in a somewhat uninspiring piece of landscape.

Trees were an essential component of any attempt to transform the landscape, and the great woodlands and occasional clusters which resulted from the extensive planting of the eighteenth century were a striking illustration of the art of integrating the twin elements of beauty and use. Timber was a profitable investment. There was a great demand for it not only to build ships but for a multitude of other purposes.[48] There was also considerable need for it on the estate itself. Philip Yorke, for instance, required timber for rebuilding the King's mill and for repairs to farm buildings on the estate. His accounts included items such as the following:

> October 17th, 1769 Edward Fabian for carrying timber &c £6/3/.
> September 25th, 1770 Yeud's Bill (pt.) for drawing Timber £2.
> December 12th, 1772 Repairs to Plas Drain – paid the men for following your team. Drawing Timber from Erthig since 10th of July. £1/15/6.[49]

As we have seen, Philip Yorke's lease agreements allowed tenants a certain amount of "timber in the rough" for the upkeep of their farm buildings and fences, and it was also required not only for building work at Erthig itself but for the construction of a wide assortment of items such as waggons, carts, tools and even furniture. Timber could also be sold to raise money in times of severe financial stress.[50]

Such considerations, however, were not permitted to intrude upon the aesthetic function of trees, particularly those within sight of the mansion itself.

It was, however, in the settings of their houses, and in those portions of the general landscape visible from favoured viewpoints and drives, that the aristocracy spared no expense in the lavish use of trees and woods to beautify the scenery.[51]

On May 28th, 1770 Philip Yorke wrote to John Caesar,

... Be very careful in the choice of Timber you cut down. That which is mature, distant and never likely more to mature. If you value my Approbation and good opinion, be careful how again you use the axe near my House, or Walls – you can offend me in nothing more.[52]

The message was the same eight years later. On April 28th he wrote,

I would have you cut down 8 or 10 good trees this Spring, for my particular Use. See if you can find them at a distance. Could not you pick so many without injury to the Richness of the Pentre Clawdd wood. They must not be taken anywhere from my demesne, or within sight of it.[53]

Again and again he stressed the need for care in felling trees. On November 1st, 1770 he wrote, "The Hurdles must not be begun till I come down, and then I will appt. some trees. Cut none ever down without first consulting with me",[54] and on March 5th, 1771, "No timber to be cut down but what I mark with my own hands."[55] His reluctance to cut down trees around Erthig was remarked upon in the 1804 survey of the estate; "...the Woods adjoining to Erthig which being so great an ornament to that place, Mr. Yorke would never injure..."[56] As a landscape gardener who owed his inspiration to 'Capability' Brown, William Emes would have been familiar with the idea of using clumps of trees and open lawns to create a natural effect,[57] a device which was employed in his labours for Philip Yorke,who wrote to his steward on January 3rd, 1772,

Near to where the old Willow Plantation grew in the French Mill Meadows stand now five Handsome Trees (viz a Crab, a Cherry, an Oak, 2 Ash). I would by all means wish these to remain, and altho' they may grow in the Awkward Line of the Old Hedge Mr. Emes (if he should get so far before I see him) might yet, I should think preserve them by raising the ground a little around them, and throwing in more additional Trees, might make together with them, a very Handsome Circular clump.[58]

On July 22nd, 1772 Philip Yorke informed John Caesar that if he needed two beams (for what purpose he did not state) he could obtain them from "... a couple of my Firs, either in the North Orchard (but not out of the Clump there), or you might take them from that end of the Avenue, in Gwern-Erthig, extending to the Gate of the Engine meadow."[59] In 1778 Emes was paid £211 for, among other things, "planting scattered trees of tolerable size ... at the foot of the Hill, west front".[60] The most striking feature of the planting carried out by Philip Yorke on the northern and western sides of the House was the avenue of beech trees along a ridge which might once have been a formal walk, and which, because of its impressive appearance, came to be known as the Cathedral aisle. The beech tree was a happy choice because, in addition to its beauty, it would withstand planting in shade and,therefore, it could be introduced late into the pre-existing woodland.[61]

One Restoration peer is reputed to have said that wood was "an excrescence of the earth provided by God for the payment of debts".[62] It would appear that Philip Yorke, whose expenses were particularly heavy in the 1770s , utilised his trees for this very purpose. Although the trees which were actually cut down were in the more distant areas of his estate, he insisted that care should be taken not to spoil the general effect. On February 20th, 1772, he wrote to John Caesar about the sale of timber in Pentreclawdd wood:

> However the most pressing business is the Care of the Timber, I have marked, which should now be put in the way to a sale forthwith - I have wrote on that subject to Mr. Vernon tonight, and I conclude you will see him, very soon, when he comes over to look at the Timber – If it be Felled this Spring I depend on you to see, that no injury is done, to any Neig'bring tree, or any of my Property, mixed with that which shall be sold; as I know how necessary it will be to watch the Timber Merchant, and his servants and officers – when Mr. Vernon has determined what is to be done and the Course of it, you will acquaint me ...[63]

On June 6th Philip Yorke instructed his steward.

> I think it would be well for you to look over the timber Fallers at Pentre Clawdd that no tree is mistaken, and that Messrs Emes and Edwards enjoy the identical trees they have purchased. I know not what choice the Timber-Cutter might make ...[64]

Unfortunately, there is no account of this sale. Records do exist, however, for the sale in 1775 of 1,864 oak trees, 63 ash trees, 11 elm trees and 19 sycamores to John Jones of Llwyn Onn and Peter Jackson, a Chester timber merchant, for £1,535,[65] and in 1778 of 643 oak trees, 110 ash trees, 24 elm trees, 21 sycamores and 2 fir trees to John Fisher, a Liverpool merchant, for £665.[66] Substantial sales of timber were commonly undertaken only in times of serious financial difficulty since, as a resource slow to renew itself, trees represented a reduction in the assets of the estate for a long time to come. Sales on the scale of these two, therefore, indicate how parlous Philip Yorke's financial position was in these years of heavy outlay on estate and house, and might explain his desperate letters to his steward to pacify his creditors and even, on one occasion, to send £50 to enable his employer to travel home.[67] It is interesting to note that the sale in 1775 just covered the cost of the new stable and kitchen block then under construction.[68]

It would seem that Philip Yorke's financial position was again not too secure towards the end of his life.[69] It is not surprising, therefore, that on March 3rd, 1803, he agreed to sell a further 461 oak trees, 16 oak cyphers, 31 ash trees, 1 ash cypher and 6 elm trees. It is significant that all these sales were of trees on the land of various tenants in different parts of the estate, well out of sight of Erthig itself. The 1803 sale was of trees at Pentreclawdd and Maes-y-Llan in the parish of Ruabon, to Ralph Manley, John Hancock and William Golbourne, timber merchant, of Chester.[70]

Philip Yorke's refusal to countenance any change to the precise, geometrical design of the garden to the east of Erthig has, in the absence of any explanation on his part, been the subject of some speculation. It has been attributed to "his strong historical sense".[71] There may be an alternative explanation. Philip Yorke, by temperament and education, was an Augustan who admired the classical virtues of order, symmetry and moderation. The creation of a harmonious whole was as essential in terms of the relationship between his mansion and its setting as it was between different parts of the house itself. To destroy the ordered pattern of the existing garden and replace it by a more modish, pseudo-naturalistic design would have been to create something which was out of keeping with the classical lines of the east front of the house.

The point has been made that, as a result of changing fashions in landscape design in the eighteenth century, houses built along ordered, symmetrical lines came to be set in informal, "picturesque" surroundings.[72] In the case of Erthig, where the house and garden both retained their formal outlines, the 'natural' landscape was confined to the parkland. It is also worth noting that in Wales generally, changes to the landscape along these lines were usually modest, either because of the owners' lack of resources, or because it was felt that the grandeur of the scenery was such that it could not be improved upon by artificial means.[73] Philip Yorke's changes did incorporate a number of features of the fashionable landscape planning of the age, but by no stretch of the imagination could they be called sweeping.

His alterations to the west front of the house and changes to the interior, the creation of a stable block, domestic offices and kitchen were much more radical, and together constitute the nearest Philip Yorke came to "turnying every thing up side down". Only one major alteration, namely a new dining room, in 1826-27,was made after his death. Otherwise, Erthig remains today much as he left it.

After a decade and more of improvements to Erthig park, Philip Yorke, in 1779, invited his neighbours "to walk in the same for their Health and Amusement".[74] What prompted him to do this? No doubt, the strong sense of duty towards the local community which Philip Yorke shared with so many of his fellow gentry[75] had a part to play in his decision. It would probably be somewhat naive, however, to suppose that his motives were entirely disinterested. His main incentive may well have been a logical extension of the underlying reason for the expensive changes to his house and park, namely to enhance the status of the Yorkes and that of Erthig in the locality. To admit the lower classes into his grounds would serve to strengthen Philip Yorke's squirearchical eminence in the neighbourhood and his reputation as a popular and benevolent landowner, whose grounds could bear comparison with those of even the most illustrious of his peers.

CHAPTER 9: Public Life

The foregoing pages have shown that Philip Yorke was no Squire Western but, on the contrary, a hard-working, hard-headed landowner who had to wrestle with the multifarious problems of running his estates and caring for a large family. Along with other members of his class, however, he also had public duties to perform. The peers and gentry were regarded as the traditional leaders of society, endowed with the power and authority to fulfil their obligations in the various spheres open to them. Thus, while he was concerned with his personal and domestic affairs Philip Yorke was also attending to his responsibilities in parliament, parish and the militia.

His parliamentary career was bound up with the Yorke interest. During the eighteenth century political life was governed by family 'connexions' and personal loyalties, and Philip Yorke was fortunate in that his illustrious relative, the first Earl of Hardwicke, who had occupied the Lord Chancellor's seat in the House of Lords, had been intent on packing the House of Commons with his supporters. In 1761 he had four sons, a son-in-law and two nephews in the House. He wrote to his eldest son,

> It is ... a good thing for you and your fraternity – for an extensive alliance in the House of Commons is a thing of figure and weight in the country.[1]

Among the seats in the gift of the Hardwickes was one of the two for the borough of Reigate where most of the 200 freeholds were dominated by the two families of Yorke and Cocks.[2] Charles Cocks represented the borough from 1754 to 1780, while the Earl of Hardwicke himself, before he acquired the Chancellorship, had held the other seat from 1741 until 1747. He was succeeded first by his brother Charles, until 1765, and then by another relative, John Yorke.[3]

The first approach to Philip Yorke was made on November 9th, 1770 because John Yorke intended to stand for the county of Cambridge. The second Earl of Hardwicke, whom Philip Yorke seemed to treat as a close friend, wrote,

> As Mr. Yorke's standing for this County will make a vacancy at Ryegate, permit me to ask if it will be agreeable to your inclination, to be brought in there. I shall be happy to shew this Mark of Regard to one of your Character and a near Relation...The Trouble and Expence are trifling.[4]

On the same day, Philip Yorke wrote to thank him for "an offer very honourable to me", and accepted.[5] One reason for the offer could have been a consequence of the Earl's earlier career as MP for Reigate, when from 1743 to 1745 he had kept a journal of House of Commons debates, later to be incorporated in Cobbett's parliamentary history. Perhaps he envisaged a similar role for Philip Yorke whose reporting skills might eventually prove useful. In the event, whatever he had in mind for Philip Yorke would have to wait for some time because John Yorke's plan did not succeed and he remained an MP for Reigate until 1780.[6]

In the meantime, Philip Yorke had stood for a seat which was in the sphere of influence of the Cust family. In Helston, which he represented from October 1774 until September 1780, the number of electors did not exceed thirty,[7] although apparently it was not as corrupt as other slightly larger Cornish boroughs.[8] The right of election, about which there was some confusion, was assumed to lie with the corporation, which consisted of a mayor, four aldermen and an indefinite number of freemen.[9] According to 'immemorial usage' the freemen were elected by the mayor and aldermen.[10] Control over the borough had lain with the Godolphin family from 1754 to 1768. When Francis, the second Earl of Godolphin, died, the interest at Helston passed to his grandson, Francis, the Marquess of Carmarthen. A series of disputes in the corporation between 1768 and 1772 seriously weakened the Godolphin party which petitioned for a new Charter.[11] This was granted in 1774 and the new corporation had a majority in the Godolphin interest. When parliament was dissolved in September 1774, the Godolphin party chose the Marquess of Carmarthen and Francis Owen to contest the borough, while the anti-Godolphin party, now reduced to six, chose a member of the Cust family,[12] Francis Cockayne Cust, a deaf, irascible but competent Chancery lawyer, and his brother-in-law, Philip Yorke.[13] It was understood that if, as expected, Francis Cust and Philip Yorke were defeated they would petition.

The first session of a new Parliament dealt mainly with voting supplies and determining election petitions alleging malpractice. Since the bills of 1770 and 1774, election petitions were heard by a House of Commons Select Committee chosen by lot, which proceeded "to try and determine the Merits of the said Election and Return".[14] The members of the Committee, chosen by an elaborate arrangement,[15] were not really competent to judge the complicated legal issues involved.[16] Little wonder, therefore, that such Committees occasionally produced some whimsical verdicts.[17] Such was the one at Helston when the Committee accepted the petitioners' contention that the subsisting members of the corporation under the old Charter had the sole right to elect the MPs[18] and that, therefore, "Philip Yorke and Francis Cust should be duly elected as burgesses to serve in the present Parliament".[19] This verdict meant that the six freemen who had voted for them were declared the only legal voters of Helston.[20] The Committee noted that the petitioners who had "at a considerable expense, brought this business for your consideration, have merit with the Public, and deserve the Thanks of the Community".[21] Philip Yorke noted in his account book for March 31st, 1775 election expenses of £2,000.[22] He kept the Earl of Hardwicke informed of the progress of his campaign and sent him his own report of the 'controverted' election which, he claimed, gave a fairer version of the affair than the official document, "for it was enveloped in all the mystery and Abridgement of a legal note, taken at the Tryal; and was moreover incorrectly copied".[23]

Philip Yorke was re-elected in 1780 but resigned his seat in June, 1781.[24] Nothing survives to explain his action, though his statement to John Caesar in the previous year that "I believe I come in myself for Ilchester without opposition" may have been a reflection, perhaps, of a growing dissatisfaction with his situation at Helston, but nothing came of the hint that the seat might have been available for Philip Yorke.[25] A second attempt to persuade him to represent Reigate was made in 1784, after he had had a lengthy experience as a Member since 1774 for the Cornish borough of Helston and had married for a second time. On this occasion his response was different. On January 21st he wrote to the Earl of Hardwicke,

> It is the circumstance of my particular situation, that now prevents my taking Advantage of yr. flattering offer, but indeed for the size of my family, I must be local, nor dare Engage in any thing that increases my Family Establishments, in the necessary journies to London and Residences there. [26]

In spite of his decision to relinquish his Helston seat in 1781 and his refusal of that at Reigate in 1784, there is a remote possibility that he harboured ambitions to represent his county in parliament. The evidence for this supposition is extremely tenuous. Nimrod stated that Philip Yorke had made an unsuccessful attempt to represent Denbighshire "during the minority of the last baronet",[27] while an entry in his account book for August 3rd, 1789 records an item of £1/13/- for "Denbigh Nomination Expenses",[28] the exact implication of which is uncertain. These two pieces of evidence admittedly constitute very slender grounds from which to argue that Philip Yorke desired to represent Denbighshire, but the possibility, however slight, is intriguing and invites speculation. The expenses referred to above arose from the need to elect a successor to Sir Watkin Williams Wynn of Wynnstay who died in 1789 after representing the county for fifteen years.[29] At first sight, it may seem puzzling that Philip Yorke, after his actions in 1781 and 1784, might have wished to resurrect his political career. His circumstances in 1789, however, were different from those in the earlier part of the decade.

In 1781 he had just embarked on the latest phase of the new kitchen and stable block and was "in a sad hobble for money". Although his marriage to Diana Meyrick in 1782 brought him two substantial new properties, this cannot immediately have eased his situation as she was herself deeply in debt. The building project was not completed until 1784 which saw the birth of the first child of his second marriage, to add to the six he was supporting from his first. Viewed against this background, the reasons he gave to the Earl of Hardwicke for refusing his flattering offer have a ring of truth. It may well be that he was reluctant to undertake frequent visits to London for another reason also, since he had just begun to devote himself once again to his genealogical studies which could be pursued so much more easily in north Wales.

By 1789, however, all his great improvements to house and estate were completed and his financial situation was, conceivably, more secure although it is true that his family had again increased. Philip Yorke may not have been particularly ambitious for a political career but, like other members of his class, he would surely have harboured social aspirations. A county seat carried more prestige than one for a borough and it has been alleged that candidates were prepared to contest a county seat because "In part, the desire to represent one's county in parliament was a fashion of the times, like planting trees and building country houses, and there is no accounting for fashion."[30] It was a social honour and by this time Philip Yorke, forty-six years old, with a property base at either end of the county, with years of involvement in its local government affairs as a JP and as High Sheriff as recently as 1785-86,[31] aimed, perhaps, to enhance his social status significantly by becoming its MP. He would also have been aware that it would enable him to gain control over the local government of Denbighshire. He might become Custos Rotulorum and Lord Lieutenant, so gaining the right to make a number of key appointments.[32] Thus he may well have seen the acquisition of a county seat as the crowning achievement of a public life.

His chances of success, however, would have been slim. Welsh MPs were less concerned with national issues than with local affairs. Great landowning families held sway in their constituencies for generation after generation, making it virtually impossible for a comparative newcomer like Philip Yorke to break the succession. "Given the nature of Welsh society, it is not surprising that most parliamentary seats became self-perpetuating gifts in the possession of landed Titans."[33] Counties, furthermore, were against any change in their representation, especially if this involved an expensive contest.

Whatever ambitions Philip Yorke may or may not have nurtured would have been doomed to disappointment, for, as the *Chester Chronicle* reported on August 21st, 1789, a meeting of the gentlemen, clergy and freeholders, held at Denbigh town hall on August 18th, elected a Wynnstay nominee, Robert Watkin Wynn of Plasnewydd, to hold the seat for Sir Watkin Williams Wynn, the fifth baronet, who did not come of age until 1793.[34] Despite their success, however, the Wynn supporters, fearing that their hold on the county seat was not too secure, were uneasy. In December 1789, Francis Chambre, the chief agent for the Wynnstay estates, expressed these fears in a letter to John Madocks of Llay Hall, an MP and KC, who had served the Wynns well since 1780.

> Agreeable to the promise I made you at Oswestry I will write this to inform you, I din'd and slept last Thursday at Chirk Castle where nothing transpired from whence any inference cou'd be drawn (even with the assistance of a Dray Horse) that the Master of the Mansion meant anything hostile agst. the House of Wynnstay at the next Election, and I am persuaded he himself does not, but

whether there may not be some other (as I have since heard) that wou'd be Troublesome (without a prospect of success) is what I can't take upon me to determine.[35]

Is it just possible that the mysterious figure referred to was Philip Yorke? Had any statement or action on his part in the preceding four to five months given rise to rumour and suspicion?

In the event, as far as the 1792 general election was concerned, any fears proved groundless, since Philip Yorke found himself representing the borough of Grantham which, with about four hundred voters, was under the patronage of the Cust family and the Duke of Rutland. The Custs had supplied one of the two MPs from 1741 to 1792,[36] when Brownlow Cust preferred his brother-in-law, Philip Yorke, to the seat. He was to hold it, however, for only eleven months, from January to December of that year, since he was acting merely as a 'seat-warmer' until his eldest son, Simon, came of age. Thereafter, Simon sat for the borough until 1802.[37]

Philip Yorke did not distinguish himself as a politician. He could be considered as belonging to a group of MPs, about two hundred in number, categorised as 'country gentlemen', and characterised by their independence and indifference to office.[38] Although he was obligated to his patrons for his seats, this did not seem to influence his political allegiances. Generally, he supported Lord North's administration, but in three divisions in February/March 1780, he, like most of the other 'country Gentlemen', supported the opposition's programme of economic reform[39] and voted against the government.[40] His correspondence gives one or two hints that he was involved in House of Commons committees. On January 31st, 1775, he informed John Caesar that "My Question in the Committee will come on early in March", a reference probably to the Committee which met on March 11th to discuss the disputed Helston election, and an undated fragment of a letter said that, since the election, he had been "locked up in a Committee Room".[41] Unfortunately, he did not elaborate on the second statement and his name is not included in the lists of committee members in the House of Commons Journals of the period.

Records of members who spoke in House of Commons debates in the eighteenth century are very unreliable. "Contemporary attempts even to list all the members who spoke in major debates are rare, and seldom successful."[42] It would seem, however, that more than half the MPs in the later years of the century did not take part.[43] According to the Reverend Samuel Strong's obituary notice, Philip Yorke, like most of his fellow gentry, was a staunch supporter of the established order who,

...loved his country and the constitution of its Government, from a conviction of their excellence, and what he loved he was always ready to support, both in his public and private capacity, although constitutional diffidence would not allow him to speak in the House of Commons.[44]

Nimrod added that "politics were very rarely a subject of conversation at Erthig, – in the social hour, never"[45] and cited as an example of Philip Yorke's moderate outlook and lack of any deep political convictions his tolerance of William Wilkinson, the radical ironmaster, who was suspected of supplying arms to the French during the Revolutionary wars. When the Reverend Samuel Strong, his most intimate friend, remonstrated with Philip Yorke about having a traitor like Wilkinson as a guest at Erthig, the squire merely decided to call him Wicked Will instead of Neighbour Wilkinson and remarked "My dear Strong...What am I to do? I cannot fight the fellow!"[46]

It would appear, indeed, that most members lacked the spur of political convictions and constituency pressures which would have enabled them to overcome the fear of rising to make a speech in a confined space, surrounded by a sea of faces.[47] One MP expressed himself "greatly awed" when he spoke, while another declared, "I have remained silent and notwithstanding all my efforts chained down to my place by some unknown invisible power".[48] In the absence of any statement by Philip Yorke himself, or by anyone else except Samuel Strong, one must assume that he too was chained down to his place by his "constitutional diffidence".

However, if Philip Yorke could not bring himself to speak in debates, he could write about them. As early as 1768, the Earl of Hardwicke had asked him to write reports for him on the trial of John Wilkes. Still politically active even after taking his seat in the Lords in 1764, the second Earl followed the Wilkes case with interest, and sought a reliable source of information about developments in such a potentially inflammable affair. The portions of the preliminary drafts of Philip Yorke's reports which are decipherable, hint at a clear grasp of the legal arguments in the case. They were clearly not the work of someone who had paid scant attention to his legal studies. Unfortunately, the final versions have not survived but the note he wrote to accompany them has done so.[49]

> It arises from your own request that your lordship is troubled with the enclosed, long, dull and (I fear) inaccurate note hastily drawn from the undigested mass before me. Mr. Serjeant Glynne and Mr. Thurloe, were the only Counsel who spoke, and the Case was universally allowed by the Judges, to have been very learnedly and very ingeniously argued on both sides. Many precedents being cited from the Rolls, and other places, which required Inspection, the decision is postponed till after a second argument in the ensuing terms, so, Sir, our Patriot must continue some time yet in durance vile.[50]

It is a measure of the Earl of Hardwicke's high opinion of Philip Yorke's abilities in such matters that he gave him a similar task ten years later when he was MP for Helston. There are two possible explanations for his request to Philip Yorke to supply him with reports, this time of House of Commons debates. Firstly, the presence of peers in and under the gallery during debates was very much resented by MPs and was subject to various limitations and indignities.[51] In these circumstances it would be a distinct advantage to have as an informant a trusted member of the Lower House. Secondly and more significantly, the standard of newspaper reporting of debates at that time was deplorable.[52] The conditions under which they were produced and the haste with which they were prepared for publication meant that they did not reflect accurately what had been said. Not until 1778 were reporters allowed into the gallery of the House of Commons, and not until 1783 were they permitted to take notes of speeches. Even then, the difficulties under which journalists worked were quite inimical to accurate reporting. Confined to the back row of the gallery and having to fight for places with members' constituents, they had to endure long hours in stifling heat, unable to hear distinctly what speakers were saying, or even to see them. As a result, speeches were often attributed to the wrong person. There was no verbatim reporting, therefore accounts of debates were much shortened and even the speeches of such leading politicians as Pitt, Fox or Burke were not given in full. Consequently, reporters often relied on the members themselves to supply them with their own detailed notes of debates, especially since before 1783 they had to rely on their memories. Some members, worried that the press would carelessly or wilfully misrepresent their words, supplied newspapers with correct copies of what they had said.

Not surprisingly, therefore, the Earl of Hardwicke turned once again to the member of his family supporters in the House of Commons who had already, during the Wilkes trial, revealed journalistic skills, to provide him with reliable, accurate accounts of important debates in that Chamber. The Hardwicke papers contain reports sent by Philip Yorke to the Earl of Hardwicke in May, 1777 and March, 1778,[53] although there is no evidence that he wrote any before or after these dates. The debates which he did report were mainly those on the budget in May, 1777 and those on the American war and Lord North's Conciliatory Bills in March, 1778. His accounts were long and exhaustive though, even so, nowhere as full as the versions given in William Cobbett's *Parliamentary History of England*, published nearly forty years later.[54] Philip Yorke's reports presented the gist of the arguments clearly and vividly and, particularly in the case of leading speakers such as Lord North and Edmund Burke, he included a great deal of detail. The preparation of these reports was no easy task. On May 7th, 1777, for instance, he wrote to the Earl of Hardwicke.

> The Parliamentary Intelligence yr Lordship was pleased to ask of me, is indeed grown so very stale, and forestalled by all the Prints, that I wished to mix with it some faint outline of the subject matter of the business of Thursday, which from our late hour of breaking up that night, I was not able to do before your departure, nor till this afternoon have I had any liesure to digest and to put my notes into an intelligible shape...

At the end of this letter, after his lengthy account of the budget debate, he added, "If I had had more time I could certainly have written better, tho' unable to have given you a fresher or fuller account".[55] On May 29th, 1777 he informed the Earl that,

I will endeavour to get a place (i.e. in the House of Commons) where I may hear early, and If I can carry anything away, I will in my manner deal it out to yr Lordship by Friday night, or Saturday's post.[56]

The debates usually went on until well after midnight and, in March 1778, after a number of such sessions, an exhausted Philip Yorke wrote to the Earl of Hardwicke,

I am almost knock'd up with these constant attendances, but I shall endeavour to hold out tonight, and will send your Lordship a note Either this Evening, or tomorrow morning, tho' I shall not be able to be at the House till six this evening.[57]

If he appears in the somewhat passive role of commentator rather than active participant in the House of Commons, Philip Yorke played a more substantial and positive part in local government. As paternalists, the gentry believed that it was their duty to rule, guide and help the lower orders. Their activities as justices enabled them to project on to the local scene the care and authority they exercised over their families, tenants and workers. As we have seen, Philip Yorke was an authoritarian, conscientious and kindly father and landlord. Not surprisingly, he exhibited the same qualities in the performance of his duties as a justice of the peace. His concern was not confined to the poor but embraced the whole community. We have already seen how he opened his grounds to the public in 1779. On another unspecified occasion he wrote to his steward at Erthig,

If the people of Wrexham have any view to their general advantage they will unitedly withstand this unjustifiable demand, which I am very glad I have been the first to Enquire into, and withstand. I shall soon have a full opinion upon it from T. Cust.[58]

Unfortunately, no further references are available to elucidate the subject-matter of this intriguing statement.

He was anxious to support local tradespeople like Miss Davies in the Beast Market, already referred to, or Hugh Roberts the tailor. On August 19th, 1778 he wrote to Jacky Caesar, "If Hugh Roberts who offers for my tayloring business, governs himself by Davies' prices, or at least does not exceed them, I shall willingly employ him, on the strength of what you say in his favour; I don't know the man myself."[59] In the following month he asked his steward, "Who sells soap in Wrexham? Your mistress thinks the business should be a little divided among the people of Wrexham".[60]

It would be unrealistic to believe that Philip Yorke's concern for the local community was his only motive for undertaking the sometimes onerous, unpaid duties of a justice of the peace. He must also have been aware that the office would greatly enhance his own prestige and that of the Yorkes amongst the old-established county families.

He was sworn in as a justice of the peace on January 15th, 1771,[61] when he was twenty-seven, and he served as High Sheriff for Denbighshire in 1785-86,[62] and for Flintshire in 1787.[63] He was also active in the administrative affairs of the local churches at Wrexham and Marchwiel. He was not one of those who, like many eighteenth century justices in Merionethshire for instance, had achieved this position after serving an apprenticeship as sheriff. By his day, the shrievalty had become an honorary, if still prestigious and expensive, office, and in practical terms had far less significance than that of justice of the peace.[64] There are no records of Philip Yorke's activities or expenditure during his time as sheriff.

Unfortunately, the justices' attendances at Quarter Sessions' meetings were not always recorded in the Minutes and we have, therefore, to be cautious about concluding that they attended only when their names appear. However, on the basis of such information as is available in the Minutes, together with the number of occasions on which Philip Yorke's name is recorded as inspecting a bridge or receiving money to repair one, it appears that his degree of involvement in local government affairs varied considerably between 1771 and 1804. A picture emerges of a very inactive justice in the 1770s (four occasions), a busier one in the 1780s (twenty occasions) and a more intermittently active justice between 1790 and 1804 (fourteen occasions).[65] His poor attendance in the 1770s can be attributed not to apathy, expense or difficulties of travel, the more usual reasons for justices' inactivity, but rather to his other preoccupations during this period, namely his 'improvements' at Erthig, his duties as MP for Helston, his militia service towards the end of the decade, and, generally speaking, his prolonged absences from Erthig. In the 1790s, as he grew older and perhaps frailer in health, he seemed to concentrate much of his time and energy on his antiquarian interests, handing over some of his other responsibilities to his son and heir, Simon. His most active period in local government occurred in the 1780s, especially after he had ceased to be an MP in 1781, and a Captain of Militia in 1783. From 1784 to 1790 he regularly attended general and adjourned Quarter Sessions' meetings at either end of Denbighshire and participated actively in the other duties of a justice. He and his fellow justices were kept busy trying to deal with the ever-growing complexities of local administration. One of the most pressing problems was that of the construction and repair of bridges which had become increasingly burdensome in the course of the eighteenth century as the number of bridges maintained by the county had multiplied.[66]

Justices had to attend many adjourned as well as general meetings of Quarter Sessions to settle problems connected with particular bridges. The adjourned meetings were gatherings of two or three justices, frequently in remote villages such as Llansannan and Pentrefoelas. As they usually met at a public house, these often became enjoyable, convivial occasions.

The records reveal that Philip Yorke's responsibilities were largely confined, initially, to the Wrexham area. Together with one or two other local justices, squires like himself, he 'viewed' and 'set' bridges and certified that repairs had been completed at the King's mill, Penybryn, Bradley, Coedyglyn and other locations in Wrexham and its associated townships. After his marriage in 1782 to Diana Meyrick of Dyffryn Aled his sphere of activity expanded to include the Llansannan area on the western side of the county.

The earliest recorded instance of his involvement in bridge repair occurred on July 11th, 1775, when the county treasurer was ordered to pay him £2/16/6 for "Additional repairs to be Due on Pont Coed-y-Glyn. Under the Direction of the said Philip Yorke a Trustee appointed by this Court for that Purpose".[67] A year later, a further £3/15/- was paid to him for the same reason.[68] At the Michaelmas meeting of Quarter Sessions, 1782, it was ordered that "Philip Yorke and two other justices do view and contract for the repair of the road at the end of Pont Bradley, Pont Plas Maen, Pont Y Capel in Gresford, Pont Felin Bulston [Puleston] and Greenbridge in Wrexham".[69]

He was also involved in the lamentable saga of the King's mill bridge which, on the main highway past his newly-constructed mill, would have concerned him as a landowner no less than as a justice of the peace. At the General Quarter Sessions meeting at Wrexham on June 6th, 1782, Daniel Poole, mason, of Ruabon, was contracted to remove the old King's mill bridge and to build a new one about 100 yards further down-stream.[70] A number of local farmers provided sureties amounting to £380 for the satisfactory completion of the task. Philip Yorke, along with William Lloyd and Thomas Boycott, kept a watching-brief over the progress of Daniel Poole who had agreed to build the new bridge before October 1st, 1782. However, by June of the following year he had not fulfilled his obligations. He had, it is true, built the arch twice but, on each occasion, floods had swept it away. Philip Yorke and William Lloyd ordered the county surveyor to cancel Daniel Poole's contract and to take responsibility for building the bridge himself at the expense of the mason and the other sureties. In an adjourned Quarter Sessions meeting, however, Daniel Poole was granted a new contract to build the bridge.[71] Unfortunately, the records are thereafter silent on the matter but it is significant that in1801 and 1803 new arrangements were made and a different mason appointed to carry out the work.[72]

Other duties fell to the lot of Philip Yorke in connection with the King's mill bridge and others in the Wrexham area. For instance, at the Michaelmas Quarter Sessions meeting in 1783, Philip Yorke, William Lloyd and Thomas Boycott were ordered

> to view and contract for the Removal of a Cottage belonging to Miss Puleston at the end of the King's Mill Bridge to strengthen the road, to see to the Repair of the pavement of the Denbighshire part of Rossett Bridge, the Battlements of Gresford bridge, Penybryn Bridge, Pentrefelin Bridge, Pont Pentre Debenny.[73]

The bridge at Chirk formed the boundary between Denbighshire and Shropshire and proved a perennial problem for both counties. Philip Yorke was chosen as a member of a committee to discuss proposals for the construction of a new bridge over the river Ceiriog and to meet with representatives from Shropshire in January 1793.[74]

In 1784 and 1785 he was involved in the negotiations for the construction of Pont Deunant near Llansannan. On November 4th, 1784,

> At an adjournment of the Court of Quarter Sessions held at the Cross Keys in Llansannan... before Philip Yorke and John Lloyd, Esquires, two of His Majesty's Justices of the Peace...the building of Pont Deunant was let to David Lewis of Lletu in the parish of Llanyffydd...[75]

On October 15th,1785, proposals to make a road from each end of Deunant bridge were signed by the same two justices.[76] The construction of this particular bridge seemed to Philip Yorke important for historical[77] as well as practical reasons since an ancient route encountered a difficult crossing here.

> ...The span of the brook is narrow, which makes it subject to very frequent high-water, and Horses have been often I understand, obliged to swim over; one short Arch will do it, but it had better then, be equal to a Carriage, as well as a Horse, and I do conceive cannot exceed forty pounds expence, when made of the fullest use to the public.[78]

These words were written on September 17th, 1791 to his friend John Lloyd of Hafodunos, the 'Philosopher', seven years after the contract had been granted to David Lewis of Llety to build the bridge. It would be another four and a half years before, once more, contracts were signed to build the bridge "from the Quarry of Philip Yorke Squire or from a quarry in the hands of the Glanywern family".[79]

Protracted negotiations of the kind relating to the King's mill and Deunant bridges were by no means unusual. The same bridges were 'presented' to Quarter Sessions again and again, and such instances reveal how cumbersome, 'amateur' local government machinery was being overwhelmed by the ever-increasing complexity of the problems with which it was confronted. This inefficiency led a number of counties to appoint full-time, salaried staff to undertake some of the duties performed by the justices. Thus in 1782 the January meeting of Quarter Sessions resolved to appoint a surveyor of county bridges, and Philip Yorke was one of those who voted to appoint Joseph Turner to the post.[80] A number of the justices, no doubt reluctant to relinquish some of their authority, had second thoughts about the appointment but, at the Easter meeting, the decision was taken, by a majority of one, not to rescind it, – a decision which Philip Yorke supported.[81] Not surprisingly, his passion for efficiency, so evident in the administration of his estate, led him to ally himself with those progressive spirits who supported the introduction of an element of professionalism into local government operations.

In addition to dealing with matters which were the direct responsibility of the County itself, the justices also had to see that the parishes performed their duties as units of local government.

The area of greatest concern to the justices of the peace was the administration of the Poor Law which, by the second half of the eighteenth century, was threatening to get out of hand. This was a sphere where the jurisdiction of Vestry and Quarter Sessions overlapped and where the organisation was proving increasingly inadequate to deal with the growing problem of the poor. After 1750 particularly, the authorities showed a tendency to shelve their responsibility by increasing the number of orders for the removal of paupers to their places of origin.

Throughout the country there was growing concern as the number of paupers increased – inexorably, it seemed – and the problem called for something at once more economical and more efficient than the usual palliative measures to cope with it satisfactorily. The idea, which had gained much currency towards the end of the seventeenth century, of "setting the poor to work", had been acted upon in Wrexham in 1743 when a workhouse was built. Like so many other enterprises of its kind, it foundered eventually because the products made by the inmates proved unmarketable and, consequently, it became an increasing burden on the rates.[82] Soaring bills for these, above all, showed the need for reform. In Wrexham in 1784 the rates reached 6/- in the pound and the parish was greatly in debt.[83] One solution attempted there, as elsewhere, was the removal of expensive paupers to their parish of settlement, but removal alone was not an adequate answer to Wrexham's problem.

The situation was complicated by the fact that the parish had to organise the affairs of thirteen rural townships, each with its own overseer, as well as those of the urban area itself.[84] It appeared to be facing a crisis in its administration of poor relief when in 1784 the overseers of the poor and the churchwardens sought Philip Yorke's advice. That they turned to him rather than to one of the other landowners who were ratepayers, or whose estates bordered the town, suggests that he had acquired a reputation for some expertise in that area. His reply to the churchwardens' request for advice, dated February 4th, 1784, began modestly enough:

> …However, incompetent and really inexperienced as I am in such subjects, I shall not hesitate to comply with your command, and to communicate with you the best manner I am able for the Public Good, and to send you the result of what I could collect in the short time that has since elapsed from Persons of much better knowledge and experience than myself.[85]

This appears to be a reference to an experiment in Shropshire (itself inspired by others elsewhere in the country), which was introduced at Oswestry, Ellesmere, Atcham and Whitchurch, among other places.[86] It had, as recently as the previous year, been tried at Shrewsbury also when a local Act was obtained to borrow £10,000 to build a House of Industry, "to furnish employment for the Poor and compel them to earn their own support".[87]

There followed a memorandum in which Philip Yorke analysed the problem in Wrexham and proposed a solution, part of which was based on the Shropshire scheme. He appreciated that sound administration was the key to success and began his recommendation with a perceptive and honest, if rather tactless, appraisal of the shortcomings of the parish officers and, by implication, of the system which imposed on them the obligation to serve.

That the Overseers and Churchwardens according to the present and usual mode of appointment and execution are incompetent to the service and good government of the Parish will scarcely be controverted. They come unwilling into office, are persons almost ever in trade, who have a more profitable use of their time, and can give no sufficient share of it to the public to answer the purposes of their creation. Their continuance in place, moreover is not of duration to give them knowledge and Experience, and in their business supposing they had diligence, ability and inclination to obtain it.

As in the area of bridge administration, he advocated the introduction of an element of professionalism into the organisation of the poor law and argued that "...an Efficient standing overseer might not be liable to the same objections" as the unpaid parish officials. In his view, the essential basis for reform was the appointment of a salaried general overseer and the creation of a unified body, both of which were necessary to end the chaos caused by Wrexham's multitude of small authorities . He stressed that the choice of the right person to fill the position was crucial; he had to be "diligent, honest, able, active and decisive in his calling", and devoted to the public interest. He should be well paid, "for *sufficient* men must be paid". The general overseer would have to ferret out abuses:

This *Overseer General* should (I apprehend) visit diligently through the parish and be personally acquainted with every poor person receiving alms in it, and by that means be guarded against the several impositions that are attempted, from false numbers of poor given in, from collusive payments of House Rents and other unreasonable and unjust demands.

He was careful to point out that such an appointment, provided that it was made along with those of other overseers, should involve little change in "the old constitution and practices of the Parish". The new official should be granted full executive power . "Unless...such a person has a *legal existence* how can he be fit as a sole distributor of the public money..." He was not to enjoy an unfettered authority however. He should have a fixed residence, "always to be found", and be prepared at all times to submit his accounts at monthly meetings of an "open committee" consisting of the members of the vestry itself, and to answer the summons of a magistrate.

Philip Yorke showed his adherence to the philosophy underlying all the Acts setting up workhouses, beginning with that granted to Bristol in 1696, namely the need to organise the labour of the unemployed in order to maintain them without fear of disorder and, at the same time, increase the nation's wealth.[88]

But among the most essential uses of such an officer (properly qualified in every respect) would be his knowledge and activity in setting the poor to work and placing some of their support at least, on their own proper shoulders equally for *their* as the Public *benefit*; and in this case money must be soon put and some always kept in his hands.

Very sensibly, he recommended that his proposals should be given a year's trial and that as much information as possible should be gathered about the operation of the Shropshire scheme. His friend and tenant, William Wilkinson, had even promised to send the officer, who had conducted the successful Shropshire experiment, to advise the new Wrexham overseer general, if such was appointed. The ever-practical Philip Yorke added that he preferred such a procedure to the pursuit of "...any speculative, unpractical system of your own". At the same time, he urged that "the written sentiments of the most capable of your Parishioners should be collected, ...and by comparing and digesting what is offered by others form from the whole, one *system* and *good plan* for yourselves".[89]

In his carefully prepared and courteously worded letter to the churchwardens and overseers of the poor, Philip Yorke had shown himself to be a persuasive advocate of the case for a more professional approach to the administration of the poor law. Aware that they might be reluctant to accept what in reality amounted to a drastic change, he cunningly stressed that his proposals, which he likened to the unified organisation of central government departments, would involve no fundamental alteration to the constitution of the vestry. He had obviously discussed the matter with his neighbours, the Rev. Henry Newcombe of Gresford, Thomas Apperley and William Wilkinson, and persuaded them to offer advice to the vestry. The tone of his letter suggested that he was greatly concerned about the plight of the poor and had given much thought to the problem of its alleviation.

A mere four days after the date of his letter, it was decided to appoint an overseer general but it was not until April 12th, 1784 that Rowland Samuel was actually chosen to fill the position. At the same time it was decided that "the Business he is to Perform & the Salary he is to receive be settled by a Committee of the following Gentlemen, Tradesmen and others".[90] Philip Yorke headed the list of nominees for this committee. Rowland Samuel, who became the first overseer, appears to be, at least as far as business experience went, one of the "sufficient men" whom Philip Yorke had in mind. A prosperous currier and later a hop merchant in the High Street, he was already a churchwarden. It seems to have been a successful appointment since it was renewed on later occasions, so that he served in all for twenty-seven years.[91]

Philip Yorke's recommendations were carried out in another respect. It is clear from the annual statements of accounts which the overseer submitted that,while he had overall responsibility for the administration of poor relief throughout this large parish, the elected officers continued to operate in each township under his supervision. A move was also made to implement Philip Yorke's proposal that one of the overseer's prime duties should be to provide work for the poor. A meeting on January 2nd, 1786, at which he was present, agreed to adopt Mr Richard Lloyd's "Plan for Employing the poor of the parish ..." and also that "a subscription paper be carried about and annexed to the plan ..."[92] Unfortunately, no details of this plan have come to light.

Yet another of Philip Yorke's suggestions was acted upon when, on May 5th, 1788, a committee was appointed "to inspect the management of the Poor etc. of Wrexham and the General overseers Accts from May 1788 to May 1789".[93] A further development in this direction occurred on March 26th, 1796 when the vestry decided to renew Rowland Samuel's appointment and, at the same time, to appoint a committee consisting of about fifty members, which included Philip Yorke and the remaining churchwardens and overseers of the individual townships, with the vicar in the chair. Its purpose was to "attend to the complaints of the poor". The committee was to meet at least once a fortnight, immediately after the Sunday afternoon service in a committee room assigned to it in the church.[94] Philip Yorke's attendance at meetings of both vestry and committee ceased after this date. The committee, which dealt with all matters of poor relief, settlements and apprenticeships for the next thirty or so years, as well as the new workhouse built by 1840, had been anticipated by him in his letter of 1784.[95]

As a JP, Philip Yorke was more consistently active from 1771 until 1803 in examining (in company with another justice) the legality of parish settlements than in any other sphere of local government. He examined seven cases between 1771 and 1774, thirteen between 1782 and 1788, eleven between 1790 and 1797, and five between 1800 and 1803.[96] This experience would have made him aware of the circumstances of numerous paupers. In one criminal case, a detailed record of which has survived, Philip Yorke acted in a way which may seem harsh to a modern reader. It would have been highly unlikely, however, that an eighteenth century justice would have allowed sympathy for the poor to over-ride a concern that the law should be applied. The justices acted in the belief that property was to be venerated and that it was their duty to ensure that those less fortunate than themselves obeyed the law.[97]

In 1795 Philip Yorke conducted the examination of Elizabeth Edwards and her sister Dorothy Griffiths (wife of Nathaniel Griffiths, a private in the Denbighshire Militia), who had been accused of stealing a piece of calico and eleven cotton handkerchiefs from the shop of Samuel Roberts, draper.[98] As a captain of militia himself, Philip Yorke would have known how miserly was the allowance doled out to the wife of a militia man. He would also have been aware of the savage sentences meted out for what were minor offences. Nevertheless, he ordered the two women to attend the Quarter Sessions at Ruthin where they would be indicted for felony. At the Hilary meeting, 1795, at which Philip Yorke was not present, Dorothy Griffiths was found not guilty, but Elizabeth Edwards, on whom the stolen items were found, was declared guilty and sentenced to seven years transportation.[99]

The exercise of authority was coupled with acts of charity consisting of payments – some regular, others ad hoc – which supplemented the relief dispensed by the parish. Thus, Philip Yorke's account book records regular donations of ten guineas to the poor of Wrexham and five to those of Marchwiel, as well as subscriptions to 'relieve' both Ruthin and Flint gaols.

There was also a payment of fourteen guineas to Chester Infirmary and of one guinea to the family of a blind clergyman.[100]

Philip Yorke's contribution to the matter of poor relief was the most significant feature of his association with the administration of Wrexham's affairs. However, he also had a hand in other developments connected with the church in the 1780s. The decision to build a gallery had been taken as early as 1776.[101] This involved the sale of a number of pews which had to be removed. Progress, as usual, was slow and it was not until a vestry meeting on December 17th, 1787, attended by Philip Yorke, that it was "... ordered that the following Gentlemen be appointed to form themselves into a Committee to superintend the Execution of the Plan for Regulating the Pews and new Flagging the Aisles of the Church, seven of whom to be a sufficient number to do Business, and to meet on 26 Inst. in Church, at 2 o'clock, and the said Committee be empower'd to Adjourn from time to time."[102]

In 1779 a new organ was built in the parish church, though Philip Yorke's name did not appear in the subscription list of those leading gentry of the neighbourhood who had promised £10 and upwards. However, he was present at the meeting of December 22nd, 1788 which appointed Edward Randles, the blind son of a Wrexham butcher, as organist at a salary of twenty guineas a year. His duties were onerous:

> Play every Sunday in the year (morning and evening), Christmas Day, Monday and Tuesday in Easter and Whitsun week, and on the day of the Judge's Sermon in the Assize week and also on Club Days, when there shall be a Sermon.[103]

In addition, he had to assist the children to sing in church. For this he received an additional ten guineas in 1793. Edward Randles was responsible for the music of the church for the remarkably long period of thirty-two years, until his death in 1820.[104]

Despite his involvement in church and parish administration in Wrexham, Philip Yorke and his family actually attended the church in the neighbouring village of Marchwiel and he played a very active part in its life. His purchase of New Sontley in 1772 included the acquisition of three pews in Marchwiel church, one of which was in the chancel, another also for the use of the Yorke family and a third for the tenants. These, together with burial rights in the chancel, were privileges enjoyed by the previous owners.[105]

It is not surprising that Philip Yorke was keen to exercise a controlling influence over the affairs of Marchwiel church. His letter to John Caesar, dated January 26th, 1775, expressed his regret at the death of the rector, Maurice Anwyl, and his urgent need to reach an agreement with the new incumbent over the tithes of Sontley.

> Between ourselves, I pushed the Bishop hard for the Living a month since, but it was long promised. It would have been very desirable to have had a friend seated there.[106]

As it turned out, he was to enjoy, over a quarter of a century, a very close relationship with the new rector, the Reverend Samuel Strong. Hailing from Devon, married to a wife who was the sister and co-heir of Sir John Chudleigh of Chelmington in Dorset, and having previously been rector of Newtown from 1772 to 1775,[107] Samuel Strong was an example of those well-connected English clergymen who were being appointed to Welsh livings during the course of the eighteenth century. The fact that, unlike his predecessor Maurice Anwyl, Samuel Strong was non-Welsh speaking would not have been likely to arouse the kind of overt hostility in an anglicised border parish like Marchwiel which such appointments engendered in monoglot Welsh communities in other parts of Wales.[108] As early as 1749 the rural dean reported that,

...the language in Church is all English, excepting the 2nd lesson which is always in Welsh, and Welsh prayers and sermon on the last Sunday morning in every month; which I believe to be a proper proportion of the two languages to be used in this Church.[109]

The dean's report for the year 1791 made no mention of the provision of services in Welsh, so presumably there was none by that date. In the absence of records for the years between 1749 and 1791, we can only speculate that this provision had ceased some while before the latter date, perhaps when Samuel Strong became rector in 1777.

As far as Philip Yorke himself was concerned, the rector was someone who shared his interest in the Classics and in local history.[110] He was invited to Erthig frequently and was the recipient of many gifts of fruit, meat and drink.[111] Appropriately, it was he who eventually, in 1804, wrote the squire's obituary for *The Gentleman's Magazine*.

A strong hint of Philip Yorke's assumption of proprietorial rights in his family church was given in a letter to John Caesar, dated June 22nd, 1775. It was occasioned by the new rector's appointment of John Cross as parish clerk, a choice approved by the parishioners also. The letter displayed a concern for the church furnishings and monuments, particularly those of the squire's family, and a detailed knowledge of how best to care for them.

As this man [i.e. John Cross] is somewhat among the rest, indebted to my Interest, I hope he will be diligent, in your directions to him, to keep the Pews clean, and if he has a Chest, to lock up the Cushions of my own seat, having well brushed them, at such times as the Family is absent; and that in regard to the Monuments, he does no more to them, than to brush off gently the dust or the Cobwebs with a Fowl's wing, or such gentle thing; and that he does not officiously wash them with water, or use Soap; all which, would ruin the Polish, and delicacy of the Marble. I would have you gravely communicate these Instructions to him early, and tell him, that if I find them regularly obeyed, I shall make him, an annual present...[112]

Marchwiel church was rebuilt in Philip Yorke's lifetime: the main body of the church in the early 1770s, an event commemorated in a window inserted in the south wall in 1778,[113] the chancel between 1776 and 1781 and the steeple in 1789, with Philip Yorke apparently bearing a substantial part of the cost. The rural dean's report for 1749 stated that, unlike so many other churches in the diocese of St. Asaph which had endured years of neglect, Marchwiel church was in a good condition, "except that the Chancel and steeple want some Flags", and that some of the seats "are irregular and project into the alley... "[114] Perhaps some deterioration in the condition of the church occurred between 1749 and 1773 when, at a vestry meeting on November 20th, it was agreed "that the Church be new paved according to the plan produced by William Worrall ... the old Pew materials to be used as far as they shall go..."[115] The money to meet the cost would come from several sources. On June 11th, 1773, a vestry meeting had already agreed to a rate of ninepence in the pound towards building the church. Three local squires, excluding Philip Yorke, agreed to pay the master mason, William Worrall, to build a new gallery, recouping their shares of the cost from the sale of a number of old pews.[116] On July 1st, 1774, William Worrall presented his account to the vestry:

For building the church	£260 . 0 . 0
Inside work	£ 42 . 14. 6
Extra for Church	£ 3. 0. 4
Gallery	£ 65 . 0. 0
Total	£370. 14. 10

Nevertheless, Philip Yorke, who was himself a churchwarden for the years 1773 to 1774[117], contributed £40, and the three other squires £20 each towards the final payment, the remainder of the cost being met by the parish.[118] Some of the money was raised by a mortgage on Tyddyn Daniel, a tenement purchased in 1626 in fee to the Crown "for the only use, maintenance and reparation of the Parish Church of Marchwiel, and to no other use, intent or purpose whatsoever".[119] The debt was finally discharged on July 15th, 1774 when, on the decision of the vestry, Philip Yorke and Charles Browne paid the requisite sum.[120]

The later phase of the 'rebuilding' programme involved Philip Yorke in a lengthy and acrimonious dispute in which he appeared to assume a leading role. Though the outcome was inconclusive, the course of the dispute is worth following because of the insight it provides into his insistence that affairs should be conducted with integrity.

The belief that the steeple of Marchwiel church was built in 1789 cannot be verified from the surviving church records apart, that is, from the statement in the rural dean's report for 1791 that "This Church and Steeple have been lately built".[121] An amusing tale about Philip Yorke, if true, told by Nimrod suggests that the steeple was unsafe and that it was due for renovation.

...he was sitting in Marchwiel Church with his back to an old gentleman, who had fallen asleep in the sermon, when one of his tremendous sneezes exploded.

Now it happened that some doubt existed at the time as to the stability of the tower of this church, which was about to be repaired; and the old gentleman, imagining that the noise which assailed his ears was caused by its fall, absolutely tumbled to the ground with affright; and, being in a weak state of health at the time, it was said he never recovered it. Mr. Yorke used to say he believed he was the only man who had ever sneezed another to death.[122]

The Erthig papers themselves reveal that the chancel was rebuilt by William Worrall at a cost of £119 between 1776 and 1781.[123] That the work on the chancel took so long to complete could have been partly due to a disagreement which arose between the three squires, namely Philip Yorke, Charles Browne and Peter Ellis of Eyton, who had contracted to divide the cost, and a Mr. Twigge who was responsible for the upkeep of a fourth part of the chancel before he sold his property in the area and went to live elsewhere. The trouble arose over this part of the agreement; Peter Ellis refused to pay his share, declaring that, as the parish occupied a third of the chancel, the parishioners should bear a proportion of the expense of rebuilding. Accordingly, on December 17th, 1781, Philip Yorke wrote to Peter Ellis,

> I understood it to be your wish, when this matter was last mooted, that a Vestry might meet to consider what interest the Parish had in the chancel of Marchwiel Church, and how far they ought to bear any Concern in the Expences of the same. My stay in Wales, was at that time so near its period that I was obliged to desire that this business might be adjourned to my return, and if it be agreeable to you now, I thought of desiring Mr. Strong to have the following notice given next Sunday. That a Vestry will be held in the Parish Church of Marchwiel on Tuesday the 8th of Janry 1782 at Eleven o'Clock in the forenoon, to consider and adjust the Property of the Chancel so far as the said Parish are supposed to have any claims on the same.[124]

This carefully worded letter elicited from Peter Ellis a swift denial that he had had any desire of calling a vestry meeting and a declaration that he thought that Philip Yorke could settle the matter with or without one.[125]

The dispute remained unresolved during the following year, with Peter Ellis remaining obdurate. Finally, on March 7th, 1783, Philip Yorke wrote to Thomas Hayman, his solicitor, enclosing with his letter "the several papers that have passed between Mr. Brown, Mr. Ellis, Worrall the builder and Mr. Boydell of Trevallin, & myself relating to the new Chancel of Marchwiel Church, from which you will draw a Case for a civil or common law opinion, which ever it may be most proper to consult". All other steps having failed to secure from Mr. Ellis what was really a modest sum of around £20, Philip Yorke and Charles Browne decided to resort to "more forcible expedients",[126] and Philip Yorke concluded his letter of March 7th, 1783 to Thomas Hayman with the following words:

> ...might you not give Mr. Ellis a line, acquainting him of the order you had received from Mr. Brown, and me, to commence a suit against him, and rather

advising him to submit to an Arbitration than to stand the Issue, and you may presume Mr. Brown's and my Consent to such a Reference.[127]

The matter seemed to hang fire for a number of years until, in 1792, Philip Yorke rejected the idea of taking the case to a 'Court of Equity', arguing that it was hardly "worth such a contention".[128] Whether or not he intended at any stage to resort to more than threats of legal proceedings it is impossible to say, but it would seem that his usual common sense finally prevailed.

We have seen Philip Yorke in the roles of a somewhat passive politician and a far more active justice. What can be said about his career as a soldier? Nimrod's picture of Philip Yorke – "the worst horseman I ever saw in a saddle" – riding furiously, a cocked hat on his head and generally clad in cold weather in an immense blue military cloak, the remnant of his military exploits in the Denbighshire Militia some twenty years before,[129] has made it difficult to take him seriously in this role. However, his career in the Denbighshire Militia, which was first formed on May 8th, 1760 and consisted of 280 men,[130] is worth some attention, if only for the insight it affords into various features of that organisation. He was appointed as a deputy-lieutenant for Denbighshire on October 21st, 1765,[131] but no records of his activities in this role have come to light. Between the end of the Seven Years' War and the start of the American War of Independence the militia was merely assembled each year for twenty-eight days' exercise and training, but the alliance of France with the rebel American colonies in 1778 made it necessary for it to be re-embodied. In company with the majority of his fellow Tory squires, he was opposed to war but saw the American revolt as an alarming threat to the established order not merely in the New World but in the mother country. As early as July 30th, 1775 he had written to the Earl of Hardwicke,

> I do assure your Lordship this most unnatural and bloody Contention in America, makes me quite sick at heart. A Continental war seems to me preposterous and impracticable, and to my Political sense (having confined their trade by yr fleets, and secured Boston as a Place of Arms and refuge to yr Friends), you must wait till it shall please God to give to that Headstrong and Contumacious People, a better sense of duty, and obedience, and a more accomodative spirit ...[132]

On August 29th 1778, Philip Yorke was commissioned Captain in the Denbighshire Regiment of Militia[133] and served until it was disembodied at the end of the American War of Independence. When the militia was embodied, it could be stationed in quarters, in barracks or in camp. Though one letter from Philip Yorke to John Caesar referred to the militia exercising at Erthig during his absence,[134] other references were mainly concerned with his military life in quarters or in camp. It was only in the camps, with their accompanying exercises and reviews, that the militia could reach a reasonable standard of proficiency.[135]

His period of service, therefore, coincided with a time of war, when the militia's main task was to safe-guard the home country, performing such duties as guarding prisoners of war, suppressing riots, chasing smugglers and protecting the coasts against attack, while the regular army was abroad.[136]

Philip Yorke, like the majority of his fellow officers, seems to have been a reluctant soldier. He qualified as an officer because he owned land worth more than £150 a year.[137] Even though the arrangements for the organisation of the militia were such as to reinforce the local power of the country gentlemen, they showed little enthusiasm for serving in its ranks and, in many cases, performed their duties in a perfunctory fashion.[138] On December 8th, 1778, an anonymous writer sent a letter to Lord Jeffrey Amherst, the commander-in-chief to inform him,

> ...that not one of the Captains (except the Ajutant) are at present with the Denbighshire Militia, quartered at Whitehaven, Workington and Maryport in Cumberland, the Major has been absent since June, and the Colonel since September, since which time only one Captain (except the Ajutant) has ever seen his Corpse, he, it is true, did stay with them till his Attendance was required in Parliament and never absented himself for more than 14 days from them; the other captain has scarsely ever seen his Company, to their great Disadvantage, and at this time there is not an officer above the Rank of Captain with them (the Ajutant excepted)...[139]

A series of letters between June 28th and September 15th, 1778[140] show that Philip Yorke was the Captain who had been with his men in their Cumberland quarters and who had returned to Erthig on his way to attend Parliament at the end of October.[141] Whatever he thought of them, it seems that he took his military duties seriously, as he did his obligations in other areas of his life. On August 20th 1780 he wrote to the Earl of Hardwicke, "I have worn away the best part of the Summer, here [i.e. in the camp, this time at Southsea]. It is a life, that the Public Good can only reconcile to a Country Gentleman, and to a man, of the least regularity of manners ..."[142]

Guarding the country in wartime meant responding to the occasional scare. It also provided Philip Yorke with the opportunity to study and describe his surroundings at Cockermouth.

> It is my fortune to trouble your lordship from such places, as have no note, or mark on the map. This is a rising town, in the Solway Firth, 14 miles to the Northward of Whitehaven. We have 150 Houses at least, where 28 years since there was but one house. They supply (with Whitehaven) Dublin with coal, and their trade has no way suffered in the late public misfortunes... I live in command here, in the house Quarters, with eternal Interrogations, from the soldiers, or one person, or the other. The Regiment being detached gives me this trouble, and Authority. The night attack on Whitehaven I suppose was the cause of our coming here; otherwise the shoals, tides and sands, set an enemy of any strength much at a distance. We camp here after a march of 220 miles from Newport in very good health and spirits last Saturday month...[143]

On September 12th, 1778 he wrote to John Caesar from Workington,

> We were moved here on Thursday on an alarm of American Privateers on the Coast, but it seems on Enquiry, to be ill founded, and we shall be ordered I conclude to Maryport very soon.[144]

Their periods in camp left the officers with plenty of leisure time and regimental life could take on the semblance of a holiday, with invitations to various functions being issued by gentry living in the neighbourhood.[145] Philip Yorke informed John Caesar from Workington,

> The Gentlemen of this neighbourhood have been very obliging to us. I have Received particular Civility from a neighbring Gentleman of large fortune of the name of Christian...[146]

The stream of letters dealing with estate matters at Erthig sent to John Caesar from various army camps during this period also attest to the amount of time on his hands which was not being consumed by military activities. He even had leisure for one of his poetic effusions entitled *Journey to Maryport, June 1778*:

> The twenty-fourth, I left my dwelling,
> and out I went a colonelling;
> Not with such joy, as lovers run,
> I hasten'd to this northern sun,
> For they have subjects softer far,
> Than the rough circumstances of war.

He then proceeded to describe the various scenes on the journey while lamenting the inadequacy of his poetic gift:

> All unfit my dogg'rel,
> Thy magnificence to sing.
>
> Keswick's lakes, demand a lay
> Equal in depth, and clear as they;
> My colourings are all too faint,
> I feel the scenes, I cannot paint.
> Cockermouth! thy ... ? ... glory,
> Speaks to the Great, an useful story;
> Once the seat of Percy's might,
> Haunted now, by birds of night.
> Dust and business, coal and smother,
> Mark thee, Whitehaven! 'bove all other:
>
> Maryport, they welcome street,
> Kindly receives my wearied feet.[147]

It has been alleged that Philip Yorke received no pay and incurred heavy expenses in pursuit of his military duties.[148] This statement is not entirely true, however. To pay and equip their regiments, officers received funds from the government and supplied themselves and their men with what they required. If they could, they made a profit, though some items of equipment were supplied by the government.[149] Food, the cost of which was met by the men from their pay, was supplied by contractors.[150] There were occasions when expenses would be incurred, especially when the pay was late in arriving or had to be used to defray urgent expenses. On July 17th, 1778, Philip Yorke wrote to John Caesar,

> To be sure you must not be without money at this time, and therefore I enclose you 60£ – at the same time I am obliged to live by London draughts, as well as you, for our pay from the 25th of last March to this time, has all been consumed in the Expences of the march of the Regiment here, and in the present the Captains made of short [?] clothes to the men …[151]

As we have seen, Philip Yorke was very short of money at this time, but the entries of expenses and receipts in his account book are too fragmentary to calculate the extent to which his militia activities were a contributory factor. In the following examples, covering the period July to October 1781, his expenses outweighed the money he received by just under £10, but the system of payment was slow and disorganised[152]and we can never be certain that Philip Yorke kept a record of every payment made by or to him.

	£	s	d
1781 - July 25th Sutler's Bill at Warley	7.	0.	0
August 24th J. to and from Margate	48.	18.	0
July 9th Received of Capt. Eyton (Paymaster)	20.	0.	0
August 18th Recd. of Captain Eyton	10.	10.	0
September 13th Recd. of Captain Eyton	20.	0.	0
September 17th Recd. from Serj. Robertson on Acct. of Thompson and Lewis	1.	19.	4
September 17th From Gartside on Acct. of Lewis	2.	11.	10
September 17th Ditto on Acct. of Thompson		10.	6
October 1st Present to Hostler at Warley		10.	6
October 16th Horses standing at Warley	10.	10.	0
October 16th Serjt. Hughes Taylor		9.	6[153]

To supply provisions for men and animals in the camp, the Treasury usually concluded contracts for bread, fuel and forage, each camp having a resident commissary from the Treasury to deal with supplies. Such arrangements gave rise to a great deal of corruption. Philip Yorke suffered as a result of this, though he seemed to accept it without undue rancour.

> … In the survey of the new Parliamentary list, your Lordship finds many fresh names. I hear (and indeed have some occasion to know) that the Treasury have not been very delicate in the manner, or in the Persons chosen to their Boroughs. Among other of their Recommendations, I find a Mr. Fitzherbert for Arundel, our Camp Contractor for Hay and Oats, who, by the bye, served my Horses with very bad ones. So that I must say of him, as Charles 2nd did of Titus Oates, that he is a Rogue in Grain at least.[154]

As this suggests, provisions for the men, and even for the officers, were frequently of poor quality and gave rise to health problems in the camps.[155] Writing to John Caesar on October 20th, 1780 from the camp at Southsea, Philip Yorke complained "... for this month past I have been considerably ill, owing as Sir George Baker tells me, to the bad wine, and to the extraordinary fatigue, and severe discipline of the Camp ..."[156] On September 7th he had mentioned that "... I was laid up last Sunday with a severe attack of the Piles, from which I have suffered great pain and uneasiness".[157] Over a quarter of a century later, his army days long since over and after the conclusion of the Peace of Amiens, he wrote that "...I rejoice on many accounts in our late Peace.."[158], and cynically,

> I pray for the Peace of Jerusalem; long may it continue. For what is there to contemplate in war says Samuel Johnson, but the sudden Glory of Contractors and Commissaries, whose Equipages shine like meteors, and whose Palaces rise like Exhalations, and, by the bye, evaporate like them too...[159]

Nevertheless, the camps, apparently, were quite grand affairs and often presented a fine spectacle, though Warley camp was not as impressive as some.

> The common on which it stood was smaller than Coxheath, the ground was not level and it was covered in wood and furze, some of which had to be cleared. The 11,000 men there (nine militia and three regular regiments) had pitched their tents in two oblongs, set at an angle to each other. There was a separate park for the artillery. The tents were less regularly arranged, the marquees were only floored with turf, the booths were shabby...[160]

Philip Yorke's periods of service in quarters or camp, to judge from the available correspondence, were confined to the period from July to the end of October 1778 in the area of Whitehaven/Maryport/Cockermouth, August 1780 at Southsea camp near Portsmouth, and August and September 1781 at Warley camp.

The note of pride in his remark to John Caesar from Warley camp, that "Our Welshmen gained great Credit, in their Review last Wednesday",[161] seems to have been justified. The Royal Denbighshire Regiment of Militia, under the command of Lieutenant-Colonel John Myddleton, consisted of five companies, one of which was Philip Yorke's, and added up to a total of three hundred and twenty men. They were reviewed at Warley camp by Lieutenant-General George L. Parker,[162] and the following extracts from the official account of the review will show how the Regiment performed.

> *Officers* – Armed with Fusils. Salute moderately well. Uniformly clothed. They wore caps.
> *Manual Exercises* – Well performed, and in proper time.
> *Marching* – March tolerable well, and arms well carried.
> *Firings* – Well performed. The front rank in making ready did not bring the Butts to the ground, as directed in the exercise.
> *Manoeuvres* – Tolerably well performed.
> *Arms* – Good. Clean, and in proper order.

Accoutrements – Good, and carry 29 rounds.

Clothing – of the year 1781. Bad Cloth. Coats had no lining. But indifferently fitted. The men wore jacked leather Caps.

Complaints - None.

General Observations – This Regiment as Militia may be said to be fit for Service, and considering how short a time the Men had been ballotted in, did their Business as well as could be expected. The officers mess together, and seem'd to live in Harmony - Had a Band of Music. Performed all the Firings and Manoeuvres according to General Lord Amherst's Instructions.[163]

The militia furnished Philip Yorke with an opportunity to extend his experience in another direction. The maintenance of discipline in the regiments was by no means easy and after 1762 the militia, whether embodied or disembodied, was subject to martial law. Courts martial were composed of officers only. Lesser offences were tried by regimental courts martial appointed by the commanding officer, while more serious offences went to general courts martial, appointed by a higher authority.[164] The panel of officers would contain representatives from a number of regiments. The trial in which Philip Yorke was involved concerned two captains of the Cambridgeshire regiment, with which the Hardwicke family had close links. Nowhere is it stated, but it might be fair to surmise, that the Hardwicke connection once again was involved in some way. In any case, Philip Yorke was to write the Earl of Hardwicke a letter relating to the court martial.[165]

The trial examined Captains Littell and Aveling on the rather vague charge of "Aspersing Characters and Conduct", and although an objection was made to the Judge Advocate, Sir Charles Gould, on the grounds that the charge should be more specific,[166] from the sparse information available no alteration seems to have been made. Unfortunately, no details of the trial itself can be found. It would appear, however, that the complainants were given an opportunity to try to justify the accusations which were the grounds for the charge, while the defendants in their turn were permitted to attempt to disprove them.[167] The case went on throughout most of July, 1781 and until the first week of August when the Earl of Hardwicke, who made an appearance at the court martial,[168] sent the dismissory letters to Captains Littell and Aveling.[169]

On August 9th, Philip Yorke wrote a letter to the Earl of Hardwicke in which he expressed his sympathetic understanding of the plight of the two men while, at the same time, deploring their tactics.

Being confined to my Bench, when your Lordship attended our late Court-Martial, I lost the opportunity I wished of paying my respects to you, on this Ground. Your Lordship has no doubt heard the Issue of that business, which has taken from this Camp, and Service, two of your Cambridgeshire Captains. Mr. Aveling seemed to me, in particular to possess Powers, and coolness, equal to such unhappy Contest; yet his judgement appears to have remarkably deserted him in the Conduct of this. Had he and Mr. Little, confessed the Avowal of their belief in the Contents of the Anonymous letter, and that in the first Instance (which in the course of the Trial, they afterwards allowed, and which indeed, was sufficiently proved against them at Hockerill) and had they then thrown themselves on the Court, under the mitigation of that opinion, being in a manner involuntarily drawn from them, I really think they might have escaped with a Reprimand for Indiscretion only; but on the other hand, taking on themselves the bold ground of accusation, under the colour of Defence, and failing in the proof of the Facts of that letter, after the most cruel and malignant Investigation, they seem to me, to have brought most deservedly on themselves, the disgrace of their present sentence. I trust, and Hope as well for your Lordship's as the Public Service that Feuds will cease in the Cambridgeshire Regiment. As far as I can Judge of the Field appearance, they do their business very well, and are very well manoevr'd by their Lt. Colonel. [170]

Philip Yorke's record of public service confirms the impression of his character which is given by his other activities. His energy and the detailed attention he gave to the task in hand are evident throughout his public life. There was, it is true, potential advantage to him in producing reports of Commons debates accurately and rapidly for the Earl of Hardwicke, but he exhibited the same thought and commitment towards the reform of the poor law administration in Wrexham and the affairs of the church in Marchwiel. Reluctant soldier though he was, it was typical of him that he should have been the only captain in his regiment to have served in Cumberland during the summer of 1778 and that he should have left only to fulfil his parliamentary duties at the end of October.

His most significant contribution was made in the sphere of local administration, where he revealed a shrewd appreciation of its inadequacies and perceived the need for a degree of professionalism. This was the sphere, too, where his natural benevolence and strong sense of public duty could find the greatest expression.

That he was able to participate so actively in public life is the more remarkable since his military and political career coincided with the period of his greatest involvement in the improvement to his house and estate. Inevitably, one wonders whether his contribution to public affairs might not have been more substantial if his energies had not been dissipated in so many areas.

CHAPTER 10: Literary Pursuits

Nimrod and the Rev. Samuel Strong noted that Philip Yorke excelled as a conversationalist, the former recalling in later life the lively, companionable and stimulating evenings spent in the company of Philip and Diana Yorke at Erthig.[1] The urbane host was also a prolific letter writer and, in the manner of the time, his letters were not unlike conversations, accommodated in tone to their recipients. Those to his stewards or to his collaborators, such as John Lloyd Hafodunos,[2] or Walter Davies,[3] concentrated solely on the matter in hand and called for action. Those to Lord Brownlow or to the Earls of Hardwicke, on the other hand, were not merely more deferential and composed with greater care, but also more relaxed in character, with a wider range of subject-matter; like his conversation, they included an occasional classical reference or apt quotation in Latin, all in the best of taste. The number of almost illegible drafts to be found in his account books and on blank pages in his hand-written copies of *The Royal Tribes of Wales* testify to the care he bestowed on his correspondence.

At times, he could be critical of others, as we have seen, but, unlike so many of his contemporaries, he was never slanderous or vicious. Nimrod remarked that he appeared incapable of thinking ill of anyone[4] and, while that is perhaps excessive praise, his letters, on the whole, do convey good-nature, moderation and commonsense, all qualities then held to be marks of good breeding.

Philip Yorke also wrote verses, as did many other members of the leisured classes of his day. "Those who have read his prose works will lament that he had not written more; and those who have perused his poetical effusions, perhaps, for the sake of literature, may wish that he had written under that 'Geny', as Antony Wood terms it, less",[5] wrote a contemporary, the Rev. John Evans, and one cannot disagree.

However,it seems that Philip Yorke himself held no great opinion of his verses. In his *Journey to Maryport*, for instance, he recognised his own shortcomings as a poet and expressed regret that his 'doggerel' was not worthy of its subject.[6] This particular poem appeared in a small volume published in Wrexham in 1802 under the title *Crude Ditties*, and John Evans remarked that "the title is an appropriate Critique of the work",[7] a verdict the author would have heartily endorsed, presumably, since it was his own choice.

In the same vein of self-mockery he appended the name of Tudur Aled or Tudur of Aled to some of his unpublished verses written after he acquired Dyffryn Aled. Tudur Aled was in fact the bardic name of one of the finest Welsh poets of the late fifteenth and early sixteenth centuries[8] who was a member of one of the gentry families of the area.

Philip Yorke's verses merit some attention, however, not because of their intrinsic quality but because they reveal the lighter, more humorous side to his nature emphasised by Nimrod, of which only rare glimpses are afforded by his letters. He seemed to compose verses on all manner of topics as and when the mood took him and they can be found scattered here and there in his commonplace books. His verses on individual servants at Erthig are well-known, as are those written by later members of the Yorke family. The following less familiar examples of his shorter poems give an impression of his style and humour.[9]

Old W . . te

In these days of encreas'd agricultural taste,
Old W . . te is grown great, by enclosing the waste;
Improvements too solidly founded, to fail;
Productory property, vested in-tail.
Hence the source of his fame, reputation, and riches.
Deservedly made, by making our breeches.

Inscription
On the broad silver rim of a very coarse earthen jug

Jug of earth, conceive not pride,
Though to rim of silver ty'd;
Rim of silver, know thy birth,
And disdain not jug of earth.

A Welsh Lady
Disputing with a Gentleman, that the Welsh were never conquered.

Quoth Mary, to Philip, in national mood,
Our Welshmen, I hold Sir, were never subdu'd;
With deference due, says Philip agen,
Your position was right, had you read Welshwomen.

To a Lady, with some Snuff

Might I humbly propose
This address to your nose,
With the sweet little tip,
Not so choice as your lip,
And in metrical stuff Present you some snuff.
 But hear sister Fan,
Who thus gravely began,
 " 'Twas made only for man,
And should not disgrace
Our more delicate face."

He was aware that humour could be used to make a point. Never one for useless adornment, his aesthetic sense could be outraged by what appeared to him offensive and tasteless embellishment which destroyed the harmony of the original, be it garden or building. In one such instance, at least, he was moved to vent his feelings in verse.

A New Brick Porch
Havinq been added to the Old stone church,
at Bangor, Monachorum

What a barb'rous trick?
With a red nose of brick,
To patch the *stone* face,
Of this reverend place,
Committing of waste in the regions of taste:
Most surely the Clark,
Was much in the dark,
That he did not prevent
Such an evil intent,
And avoid the disgrace
That attended the case.
Some Bricklay'r was Warden,
(A choice flow'r in that garden,)*
Had he been but a Mason,
'Twould have had a stone case on.

O ye men, of renown,
Who inhabit this town,
Where,where,were you dosing,
When this porch was composing?
For neither were ye, slumb'ring seen
Gently snoring on the Green;
Nor on Gwernhayled's favor'd top,
Nor upon the neighb'ring cop,
When this excrescence, filthy,vile,
Was stuck upon your ancient pile;
This barbarous compound of mortar, and brick;
Oh! rise River Dee then, and wash it off quick.

* See Epitaph in Wrexham Church

The light-hearted spirit which inspired Philip Yorke's verses contrasted sharply with the seriousness with which he approached his antiquarian pursuits. It is possible that his love of the past may have first been aroused when, as an undergraduate at Oxford, he read classical and medieval history. Certainly, as early as 1768, he was elected a F.S.A.[10] which was a further indication of a burgeoning interest in the past. A few years later, it seems that the environment of his own region was engaging his attention, and he joined those hardy travellers who rode through Wales in search of the sublime and the picturesque.

By 1773 he had already undertaken two such tours[11] and in 1776 he planned a third, [12] part of which he accomplished in August, with members of the Cust family and "Mr. Kent, the descendant of our first modern Gardener". The difficulties which travel involved clearly did nothing to dampen his enthusiasm since, in a letter of September 24th, he tried to persuade the Earl of Hardwicke to visit Erthig and accompany him on a similar journey.

> I beg leave to assure your lordship, that it would give Mrs.Yorke and me, the highest pleasure to wait upon you and my Lady Grey, at Erthig, and to be able to attend you, to our more capital objects. You would do us great honour, and I hold myself rather a good Guide, having twice completed the Tour of North Wales.

He tried to shame the Earl of Hardwicke into agreeing by extolling the courage of the aged Lord Temple, "so infirm upon his legs", who had visited Erthig and had been

> at the foot of Snowdon, but did not venture to ascend, but surveyed that mighty mountain from the lake at its foot, a handsome piece of water, and navigable. He visited several of our ancient Ruinated Castles (as his lordship is pleased to say) with great pleasure and surprize. And now, may I be indulged in a hope at least, that your lordship, who moves under none of those difficulties my poor Lord Temple doth will sometime incline to a Welsh Journey.[13]

This quotation conveys a hint of Philip Yorke's visual interest in the landscape and his sense of awe when faced with the rugged grandeur of Snowdon. The references to "our more capital objects" and "our castles" suggest also his identification with the country to which he had no ties of blood.

When he was on holiday in Prestatyn in the Autumn of the same year[14] he made another attempt to interest the Earl of Hardwicke when he wrote,

> I made a visit of a day and night last week, to my friend Mr. Pennant[15] whose house at Downing, is seven miles from hence. He was very obliging in communicating to me, so much as he had written on the Marches of Wales which he talks of Publishing the next Spring. His bookseller (White), presses him to it earlier, and says, the Town will relish a piece of Goat's Flesh in the Winter – savoury meat in patriarchal times. Mr. Pennant has wove into this first British volume, the History of Owen Glendwr. He has digested his life into Annalls, and I thought it formed, as far as it went, an interesting episode.

This qualified approval of what was to be a major factor in the rehabilitation of Owain Glyn Dwr as a Welsh hero[16] did not stop Philip Yorke from relating his career at considerable length and adding, by way of apology,

> I beg your lordship's pardon for running so far into Welsh Antiquities, but I have been led into them lately, from a promise I made to Mr. Pennant, to investigate those of my neighbourhood, and I have been fortunate in picking up some papers which Mr. Pennant thinks of value.[17]

This connection with Thomas Pennant was to be crucial to Philip Yorke's development as a student of Welsh history and genealogy. On December 3rd, 1776 he sent Pennant an account of part of the journey he had undertaken the previous August.[18] It covered the initial stages in the Wrexham area and then proceeded to an outline of the history of Bromfield and Yale which focused on the leading families of the Lordship – an early indication of the direction his interests would follow in the future. At the same time, he revealed his curiosity about the surviving historical monuments in the locality. He described how, on their journey, the travellers

> ... passed, in primo lumine, the inscrutable Remains of Wat's Dyke ... Our Traditions, for we have no written memorial, that it was a Contemporary Work, with Offa's Dyke, which for a considerable way, runs parallel with it, at unequal distances, but here, within two miles, the intermediate Country is supposed to have been neutral ground, set apart for Treaty, and Traffick, and it was a law to each Nation, that if a Saxon was taken armed on the Western side of Offa, or a Welshman to the East of Watt, he forfeited the loss of a Member ...[19]

Then followed the account, complete with foot notes and references, of the main historical developments in the Lordship of Bromfield and Yale from the year 870 A.D.. One can only regret that Philip Yorke did not emulate Thomas Pennant, whom he so admired, and produce a detailed topographical account of his tours, combining historical and geological elements with natural history, the whole seasoned with his own insight and experiences. The "papers which Mr. Pennant thinks of value" and Philip Yorke's subsequent investigations at the British Museum provided, it appears, the historical element in his account of his 1776 tour, as well as some of the background material for Thomas Pennant's *Tours in Wales.*

The early influence of Thomas Pennant on Philip Yorke, as well as on other students of Welsh history, cannot be over-estimated. He was the leader of a small group of antiquarians, drawn from the gentry and clergy of north-east Wales, who became prime contributors to the late eighteenth century renaissance in the study of Welsh history. As we have seen, Thomas Pennant's request to Philip Yorke in 1776 first involved him in such investigations and, on December 8th. of that year, we find him writing to John Lloyd of Wigfair and Hafodunos, MP and bibliomaniac, who was dubbed the Philosopher,[20] and whose assistance he sought in tracing the descent of the lordship of Bromfield and Yale. "I have been putting together some old notes for my friend Mr. Pennant, and I trouble you at this time that it might be something more accurate." He had, he said, consulted the historians David Powel[21] and William Camden,[22] but was rather wary of their conclusions.

> I believe it is clear that Sir W. Stanley enjoyed the Honour, Castle and Lands of Chirk by the bounty of Edw. 4; I wish I could be assured that Bromfield and Yale was given at the same time. [23]

Presumably, he thought that John Lloyd could find the information he sought in his huge library of books, manuscripts and maps. By 1777 it appears he may have become dissatisfied with John Lloyd's efforts, for it was then that he went to the British Museum and took the research on the history of Bromfield and Yale into his own hands. His detailed notes included a section on the lordship's development, lists of its manors and townships and of relevant source material at the Museum.[24] The meticulous research was typical of his whole approach but this visit to a museum to carry out his own investigation was one of the very rare recorded instances when he did not rely on the efforts of others to provide him with his raw material.

In the same year he found himself playing the role of unofficial critic of work which Thomas Pennant had submitted to him. Philip Yorke's remarks on the two Dykes, Offa's and Wat's, were better informed than those of a year earlier and show him making his own appraisal of the site and the function of the earthworks.

> The Dyke I apprehend was clearly a boundary, and not a work of defence, yet there are near upon it large Entrenchments seemingly to command it. It is the same with Wat's Dyke; To Sport a conjecture; might not the Dyke or rampire, properly speaking of this Foss, which was clear amidst a surrounding country of wood, act as a road or communication from North to South to be cast to a double use.[25]

He offered some words of criticism of Thomas Pennant's text. Concerning one line, for example, Philip Yorke suggested that "the word Castle is improperly repeated", and of another he enquired "Is not this part of the maid's story, too funny and gay for a grave and distinctive work?" The fact that Thomas Pennant, previously his mentor, was prepared to submit his work to Philip Yorke's scrutiny is surely significant as an indication of his growing stature in this field. In thanking Thomas Pennant for sending him his work he declared his impatience for "another of your most entertaining volumes, I can pay you but with thanks, the poor man' s exchequer" .[26]

The correspondence did not stop there. On November 17th, 1777, Philip Yorke informed Thomas Pennant that the vicar of Gresford had dined with him at Erthig,

> … and he encourages me to dislodge that ancient Briton from his snug situation under the wall of his church. My mason (who is a careful Person, and like his master, having a due veneration for Antiquities) will go over with me for that purpose, and we will serve Wilkinson the Herald with notice, if he should be at leisure to attend us in the Course of the next week.

After consulting David Powel's *The History of Cambria* (1584), Philip Yorke thought that the monument could be that of Madoc ap Llywelyn ap Gruffudd, the great-great-grandfather of Owain Glyn Dwr. He then proceeded to trace the history of the family in some detail.[27]

A year later he furnished Thomas Pennant with a meticulously detailed account of some Roman remains which had been excavated near Netherhall camp and included copies of the inscriptions.

> Mr. Senhouse is so kind to sit near me, and from his dictating, I make you the following Communication of such things as have been found in and near the Camp, since you were in this Country.[28]

Philip Yorke, therefore, had some first-hand experience of an investigation which arrived at conclusions based not on preconceived ideas drawn from ancient myths but on a study of surviving evidence, an approach pioneered by scholars such as George Owen of Henllys and, above all, Edward Lluyd,[29] and continued in his own day by his friend, Thomas Pennant. Though Philip Yorke's chosen field would ultimately be genealogy, his investigations would be marked by similarly close examination of his source material.

The years 1776 to 1778 see, therefore, Philip Yorke's introduction to the field of Welsh antiquities and his progress from an enthusiastic beginner to a relatively experienced and disciplined researcher, whose opinion even Thomas Pennant appeared to value. This burst of activity was followed, it seems, by a lull which lasted until 1783, though it is always possible that other correspondence has not survived. It would, however, be understandable if other matters took priority over research in those years. In 1779 his wife Elizabeth had died in childbirth, leaving him with a family of small children for whom he had to make arrangements.[30] At the same time, he was busily engaged in improving his estate and in pursuing his political career and militia activities.

This first phase of Philip Yorke's career as an investigator and antiquary and, in particular, his correspondence between 1776 and 1778, provide a good example of the collaborative nature of contemporary historical research.

Most written source material was located in the libraries of the gentry, such as those at Wynnstay, Hengwrt, Gloddaeth, Mostyn Hall, Hafodunos with its ten thousand items and, of course, at Downing, the home of Thomas Pennant, which was said to house over five thousand volumes.[31] Mention should be made in this context of Philip Yorke's own library at Erthig, with its catalogue in his own handwriting and a page listing the books which he had loaned to his fellow antiquarians. From it we learn that "Mr. Pennant", for instance, had borrowed the 1751 volume of the *Gentleman's Magazine* on January 9th, 1779, while "Mr. Warrington" had taken out the *Chronicles* of Baker, Holinshed, Matthew Paris, Speed, Stow and Fabian, together with Blair's *Chronology* and *Leges Anglo-Saxon*, all source books quoted in his *History of Wales*. The word "Returned" appeared after each loan![32] Thus the resources needed by the antiquarians were available in these and other widely dispersed repositories. However, travel was difficult, time-consuming and tedious in those days, especially in winter, and, therefore, mutual assistance was a prerequisite of historical investigation. For instance, when Thomas Pennant was collecting information for the account of his tours of Wales and Scotland he placed a questionnaire in the Chester newspapers, appealing to the Welsh gentry to supply him with material about the antiquities of their parishes.[33] Philip Yorke inserted a similar plea as an Advertisement in his first publication, the *Tracts of Powys*.[34] Each sought the help of the other and of like-minded individuals, such as John Lloyd of Hafodunos, Walter Davies and the Rev. John Lloyd of Caerwys,[35] as well as of a host of lesser lights. John Lloyd of Caerwys played a significant role behind the scenes as scholar, copyist and translator for more prominent and socially elevated figures like Thomas Pennant, William Warrington and Philip Yorke himself. He supplied them with a great deal of historical and genealogical information, and accompanied Thomas Pennant on many of his journeys. Pennant acknowledged John Lloyd's contribution to his work; "to his great skill in the language and antiquities of our country I own myself much indebted".[36] Philip Yorke called him "my worthy friend, that excellent historian and antiquary", and nicknamed him 'Bloddy', a corruption of Blodeu Llanarmon. The bestowing of irreverent nicknames like 'Bloddy' for blodeu and 'Double-Ned' for Edward Edwards, a Wrexham curate,[37] seems to indicate Philip Yorke's affection for these individuals and reflects his quirky sense of humour. The Erthig papers contain a number of letters on genealogical subjects written by Bloddy and copies by him of a seventeenth century life of Owain Glyn Dwr, Robert Vaughan's *British Antiquities Revived* and several other works.[38]

Philip Yorke's extensive knowledge of both general and local history also influenced his study of genealogy. In some of the instances cited, it was his fascination with surviving artefacts which led him to direct his enquiry into family history. Even when he was not primarily concerned with scholarship he would often introduce a historical perspective. For example, a letter to Ellis Yonge of Acton, thanking his wife for making him a present of portraits of the notorious Judge Jeffreys and his brother, was the occasion for declaring his views on the significance of Judge Jeffreys in the political disorders of his time.[39] Again,when in his role of JP he was concerned with the building of a bridge over the river Deunant near Llansannan, he appealed to history to support his case.

I find by some ancient papers at Dyffrynaled, that there had formerly been one, and indeed the side walls still remain, and the reason given there, for its existence, as being the high Road for the conveyance of stores and ammunition to his Highness's Castles of Conway and Carnarvon – nor can the reasonableness, not to say necessity, of one, be at present, doubted. It is a great thoroughfare; of lime, particularly ...[40]

When the new rector of Marchwiel was appointed, Philip Yorke sought a new agreement with him on his tithes. His instructions to John Caesar provide a good illustration of his precision over detail (especially if some matter of economy was at stake) and his tendency to seek out the historical roots of any problem or situation.[41]

Speaking of the Church, the Question of Tythes naturally occurrs; and by an ancient and authentick Paper, I think I trace the origin of the Parson's acceptance of the Eleventh instead of the 10th Cock: It was usual (as my Document says) in Queen Elizabeth's time, for the Farmers, not to bind up their Corn in Sheaves, but directly as they reaped or mowed it, to put it into Carts, and convey it into their Barns.

When the present improved practice came in, the Parson certainly stipulated to accept the Eleventh Sheave; and the Farmer prepared and bound it for him with the same extraordinary Labour, with which he did his own, as an acknowledgment for the same; Consequently, if the Parson will insist on the 10th he must take it according to the primitive Use: But you understand, that if we do not agree Pr. Acre for the Hay, with Mr. Strong, I do not mean but to make it for him, at present:

Not surprisingly, in view of his particular cast of mind, he sought to embellish and enliven with what he termed 'anecdotes', the genealogical studies which, before his time, had consisted of little more than lists of pedigrees. Thomas Pennant similarly looked for 'anecdotes' for the accounts of his tours; "I look up to my friends for history and anecdote latent among their papers", he wrote in the advertisement included in the first volume of his *Tours in Wales* .[42] The word 'anecdote', as used by both men, referred not only to the stories as such, but also to details about the background, historical or otherwise, to a particular event, place or person. It has been claimed that it was the amount of historical anecdote included in them which distinguished Thomas Pennant's *Tours* from those of his contemporaries.[43] The same comparison might be made between *The Royal Tribes of Wales*, Philip Yorke's major work, and its predecessors in that field. The earlier works, as sources of material, were woefully inadequate. In one of his notebooks Philip Yorke wrote,

> The little we read with any confidence, respecting the *Tribes of Wales*, is to be found in a Book, printed at Oxford, in the year 1662 by the Title of *British Antiquities revived* the work of Robert Vaughan of Hengwrt in Merionethshire, who died in the reign of Charles the first and was the most eminent Antiquary and Welsh Genealogist of that Age ... [44]

Yet some years later he informed Thomas Pennant that "Vaughan of Hengwrt's account is dry, short, and unsatisfactory".[45] Philip Yorke did not have a very high opinion either of two other early works: *A Display of Heraldry of most particular Coat Armours, now at use in the six Counties of North Wales* by John Davies of Llansilin, 1716, and, by his nephew John Reynolds of Oswestry, *The Scripture Genealogy, beginning at Noah and to which is Added, the Genealogy of the Caesars, and Also a Display of Heraldry of the particular Coat of Arms now in use in the Six Counties of North Wales.* The latter was described by the editor of the 1887 edition of the *Royal Tribes of Wales* as "a very imperfect compilation" of manuscript materials left by his uncle "and put together with very little Knowledge of the subject".[46] Philip Yorke himself called Reynolds' work "an ordinary performance", and in his preface to *The Royal Tribes of Wales* referred to them both as "two poor books".

On another occasion, he summed up the situation with the comment, " What we have abroad, is without anecdote, imperfect and uninteresting ... "[47] Yet, however inadequate they were and difficult to obtain, Philip Yorke, years later, noted that he had had to consult these books for information on both the Five Royal Tribes and the Fifteen Common Tribes of Wales.[48] The dearth of studies in historical genealogy could be one reason why he chose to focus his attention on this area. There was a gap to be filled, a field which he could make his own, especially since, as he wrote to Thomas Pennant, "You have gathered the Welsh Harvest of History so close, that there is scarce any thing to Glean after you, especially in greater matters". There was a hint of flattery in this remark but that was frequently Philip Yorke's way when, as in this letter, he was trying to elicit information for his own use.[49] Likewise, the sincerity of his comment on another occasion, that he often wished that Thomas Pennant "had thought of it",[50] (i.e. investigating the Five Royal Tribes) is extremely questionable.

By 1783, Philip Yorke had returned to his investigations. His renewed activity in this year would, at first sight, tend to support the notion that it was Philip Yorke's alliance the previous year with an illustrious Welsh family which sparked off his studies into the Royal Tribes of Wales.[51] After his marriage to Diana Meyrick (née Wynn), he spent more and more time at Dyffryn Aled, the ancestral home of the Wynns, who were descended from Marchudd ap Cynan, founder of the eighth noble tribe of North Wales and Powys.[52] It would be truer to say, however, that it gave his interest in genealogy, already aroused, greater impetus and focus. Philip Yorke sought help "to unravel the Dyffryn Aled alliances". He wrote first to ask John Lloyd of Hafodunos , on June 11th, 1783, to finish what he himself had begun and to identify the coats of arms of the families concerned, which were to be painted by Moses Griffith.

> I enclose you a very coarse card of the Dyffrynaled alliances, so far as I am able at present to recover them. You see how much is wanting by it, to compleat them, and to make them worthy of Moses's Brush[53]; If at your leisure you can fill all or any of them, I shall be much obliged to you...[54]

The letter to Bloddy on June 30th., 1783 informed him that,

> ... with the assistance of Moses Griffiths this spring, I sett a handsome load of 12 Coats, over the Chimney of my lower Hall, at Erthig, where, if we live till the proper season comes, I hope, I shall blow a pipe with you ...

He wanted to do something similar at Dyffryn Aled for the Wynn family.

> ... I enclose you a very loose paper, that hath been all that I have been yet able to collect to this purpose; much you will perceive is wanting to it ... If you can do any-thing at your leisure, to help me out of this difficulty, I know you will; and you have the Salisbury Pedigree Book, near you.[55]

These letters exemplify the manner in which he conducted his subsequent investigations. He expected a great deal of his collaborators; indeed, "research assistants" might be a more appropriate term. They were to undertake research and furnish him with documentary material and thus supplement and, if necessary, correct, his own preliminary investigations. This procedure was time-consuming and, since the study absorbed him to the point of obsession, frustration caused him at times to lose patience and apply the relentless pressure and adopt the badgering tone which he employed towards his steward when estate business moved too slowly for his liking. The survival of a considerable body of correspondence allows us to trace the course of his enquiries and to follow in his own words the evolution of his thinking in this field.

A more intensive period of investigation of the Royal Tribes began in 1791 when Philip Yorke's letters took on a note of greater urgency. On February 3rd, Bloddy, in his role of supervisor, had returned some papers to him, "having made some few corrections, chiefly with respect to orthography..." He considered the genealogical content of the papers to be accurate enough, "till you come to the House of Mortimer, where you make sad work of it..." He referred Philip Yorke to the correct sources, including his own "little black Book of Pedigrees".[56] Philip Yorke was dissatisfied, and on March 21st wrote asking Bloddy for information on a number of families including the Mortimers. "...I cannot be exact in respect of this great house of March, for want of Dugdale's Baronage, which you will consult at Downing ..." He expressed his disapproval of "the Gwidr History", and considered that "...the printed note in your Black Book, quoting the White Book of Hergest, is a strange, unintelligible piece of nonsense..." At the same time, he sent Bloddy "four Pedigrees to examine, fill up, and make authentic ..." and to "... write them over, fair, and send, properly spelt and pointed..."[57]

A reference in 1791 to "the Tribe Room" and to printing some of the material "on the Beam Compartments" indicates that his feet were set on the path which was to lead to his two publications in 1795 and 1799. He obviously had in mind a study of the five Royal Tribes and not merely of the third Royal tribe which constituted the substance of his *Tracts of Powys*. He urged Bloddy to send him information on the various tribes. On June 6th 1791, he wrote "... it is really a very good arrangement of a subject if it could be filled up and you could cover the skeleton with wholesome goat's flesh".[58] Later in the same month he tried to persuade John Lloyd of Hafodunos "to throw out any anecdotes not common, that relate to our eminent Welsh, and of which, I know from experience, that you have great and good store..."[59] Exercising all his powers of persuasion, he introduced the name of his eldest son, Simon,

> The fact is, my son Simon has left me an exercise, which altho' in its nature, certainly a good subject, yet fresh materials are much wanting. We would give you an account of each Tribe and its several descendants of Distinction, as they stand drawn out in my room at Erthig; you know very well from memory the Chief Families that descend from each – can you recollect which of the Kyffins of Maenan, translated a play, from Terence; was it the same, that fitted up the antique

Parlour there; you know a great deal of the Wynns of Soughton, and the Bishop especially; Do they come under the head of any Tribe ...?[60]

On July 19th, Philip Yorke turned to Thomas Pennant for assistance

I know your books will answer these questions in an instant, if I could get over to them. As I cannot, at present, determine that time, so I wish this information by letter, for I stop for want of it ...

A sign, perhaps, of Philip Yorke's growing frustration was the reference to Bloddy which followed: "Bloddy will only write from his pate, and good memory, and will not sit on a Chair, and consult Books, otherwise I had not troubled you, as above ..." There was, one suspects, amusement as well as irritation in this seemingly uncharitable remark because, later in the same letter, he called Bloddy "a worthy man, and excellent Welsh Genealogist ...; he is a liberal and living light to all who pry into pedigree."[61]

By October 8th 1792, Philip Yorke was writing to John Lloyd of Hafodunos seeking his help in finding

... a qualified person, to copy for me at the Museum [62] ... I remember a great many Welsh mss, I mean in English, of Welsh Families in that Collection, which will touch the tribe descendants. The subject is indeed a good one, if it was in better hands ...[63]

Evidently, John Lloyd did not reply quickly enough, for there was a note of great urgency in the letter which Philip Yorke wrote three weeks later:

... pray let me know if you received my letter, as I have no time to lose. The subject is an excellent one, if materials could be more easily found, which certainly exist.[64]

For whatever reason, there is another annoying gap in the correspondence until 1795 when the *Tracts of Powys* was published. This year also saw the start of a veritable flood of correspondence which made what had gone before seem a mere trickle. It continued virtually unabated until the publication of *The Royal Tribes of Wales* in 1799 and then gradually diminished, until it came to an end in 1803. *Tracts of Powys* was really an account of the third Royal Tribe and as such it was incorporated in *The Royal Tribes of Wales*. Perhaps a remark in an undated letter to Thomas Pennant might explain why Philip Yorke published his small tract first, without waiting until he had finished the larger work.

If it [i.e. the *Tracts of Powys*] eventually gets me some authentic information, it is all that can be expected of it ...[65]

1795 was also noteworthy because of the arrival on the scene of a figure who was destined to play an even more significant role in Philip Yorke's subsequent researches than Bloddy, the Philosopher and Thomas Pennant had in his investigations before this date.

Chapter 11: The Royal Tribes of Wales

Such was the extent of Walter Davies' contribution to *The Royal Tribes of Wales* that a reader of *Bygones* enquired whether he had actually written the book. [1] The journal recorded no answer. A modern historian has called Philip Yorke "the editor of the book", [2] while he referred to himself modestly as the "historical collector" of its contents.[3] The following pages will attempt to resolve the question.

In addition to writing his famous reports on the agriculture of north and south Wales, Walter Davies (1761-1849) made a name for himself in the world of letters as a poet, antiquarian and adjudicator. His interests also included medicine, astronomy and, more importantly, as far as Philip Yorke was concerned, genealogy. Like Bloddy, Walter Davies was a clergyman who held a number of livings during the course of his career.[4] Apart from his own considerable output, this "Goliath of literature", as Angharad Llwyd called him, gave enormous help to other writers in preparing and publishing their work.[5] The claim was made by Richard Williams in 1876 that "...few books relating to Wales and its borders appeared during the first half of the present century without receiving the benefit of his valuable aid".[6] Because of the collaborative nature of historical research at the time, authors like Thomas Pennant, William Warrington and Philip Yorke himself all acknowledged their debt to others. [7]

There is no record of how and when exactly the association between Philip Yorke and Walter Davies began but, shortly before the publication of *Tracts of Powys*, the latter received several requests for information about the Tribes of Wales and drafts for him to "correct" and "enliven". On April 14th, 1795, for instance, Philip Yorke wrote, "...I shall be highly obliged to you, if you will not only try the dates and facts by your valuable books and mss. but where you can, throw in some fresh and curious matter..." He asked Walter Davies to send him some books to consult and to return the sheets "in separate single covers of not more than an ounce each, directed to my son, S. Yorke Esq., MP, no.14, Parliament Street, London".[8]

The *Tracts of Powys* was merely the first phase of a far more ambitious project, "a Biography of Wales, a Country which hath never been wanting of great men and correspondent events through many generations." [9] After the publication of *The Royal Tribes of Wales* had provided a second instalment of this, he discussed more fully his objective,

... a continuation of Welsh Annals ... to the present Period; in the Characters (and incidents) and accounts of extraordinary men, descended from our ancient Princes, and distinguished Ancestors; who really appear utterly extinct, as in their former power, so as to their present Descendants; for indeed, our general History breaking off most unsatisfactorily with the English Conquest, and a slight account of the succession of the Anglo-Saxon Princes. There may be many opportunities in the notes, if not in the Text, to throw in some Celtic information, and suggest modestly, some improvements for the advantage of the Principality itself. Sure I am, with some good labour, and some Welsh Zeal (which is seldom wanting among our Countrymen) the work may be made useful, and respectable.[10]

It is striking that Philip Yorke, born in Erthig but of an English family and having but a slight acquaintance with the Welsh language, should identify so closely with Wales and its traditions. In *The Royal Tribes of Wales*, indeed, he refers to himself as "a good Welshman". [11] The fact that, with the exception of William Warrington, the other North Wales based scholars engaged in promoting Welsh studies would appear to have been of Welsh extraction does not necessarily mean that they were all equally familiar with the language.[12] Philip Yorke obviously shared their "Welsh zeal", although he had to rely on translations of Welsh sources by Bloddy and Walter Davies. He sang the praises of early and medieval Welsh poetry, quoting the words of Lewis Morris and Goronwy Owen in support, and was proud to proclaim that"'the Britons taught the Saxons to read ..."[13] Nor was he unaware of one of the Welsh language's most distinguishing features, namely, the mutation of initial consonants, as in:

> ... to the share of Madog, was that division of Powys given, from him named Powys Fadog, a mutability in initial consonants to harmonize and vary the diction, very frequent in ours, and not unknown in other languages.[14]

His concern for "our language" and "our country" and the preservation of its culture was very evident in a letter which he wrote to Walter Davies on December 20th, 1797, in which he commented on the first volume of the *Cambrian Register* which had been published in 1796 with the aim of safeguarding Welsh oral culture.[15]

> I should tell you that I have lately gone pretty carefully over the *Cambrian Register*. I approve much of the execution, and design, and particularly like the intention and beginnings of the Welsh historical Translations, giving our own language, and original, with the English version; now might not this plan be also followed through our Welsh Latin writers in the same manner, and begin with Giraldus and so on to Humphrey Llwyd and Dr. Powel ...[16]

In the following year he lamented that William Owen Pughe's Welsh dictionary had not been published. [17]

Philip Yorke's anxiety to bestow upon Wales a glorious past conflicted with his desire as a historian and antiquarian to evaluate evidence in an objective fashion. Initially, in the *Tracts of Powys* and again in *The Royal Tribes of Wales* (albeit in a footnote, the substance of which did not affect the main text) he subscribed to the old-established 'British' history myth, tracing the origins of the Welsh through Gomer and Japhet to Noah and giving credence to the connection with Brutus and the fall of Troy.[18] These claims and the stories of Arthur, propagated by Geoffrey of Monmouth,[19] had been fiercely contested by the sixteenth century Italian historian Polydore Vergil,[20] and William Camden in his *Britannia* of 1607. Yet they were still given credence and, indeed, became more widely accepted in the eighteenth century through works such as Paul-Yves Pezron's *L'Antiquité de la nation et de la langue des celts (1703)* and Theophilus Evans' *Drych y Prifoesoedd*(1716).[21] In 1791, Philip Yorke warned Bloddy against placing too much faith in Polydore Vergil,[22] while in 1795 the appendix to the *Tracts of Powys* contained an eighteen page attempt, based on his own translations of passages from Roman historians, to disprove Vergil's views.[23] In 1799, *The Royal Tribes of Wales* showed no sign of a change in his attitude.[24] Ultimately, however, the sceptic in him began to overcome the romantic. In 1802 he wrote to Walter Davies, "I had a letter lately, from Mr. Williams of Treffos, with the Apocryphal Pedigree of Brutus..."[25] The following year, moreover, another letter to Walter Davies stated:

> I should like (where it may be proper to introduce it) a refutation of the Trojan nonsense. It has wholly sprung out of the poets, tho' I allow, the Antiquity of its propagation is considerable. If the Ancient British had had any such tradition, Caesar must have heard it; and his Vanity (on many accounts, his own descent, particularly) would not have suffered him, to have omitted it.[26]

During the years 1795 to 1799, between his two publications, he bombarded Walter Davies with a stream of letters and sheets of manuscript for correction. The impatient squire was not slow to express his frustration at his inability to obtain the information he needed quickly enough.

> I can attempt no more than to say, where each family began, and ended, or where it is still extant, in the male line, which is rare ...[27]

A few weeks later he sent Walter Davies more sheets to correct and asked him to "...add any information or entertainment to enliven them. This you must do on a separate paper, as the margins are as narrow as the sides of our mountain roads".[28] On one occasion he complained that "...information comes as slow as distillation",[29] on others he remarked that he was keeping busy at his investigations because "...the weather here does not suffer me to stir abroad after other amusements",[30] and "In this gloomy season, and bad weather, Antiquities enliven me".[31] The last two letters despatched from Dyffryn Aled, reflect the dreariness of this remote area in December. In one instance, Philip Yorke was driven to employ heavy sarcasm, "Not a morsel of antiquities, nor I think one scrap of Welsh paper the last six weeks, so you need not be fearful of my having too soon done".[32]

Delays due to the vagaries of the postal service placed further strain on their relationship. For instance, on November 1st., 1796, after several fruitless requests to Walter Davies to return a number of sheets, Philip Yorke gave vent to his exasperation in the third person: "Mr. Yorke will be obliged to Mr. Davies, as he finishes the sheets, to send not more than two or three covers by the same post to Mr. Simon Yorke".[33] That this kind of difficulty was not unusual is suggested by Walter Davies' reply on another occasion: "If there are some other papers different from those which I now describe I never saw them; if not, you have certainly received them back..."[34]

The few letters of Walter Davies to Philip Yorke which appear to have survived are filled with detailed answers to the questions posed by the latter, and English translations of Welsh verses.[35] One letter contained an important clue to the nature of their collaboration:

> You wish me to enrich your sheets. I can only say this – that I am at your service to copy the whole over again, and whatever additions may strike me at the time I shall insert; without deranging your own stile of writing, but as little as possible.[36]

This suggests that, while Walter Davies' help was considerable in embellishing and correcting Philip Yorke's text, he did not actually write *The Royal Tribes of Wales*. It also suggests that the latter was rather more than a mere editor or, as he called himself, a collector. In fact, the collaboration resembled very closely the earlier association of Philip Yorke with Thomas Pennant, Bloddy and the 'Philosopher'. A letter of Walter Davies', dated January 7th, 1799, containing comments on Philip Yorke's script, shows him playing a role very similar to that of Philip Yorke as critic of Thomas Pennant's work referred to earlier. Walter Davies examined the draft with close attention to accuracy, style and scholarship; for instance,

> Page 2 "Hwlkyn left 4 sons". – In fact it was Rhys his grandson.
> Page 9, line 6 "was his probable residence". better probably was his residence.
> lines 9 and 10. Wele should be Gwele.
> "Llowarch" – I would prefer Llywarch being derived from Llyw-llywyd– a Ruler...[37]

Most of Walter Davies' letters provided lengthy "scraps of anecdote" on a wide variety of families and places. On occasion, he referred Philip Yorke's requests to others, such as a Mr. I Owen of Penrhos —

> Mr. Davies having acquainted me that your plan was partly Biographical, perhaps you might think some particulars relative to Sr John Owen, not generally known, not entirely unworthy of your notice.[38]

Another contributor was David Thomas, 'Bard', a customs officer from Red Wharf in Anglesey.[39] Philip Yorke, in *The Royal Tribes of Wales*, acknowledged the assistance given by John Kynaston Powel of Hardwick, the Rev. Samuel Strong, rector of Marchwiel, the Rev. Edward Edwards, curate of Wrexham, then vicar of Llanarmon-yn-Ial, the Rev. Edward Davies, rector of Llanarmon Dyffryn Ceiriog, the Rev. John Williams of Llanrwst and, of course, the leader of the group, Walter Davies himself, together presenting a picture of squire and educated parson allied in the pursuit of their antiquarian interests.[40]

It is obvious that Philip Yorke depended heavily on the support of Walter Davies in particular and was quite relentless in the demands he made on him, even though Davies was busily engaged in compiling his own report on the state of agriculture in north Wales during this period. It is true that Philip Yorke gave him some assistance in this time-consuming task from time to time, but still expected him to turn his mind occasionally to the *Royal Tribes*. Indeed, he hoped that Walter Davies' travels might serve a dual purpose.

> During your leisure, you will probably pick up some tribal information, and when in the Dolgelle neighbourhood, see if you can make anything of Roberts the surgeon. I should not be thrown out of the Nannau & Hengwrt families & such anecdotes as they afford. Besides you may pick up somewhat as to the Fifteen also in your long course of peregrinations.[41]

In a number of letters, requests for information were intermingled with pleas for Walter Davies to meet him at Erthig or Dyffryn Aled to discuss matters concerned with the progress of the investigations. On March 5th, 1797 he wrote,

> Could you contrive to get one Sunday's furlow, and meet me at Erthig at the March Fair (Wrexham). I would send a horse if you liked to Meivod at that time.[42]

Just over a year later the appeal was more urgent:

> I want a line from you, and to know whether I have a chance of seeing you after the 28th inst. at Erthig, and whether I shall send for you, and so forth. I am at the end of my tether; Lord Macclesfield is so good to answer if he can from his Welsh papers, some queries I have sent him, and I expect them shortly. I found them costive about the Sebright papers and not inclined that my proxy should see them. I have never been able to get any information out of South Wales. If you can get at Vaughan's Antiquities revised, do tell me from thence what is said about the Vaughans of Trawscoed; I have a fine engraving of the Chief Justice and law author of that house and must bring him in, some how, or other...

This particular letter also contained an example of Philip Yorke's critical attitude towards his source material:

> Warrington holds that Rhys ab Gruffydd ab Tudor of South Wales founded Stratflur, and was buried at that Abbey. The Paxton papers say the abbey was founded by his grandfather Rhys ab Tudur, and that the latter Rhys was buried at St. Davids, where (they say) his tomb remains. Who is right here...?[43]

As the time for the final assembling and printing of *The Royal Tribes of Wales* drew nearer, a distinct note of panic crept into Philip Yorke's letters. Impatient and worried at the best of times, he became more and more frustrated at Walter Davies' apparent lack of urgency. Between March 14th, 1798, the date of the letter quoted above, and May 28th, repeated requests were made to Walter Davies to visit him. That of April 10th, for instance, read,

> I have your kind letter of the 2nd and am certainly anxious to see you, as

nothing can stir without you. Give me a line directly from Meifod to say the day. I shall send my horses for you, and at all events excuse yourself over one Sunday at least...[44]

On April 21st, Philip Yorke renewed his appeal, pointing out that he could not stay at Erthig for long. He was not able to obtain the information he needed on the South Wales families: "... not even from the Goldengrove family, which of course I must leave out. But I must somehow by note or otherwise introduce the Trawscoed Vaughans (Lisburnes) to justify Chief Justice Vaughan's print. I once knew how it was to be done, when I ordered the engraving, but it has again escaped me ..."[45] On May 17th, he announced, "My Engraver wants his money, and is in a hurry that I should get the copy on. So I am obliged to begin, and without seeing you, which much disturbs me ..."[46] Then in June he wrote to say that he was pleased to hear that Walter Davies could pay him a visit "... and I hope your stay may be prolonged to the latest moment".[47] In another letter dated the same day he wrote, "I shall send the horses early tomorrow morning, and as I know you are an early man, you may get here easily to dinner at 3 on Tuesday."[48] Walter Davies appears to have stayed for just over a week, for on June 27th, Philip Yorke wrote, "I hope you got home safe, and was much obliged to you for the time and assistance you gave me. Perhaps you may start a little more before I conclude, particularly as to the Whittington Park and Goldengrove families."[49] Time had obviously run short when, on October 7th, 1798, he told Walter Davies, "I think the Book will not exceed 200 pages. Therefore the Public shall trust to their memories, and do without an Index".[50] By November 4th, however, he had changed his mind.

Your letter reached me yesterday and gave me much pleasure in the hope of seeing you, and I will send horses and a servant and male pilion, to be at Meifod on Sunday night, the 18th instant, and if you find it too far to come through the next day, you had better divide the journey by Bala, which is I think the only roosting place on the road.

It appears that the reason for the change of mind was not a matter of the index alone.

I approve of an Index, since you are so good to come here to make it, and my printer has my special orders to have all the book ready cut, and dry here, against your arrival ... Will you think of preparing something prefatory against your coming, touching the subject in particular, and Welsh history in general ... If you set me on, I think I could go off ...[51]

In his letter of November 6th, Philip Yorke expanded on some of his previous remarks and revealed his awareness of the need for a wider and more accurate range of source material to be made available.

In the prefatory discourse I suggested to you, might not the state of our subject as it now stands, be properly mentioned; and the two poor books in print that relate only to it – Price of Llansilin,[52] and Reynolds; and then say that almost the only source of information was from the families themselves. Might we not express a wish also that the Brut and Triades should be fairly translated, and the Welsh history by these means be cleared from the Errors of foreign translators. I am anxious you should think of something for a preface, which I will help out as well as I can ...[53]

Walter Davies might have visited Dyffryn Aled from Ysbyty Ifan, where he was by now a curate, for Philip Yorke wrote on December 22nd, "I shall be glad to hear that you are well and no worse for your last coarse mountain journey ..."[54] Even on Christmas Day, 1798, the much-tried Walter Davies was involved in correspondence on the matter but, perhaps, was tiring of the demands for he, with some asperity, suggested that Philip Yorke might care to make translations from Latin works himself. Thinking, no doubt, about his translations from Roman historians in his attack on Polydore Vergil, Walter Davies said:

> As to translations from our Latin Historians, you have already given a specimen that it is feasible; and were you at some future leisure hours to proceed in the same elegant manner you began, it must be received with the approbation of the public.[55]

The Royal Tribes of Wales, when it was published in 1799, did contain an index, and a preface along the lines suggested by Philip Yorke. Unfortunately, there is insufficient evidence for an assessment of the relative contributions of Walter Davies and Philip Yorke himself to these sections of the work, though the correspondence concerning the preface suggests that the former acted as mentor, if not as ghost-writer, for that.

It seems, however, that help did not flow entirely in one direction. Apart from some assistance in compiling the *Report on the State of Agriculture in North Wales*, Philip Yorke in February 1799 offered help in obtaining payment for his friend from the Board of Agriculture over which Walter Davies was apparently having difficulty. Simon Yorke, now MP for Grantham, was also, it seems, involved in the attempt, since he had elicited the not very encouraging information that payment would be made by the Board "when the minister can give them a little money". Philip Yorke was obviously willing to pursue the matter further, however, and to use any influence he could exercise on Walter Davies' behalf, for he continued, "... I think I have a friend at Court, that I can apply to to assist you, if you call for it ..."[56] Unfortunately, the final reference leaves the matter unresolved when Philip Yorke wrote "... I shall be also glad to hear that the Agricultural are able, and willing to do what is right respecting you".

The publication of *The Royal Tribes of Wales* in the Spring of 1799 was by no means the summit of Philip Yorke's ambition. Even before this work was completed he was thinking ahead to the next phase of his grand design, *The Biography of Wales*, and we have seen that as early as June 1797 he was recruiting Walter Davies' help in investigating the Fifteen Common Tribes. These requests continued during the next few years but he also sought information by inserting an advertisement in *The Royal Tribes of Wales*.

The Author of this small work would attempt to hazard another publication (correcting the errors of this), with some additional Engravings, if the Families descended from them were pleased to communicate their Pedigrees, and what biographical matter and anecdote belonged to them. This is the more necessary, nay indispensable, as the Founders of the Tribes have little, or no notice taken of them in History.

After a gap in the records for 1800 to 1801, the saga of the *Tribes* re-emerged to take another interesting, if not entirely unlikely twist. In a letter to Walter Davies, dated January 8th, 1802, Philip Yorke revealed that he had been busily making alterations and additions to his work on the Royal Tribes, omitting the appendix, so shortening the work, and making "another copy in my own hand-writing".[57] More importantly, in the same letter, he announced his latest plans for the continuation of the Fifteen Common Tribes.

I know, if the attempt was agreeable to you, you can succeed in it; and with improvement to the Royal, give us the Special Tribes also. I should like to live to see such a work, and you really can do it; but I can think of no other, that can. In that case you shall be heartily welcome to the copy right of my small work, and I would communicate with you sheet by sheet; and I think our stile would soon be made to assimilate, and form one whole. I conceive the work would bear a full octavo, without Engravings; you need not print more than were subscribed for; and I think Mr. Painter[58] would execute his part in the fairest way, and even take a share in the hazard. Pray consult your friends on this subject ... You will be at full liberty in public, or in private, to mention what I have said to you. I foresee a good deal of our matter bursting forth, and we can easily reach Mr. Panton, and Mr. Williams of Anglesey who are very liberal and generous in their Communications, and I would freely undertake a part in that matter.[59]

This letter sets the tone for all subsequent communication on the subject. Philip Yorke, obviously consumed by his desire to complete the *Biography of Wales*, used all his powers of persuasion to manoeuvre Walter Davies into undertaking the major responsibility for the task. In the new relationship he proposed, he would himself play the minor role of dealing with the "Collecting correspondence", if Walter Davies would become the author-in-chief. As the correspondence continued his entreaties became increasingly urgent. His insistence that only Walter Davies could fulfil the task satisfactorily may not have been merely flattery. With all his knowledge, his contacts and his experience of working with Philip Yorke on the *Royal Tribes*, it was perhaps natural that he should be seen as the only choice. Philip Yorke used every resource he could muster to pressurise Walter Davies to agree: the claims of long friendship, duty to his country, the gift of the copyright of the *Royal Tribes of Wales*, the offer of payment, the implication that Painter was irrevocably committed to the project and would himself offer Walter Davies a financial inducement, and even, perhaps, an attempt to play the two men off one against the other.

He began his assault on John Painter on the day after he had written to Walter

Davies in January 1802. Having related the contents of the earlier letter and stressed that "No one can do it but Walter Davies", he went on to say

> ... that I was sure according to the Rules of your trade, you would print not only on the fairest grounds for him, but probably take some share in the hazard, as I have stated it. I wish together you would undertake it, and the present is a time that communications are reviving. Would you think it right to give Walter a line on this subject round by Mr. S. Yorke here.[60]

No record has survived of John Painter's reply but at the end of January Philip Yorke informed Walter Davies that the printer was "anxious that you should undertake and complete the *Royal Tribes*, through the Fifteen; and I see by him, that he would make the business as easy and acceptable to you as possible, in the way of publication". As further inducement he added to his promise of the full copyright of his previous work the offer of "sixty pounds for your labours". He himself would also deal with the "Collecting Correspondence",[61] improve *The Royal Tribes of Wales* and help with the actual writing of the new work.[62]

Further letters in the same vein followed in March and April. In December, writing from Bath, he was informing Walter Davies that Mr. Painter had determined on publishing the twenty Tribes of Wales and was offering "... Forty Copies of the smaller half guinea, and ten of the larger guinea edition, for your assistance in that business ..." Philip Yorke expressed a wish to meet Walter Davies and Mr. Painter at Erthig in about seven weeks, when he would take up residence there again, to resolve the matter. "If you settle that we should undertake this business, the sooner you begin to turn your mind to it, the better."[63]

In a letter of March 2nd, 1803 to John Painter he discussed the project in general and assured him:

> I am satisfied you will do your part to make the work respectable, or I would myself have nothing to do with it. It is possible Mr. Davies may have this year before him, pretty free from incumbrances on his leisure. He is a friend of Welsh literature, with the aid of various information from Welsh MSS, and an ingenious mind. I do confess it would give me great pleasure to live to see a work of this sort, well-finished; and it will be very much with you, to give activity to it; nor less with Mr. Davies; you are both equal to it, in your several ways ...[64]

In April, having recovered from an attack of influenza which had "made dismal slaughter among the old and battered Constitutions in the Wrexham neighbourhood", he wrote to Walter Davies to say, "... I am pleased to hear you will undertake our Tribes, in toto".[65] But the next few letters would appear to suggest that his confidence was ill-founded. He reminded Walter Davies frequently that they were both committed to the project and even appealed to his patriotic feelings.

> Indeed we both too, seem already in some degree, committed in it. I know you can do it, and well, if you will, and I shall not forgive you if you don't. It has a

peculiar claim on your nationality, *nec vires, deficiunt.* I will set all my sails on flying, but you are master of the wind ...

He informed Walter Davies, with great enthusiasm, of source material to which they could have access and mentioned John Painter again to apply even more pressure and to provoke him into action.

> Painter has filled his subscription to his satisfaction, and I believe made other preparation. I wish whilst you were in London, you had had the time to overlook the Welsh MSS. in the Museum; You must now get some friendly Welsh spectacles to see what is there for you; so too, you should turn your eyes back to your old study, the Bodleian; so that we may give them something that may not disgrace ourselves, our Progenitors, nor our Posterity : to them it would be hard indeed as to our Ancestors, to suffer.[66]

In his letter dated August 14th, Walter Davies was addressed, not as "Dear Sir" but as "Dear Walter"; the message, vividly expressed as a military metaphor, however, was very much the same as before.

> I do hope you will drill and form the Fifteen Battalions of Tribes, this winter; and as you may send me detachments, I will renew them, as well as I am able ... and indeed poor Painter has prepared himself for it, and has in a manner committed himself to produce it.

He envisaged only slight changes to the preface, "omitting only what partially relates to myself, and former assistants". Two other changes indicate how he was prepared to modify his ideas in the light of greater knowledge and understanding. The first of these, namely "a refutation of the Trojan nonsense", has been referred to already. It would be very difficult to disagree with the need for the second change.

> "You seemed to think with me, that the notes will come in best at the End, with the necessary References ; they certainly encumber the Text, as they now stand".[67] The last surviving letter to Walter Davies on this subject was dated December 16th, 1803. Vowing to send him copies of John Davies' and John Reynolds' books, he concluded,

> I am really anxious you would begin, and send me some of the first Tribes; as our names are in some measure committed to the Public. When I can assure my Correspondents that the thing is going on, they may probably answer me better.[68]

Philip Yorke's desperate anxiety to see the final instalment of his ambitious project completed comes over very powerfully. Yet though his enthusiasm was undimmed he clearly felt unable or unwilling to undertake the task himself. A letter of July 1801 suggests that he may have been concerned about the cost. Referring to Bingley's *Tours*, he wrote "I hope they have paid better than the *Royal Tribes of Wales*, but Goat's Flesh, tho' allowed to be savoury meat, is not the food now in fashion".[69] Again in December 1802, writing to the Earl of Hardwicke, he commented that "It is high time I should have done with scribbling for the Public, and losing three hundred pounds by it, as stands the account, or very near it, I believe at present ..."[70] Certainly he appears to have involved Painter in filling a subscription list as some protection against substantial loss on the projected work. Yet financial considerations can hardly have been uppermost in his mind, for he was prepared both to pay Walter Davies and to relinquish the copyright of *The Royal Tribes of Wales* to him.

Maybe his references to "having done with scribbling" and to "Goat's Flesh" being out of fashion betray disillusion with the reception of his previous work and weariness of the full burden of authorship.

The recurring allusions to his longing to live to see the work on the Fifteen Tribes completed, however, may well be the key. There are indications that his health may have been failing in these years. He had holidays in Bath, taking the waters, in Aberystwyth, considered then as a health resort and in the Hot Wells in Bristol.[71] His last letter on the Fifteen Tribes was written only eight weeks before he died. A fear that he had not long to live would certainly explain his sense of urgency, his frustration with Walter Davies' lack of response and his almost obsessive attempts to force him into action.

In the event, he was to be unsuccessful and the final instalment of the *Biography of Wales* was never written. How can the work which he did produce be evaluated?

There did not appear to be any clear-cut distinction between so-called antiquarian, genealogical and historical studies in the eighteenth century. Thus, while the framework of Thomas Pennant's *Tours in North Wales* was topographical and that of Philip Yorke's *Tribes of Wales* was genealogical, the completed works were not unlike that of the historian William Warrington, whose *History of Wales* was based on a chronological structure. The emphasis on 'anecdote' at every possible turn, the urge to embellish the person, place or event under consideration with historical detail, created these resemblances. Therefore, in the same way as Pennant's *Tours* were superior to other similar contemporary publications because of his more detailed, colourful descriptions, it might be claimed that Philip Yorke's 'anecdotal' account of the Royal Tribes enlivened a subject which had appeared arid in the bare narratives of his predecessors.

One obvious feature of *The Royal Tribes of Wales* is the marked imbalance, firstly, in the amount of space devoted to each tribe and, secondly, in the length of footnotes compared with that of the main text. The most detailed account, by far, is that of the third Royal Tribe which, significantly, was the subject of his earlier work, *Tracts of Powys*, published in 1795 and incorporated into *The Royal Tribes of Wales* four years later. This account occupied eighty-five pages, the first Royal Tribe twenty-nine pages, but the three South Wales tribes merely thirteen, five and two pages respectively. Philip Yorke's complaints about the difficulty of obtaining information on the South Wales tribes provide the explanation for this. As he pointed out, the absence of illustrative detail rendered the account less interesting.

The merit of the overlong footnotes was that it left the main text comparatively uncluttered and concise; the drawback arose from Philip Yorke's disapproval of genealogies which were mere catalogues of names. "I know you hate these lists", wrote Walter Davies after providing him with just such a list of the descendants of Iestyn ap Gwrgant.[72] His anxiety to enliven his genealogical details with as much "anecdote" as possible tended to overload the footnotes with material not always directly related to the theme of the main text. In his account of the Parrys of Plas Newydd, for instance, he referred to Richard Parry, Bishop of St. Asaph. This was the cue for a long footnote on William Morgan, Richard Parry's successor as Bishop, on William Salesbury and others involved in the Welsh translation of the Bible, and on Gabriel Goodman, founder of Ruthin school; it concluded with a lengthy quotation from William Morris' attack on William Camden.[73] In a few extreme instances, there was a footnote to a footnote, as in the case of Gwenllian, the heiress of Dyffryn Clwyd, who merited a further note to explain the meaning of her name. "Gwenllian – *id. est*, White Linen. Linen was so rare in the reign of Charles the Seventh of France, who lived about the time of our Henry the Sixth, that the Queen of France could boast of two shifts only, of that commodity."[74] Philip Yorke himself acknowledged that the footnotes were too long after he had seen the work in print.[75] Nevertheless, clumsy though the method may appear, it did enable him to weave into the narrative the kind of background detail required to create a more general historical study or, as he termed it, a *Biography of Wales*. Because of the extent of Walter Davies' contribution to Philip Yorke's work and the collaborative nature of contemporary historical research, the suggestion has been made that he himself was not the author of the two books.[76] Since a few of the letters from the antiquarians who supplied him with information survive in the Erthig papers[77] it is possible to compare them with his own text. It is plain that there is no evidence of plagiarism; clearly, while the letters were an essential source, he interpreted the material they contained in his own way and clothed it in his own words.

For most of the general historical background he relied on a wide range of authors from Geoffrey of Monmouth and Giraldus Cambrensis to David Powel, John Wynn of Gwydir, Thomas Pennant and William Warrington. Here again, Philip Yorke used, rather than merely transcribed, his sources and, in fact, as the years went by, he submitted the often fanciful accounts of the earlier writers to an increasingly sceptical scrutiny. The evidence points to the conclusion that Philip Yorke did actually write *The Royal Tribes of Wales* himself and that he was more than a mere editor or collector.

In *The Royal Tribes of Wales*, as we have seen, Philip Yorke adhered to the 'British history' myth and the glorious descent of the Welsh from Noah, though he subsequently rejected them. Initially he also accepted the traditional explanation of the origin of the Royal Tribes, ascribing it to three thirteenth century princes. "Gruffydd ap Cynan, Rhys ap Tewdwr and Bleddyn ap Cynfyn had ordained that there should be five Royal Tribes, one of which each founded, and fifteen Noble tribes, from whom most of the gentry were descended."[78]

However, these long-established views and, indeed, the practice of the historian himself, were already being subjected, in Philip Yorke's day, to a more critical examination. William Warrington, for instance, in his *History of Wales*, published in 1786, complained that no previous historian had attempted to analyse the motives of policy or to deal with matters of causality, and then announced that he himself had carefully examined his sources and had not "servilely transcribed, or implicitly followed the modern historians".[79] He had drawn on a wide variety of sources, chronicles as well as the writings of older historians, and revealed his attitude towards the mythical elements by simply ignoring them. Other contemporaries of Philip Yorke also rejected the myths and legends after a critical evaluation of them in their work. B.H. Malkin, for example, in the first chapter of *The Scenery Antiquities and Biography of South Wales*, scrutinised the Arthurian and other legends in an endeavour to reveal the relationship between myth and reality.[80]

Philip Yorke had shown himself in this sphere, as in estate and local government matters, to be on the side of change. He was innovative in his presentation of genealogical material and, in the last years of his life, his more critical attention to its sources led him to reject his earlier beliefs on the origin of the Welsh. One can only speculate that, had he lived long enough, the account of the Fifteen Noble Tribes, which he was so anxious to see published would have reflected this more mature viewpoint.

CHAPTER 12: Leisure Activities

In none of the surviving documents does Philip Yorke declare his preference for life in the countryside rather than in the town, so one cannot be certain that Mingay's generalisation that the gentry preferred the pleasures of their neighbourhood and estate to the attractions of London or Bath[1] is valid in his case. Nevertheless, his personal account books and letters do provide some insight into his social activities over a period of thirty years from 1770 to 1804.

When he was at home in Erthig, Philip Yorke, like others of his class, immersed himself in the social life of the neighbourhood. Apart from the rare grand event, his main sources of entertainment came from visits to the houses of the local gentry and clergymen, the occasional race meeting or hunt and some shooting. In addition, there were the meetings in various towns or villages of Quarter Sessions and, less frequently, of the Assizes, which were as much social as judicial or administrative gatherings. The evidence for these activities consists, for the most part, of scattered entries in Philip Yorke's account books. However, there are an unusually high number of these in a notebook for the winter of 1781-82, which give some idea of the hectic schedule he set himself, over a comparatively short period, to satisfy his need for leisure and entertainment. The accounts, of course, only record the occasions when chaises and horses were hired – presumably to supplement his own resources – and thus do not give a complete picture of his activities. The fact that Mrs. Cust and his daughters (who were being cared for by his sister-in-law) were presumably staying at Erthig for Christmas and much of January may account for the need for additional transport and may have increased the social activity. If, however, this represented the normal pattern for other years, then it would seem that his stays at Erthig were far from restful.

1781 November 24th Red Lion. I had a chaise the whole day to Whitehouse's a shooting.

27th Red Lion. Had a half chaise to Ruthin with Wm. Lloyd.

December 14th Red Lion. Half a chaise to and from Wrexham. Present at Wrexham Hunt.

December 16th (Sunday) Had a chaise and 2 Horses to Marchwiel church.

December 21st Had a pair to Pentrebychan.

December 23rd. (Sunday) Had a pr. (pair) to church.

December 25th (Xmas Day) Red Lion. Pr. horses to Marchwiel, retd. by Wrexham.

December 28th Did not go to Red Lion hunt, but sent half a crown myself.

December 30th a pr. to Wynnstay.
December 31st Horses to Plas Power.
1782 January 4th Horses to Gresford visiting Mr. Newcome. (i.e. Rev. Henry Newcombe, the vicar)
January 5th a pr. (Eagles) visiting at Little Acton.
January 6th a pr. (Eagles) visiting at Marchwiel.
January 8th pr. to Wynnstay play.
January 11th pr. to Wynnstay play.
January 13th Pr. to church afterwards visiting Wrexham with Mrs. Cust.
January 18th a pr. of Horses came to go to Broughton, staid at Erthig till 3, took us to Plasgronw, and retired.
January 19th Post Horses to Ruthin. T.W. pays half.
January 21st Horses to Whitchurch.
January 21st My children and Mrs. Cust retd. to London.[2]

Visits to local families obviously ranked high on Philip Yorke's list of priorities. On September 27th, 1777 he noted that he had "a pair of horses and chaise to Wynnstay – 4 times in all since I came down", and on October 23rd. that "I had a pair of Horses to my own coach to see Chirk Castle with Mr. Pennant".[3]

Although Nimrod wrote that Philip Yorke on horseback was a "figure of fun", he did have some involvement in the hunting scene. In fact, an advertisement in the *Chester Courant* of January 12th, 1779 referred to him as the Comptroller of the Wrexham Hunt and he was obviously prepared to travel some distance and spend quite considerable sums in order to participate. His accounts for December 2nd, 1782, for instance, show his expenditure for attending the Hunt at Ruthin to be as follows:

Bill at White Lion, Ruthin £19/18/
Further Expences Ruthin Hunt £10/10/
Extraordinaries at Ditto and Travelling £15/15/-

A few years later, on October 30th, 1785, he joined the Bettws Hunt at a cost of 12/-.

There are also some references to shooting, though these appear only occasionally, distributed over a decade in his account books. They include such entries as:

June 6th, 1774	Mr. Newton– pd. for a Gun	£7/11/
May 20th, 1775	My last Gun, to repairs of	£7/5/
January 3rd,1780	Bill at Gunsmith's	£1/1/6
January 1st,1784	A lock to my own gun	£1/11/6
June 2nd, 1786	Shooting Meet and Buttons advd.	£37/16/
August 11th,1787	Shooting Certificate	£2/3/- [4]

When he did go out with his gun, his mother welcomed it for the benefit to his health as well as her table. On January 1st, 1772 she wrote,

I am glad ... that you now and then take the exercise of shooting ... I am sure I fare well for it, but above all things I thank you for your garden ducks.[5]

Other references to Philip Yorke's social activities include:

October 27th, 1781 Lost at cards   £2/2/-
March 26th, 1782 Ball and Supper at Mold   £13. (in connexion with Assizes)
February 12th, 1785 Eagles, Mr. Dean's meeting   12/-
Assemblies, Eagles and R. Lyon   £1/1/-
September 9th,1785 Races at Oswestry   £4/4/-
October 12th, 1785 Bloddys Daughters Xening   £5/5/-
June 2nd, 1786 Col Myddleton's Cup Prest.   £8/15/-[6]

None of these entries suggests lavish expenditure on his recreational activities and to judge by their evidence Philip Yorke seems to have exercised the same financial restraint in this as in other spheres of his life.

Nimrod remarked on the warm welcome and excellent conversation to be had at Erthig during Philip Yorke's time. Nevertheless, he stressed that the lifestyle pursued at Erthig was not extravagant. "No French cooking; no champagne; no, not even claret; but port, sherry and madeira,– all excellent of their kind, and the best of home-brewed ale".[7] Philip Yorke's account books show the very occasional item, such as,

June 20th,1776   Mr. Ireland Wine   £9/2/-
June 28th,1779   Woollam Wine   £4/5/-[8]
February 22nd 1780   Wine Merchant (London)   £17/9/-[9]

Not until 1795 do any substantial wine bills appear and even these are few and far between.

June 27th1795   Mr. Harley's Wine Bill   £158
October 2nd,1798   To Mr. Jones on Acct of Woollam's Bill   £192/12/-
May 25th, 1799   To Mr. Harley on Acct Wine   £115/12/6[10]

Nimrod also pointed out that Philip Yorke called the wine he bought from Alderman Harley, "The Harleian miscellany".[11]

A good example of Philip Yorke's insistence on economy was the instruction he sent to John Caesar on August 9th, 1781 about the impending visit to Erthig of the High Sheriff who was attending the Assizes at Wrexham. Having dealt with the arrangements for his accommodation and that of his servants, Philip Yorke then turned to the question of provisions.

Newns will write to you about some Ale, and there should be at the same time some Cold Meat, and Bread and Cheese in the House; Mr. Fitzmaurice should be asked early after his Arrival if he can dine one day at Erthig, and if he and Lady Mary can do so, Mary Rice will with the Inspection of your wife, who I must get to be a little about Erthig whilst the High Sheriff is there, make a pretty sort of dinner; not a great deal, but nice; and in that case you should get a couple of

Bottles of Port and a couple of Bottles of White wine from Mr. Woollam for that occasion. If Mr. Fitzmaurice brings Tea, and Coffee, you need not provide it, but everything that is found necessary, I know your wife will look to supply with Economy; and if Mr. F. can on being asked sup any night at Erthig, the same niceness, and provision of wine, as at dinner, should be used...[12]

Ten years earlier he had sent instructions, couched in a similar vein, to John Caesar about celebrations at Erthig on the birth of his first son which had taken place in London.

> ... I would dedicate to this joyful occasion a Hogshead of my Strong Beer; You will observe the orders I shall give about it. It is marked No 1 Letter B in the Vault. As I would above all things avoid having my house crowded, or many People about it in my Absence, you will not give out that I mean any such benefaction, but only call in the workmen some day after they have finished their work and give them a quart of Beer to drink their Mistress' health.
>
> If any Tenants should call in, or Neighbours' servants to enquire after us, you will give them a draught, and you may have some Bread and Cheese by you for the same occasion. But as I mean no ostentation, you will be able to manage this with great regularity, according to our desires; If any Ringers should come to ask for money you will acquaint me in your next, but you won't put the thing into their heads.[13]

Twenty-one years later, when this same son, Simon, reached his majority, it was a very different story. The occasion was celebrated on July 27th, 1792 by a banquet for one hundred and thirty-three gentlemen and ninety-one ladies of the neighbourhood "with great Rejoicings".

The Tables were spread in the Entrance Hall and under an awning on top of the steps. "The Marble Tazza in the Hall was filled with Punch". [14] If we are to believe Nimrod's account, it was all rather too much for one member of the family:

> On the late Mr. Yorke (i.e. Simon) attaining his majority, one of the grandest entertainments ever heard of in these parts was given at this mansion ... In the entrance hall of Erthig is a remarkably handsome cistern, holding, I may say, at least twenty gallons. This was filled with exquisitely made punch, of which I, amongst others, partook so liberally, as to be put to bed in the house, and in the same room with one of the sons of the house, then at Eton, and who fell with such force against the castors of the posts of his bed, as seriously to injure one of his eyes.[15]

It was Philip Yorke's custom to send presents of fruit to his friends and neighbours as well as to invite them to Erthig. On September 15th, 1778, for instance, he instructed that a gift of venison should be sent to Samuel Strong of Marchwiel and of fruit to Plas Power.[16] He even remembered the children of his friends, since on July 20th, 1780 he informed his steward:

> I will get Nelly to make some Raspberry Jam, & Currant Jelly, and whilst the Fruit is in perfection I wish Nelly to ask Mr. Strong's children & the little

Apperleys one day to Erthig, and she and Betty Thomas will take care they do not make themselves sick.[17]

A major source of entertainment for the gentry, particularly in the second half of the eighteenth century was the theatre.[18] The Wrexham area was very well served in this respect. The Chester newspapers advertised performances in the city's theatres, Wrexham had its own,[19] but most significant of all was the theatre at Wynnstay, founded by the stage-struck Sir Watkin Williams Wynn,[20] where, from 1770 onwards, a wide variety of plays, ranging from Shakespeare to contemporary farce, was performed. During the period 1773 to 1787, one week each year was earmarked for the production of four plays and considerable care was taken over the booking arrangements. The following advertisement appeared on January 11th, 1780:[21]

> Sir Watkin Williams Wynne requests the favour of the Ladies and Gentlemen who intend honouring his Theatre with their company this Christmas, to send for or bespeak their tickets at least the Day before they intend coming, in order that there may not be a greater Number issued for each night than the Theatre can conveniently hold. Sir Watkin also likewise begs that the Ladies and Gentlemen who send for Tickets will specify the name of each Person belonging to their Party, that it may be inserted on the Back of the Tickets, to prevent their being transferable.

In 1777 the leading actor of his day, David Garrick, visited the theatre for about a fortnight. The performances were given by a cast of amateurs, namely members of the local gentry and a number of Wynnstay servants. Nimrod wrote,

> The performances in the Wynnstay theatre were of the very best description, principally of Shakespeare's plays; and from the ready access to them of the neighbouring gentry and others, they had the best effect in refining their manners and their taste.[22]

Not everyone agreed with this fulsome description. George Colman, for instance, who had been the manager of Covent Garden for seven years before becoming the owner and director of the Haymarket, attended the performances over a number of years and took it upon himself to try to make them more competent. Apparently, Sir Watkin himself was held to be the best of the actors, although not in everyone's opinion.[23]

It is very difficult to say how regularly Philip Yorke attended the Wynnstay performances. His mother informed him of Sir Watkin's plans in 1770,[24] and he acted in one, if not two, Shakespearian plays. He certainly played Antonio in a production of *The Merchant of Venice* in 1778[25] and he was, presumably, the Mr. Yorke who took the role of King Henry in a production of *Henry IV, part I*.[26] Unfortunately, no comment is available on his performances but the following letter from Frances, Lady Brownlow, to her mother, suggests that he was a regular participant.

> I mentioned in my last that we were going to Wynnstay, we staid all night, &

returned yesterday to dinner, Sr Wtakin was so obliging to have the Theatre illuminated & shew'd us all the Scenes, of wch there are great variety and extremely pretty, I should have liked very much to have been present at the plays, wch have been performd there about a month ago, in wch Mr. Yorke was an Actor, and Garrick a spectator. There are to be plays again at Xmas in wch Mr. Y. is to have a part, Sr Watkin takes great delight in the stage tho I find he is but a moderate performer, and Lady Wynne never acts herself.[27]

Plays were also performed at Erthig itself, with roles being played by the children. In January 1786, *Henry V* was presented, for which Philip Yorke wrote a Prologue to be spoken by his son, Brownlow, then nine years old. This charming prologue which was eventually published in his collection of *Crude Ditties* in 1802,[28] seems calculated to serve two purposes apart from its dramatic function in introducing the play. Written from a child's viewpoint, it was meant to gratify the servants in the audience and, at the same time, to teach his children to be mindful of the efforts of the servants on their behalf.

> Prologue to Henry the Fifth,
> Played by the Children at E ... g, January 1786.
> and spoke by B.Y.
>
> To please you all, from Eton, have I run,
> Through mire and dirt, to kick-up Christmas fun:
> To be the Prologue to my Brother's play,
> And make you, as the season asks, be gay.
> You cook for me, and shall not I again,
> Give Mary Rice* some pleasure for her pain:
> Her pies indeed, are excellent, and good,
> And I will pay her in dramatic food.
> To Gard'ner John, I owe but little less,
> I prog his peaches, and his apples dress;
> His fairest apricots, I pull, and plunder:
> That boys love fruit, pray where the mighty wonder?
>
> To Betty Jones+ I am as much in debt,
> I daub her hearths, and give her many a sweat;
> Thro' me, her stairs, require successive scrubbing,
> And all her floors, reiterated rubbing:
> For so much mischief, you must charge my years,
> And I in time, will pay you all arrears.

Philip Yorke complemented the social life of Denbighshire by a substantial number of visits to other areas including, of course, London. It is interesting to see how the changing pattern of his social activities largely reflects the changing circumstances of his life.

Table 17 reveals how the range of Philip Yorke's journeys narrowed after 1782 when he married Diana Meyrick. During the 1770s visits to London and to family residences belonging to the Hardwicke, Cust or Hutton connection, such as Belton House, Wimpole, Overstone, Newnham, Lockinge and Baldock, occupied a good deal of his time.

Although conditions of travel had improved by Philip Yorke's day, they were still uncomfortable, hazardous and expensive. According to the entries in his

* The Cook at E....g.   + The Housemaid at E....g.

Table 17: Number and Location of Visits made by Philip Yorke from Erthig and Dyffryn Aled (1772-1803) [29]

Year	London	Family Homes (England)	Spa & seaside resorts (England) & Army camps	Tours of N.Wales, seaside resorts & other venues
1772	3	-	-	-
1773	2	4	1	1
1774	3	-	-	-
1775	4	2	-	1
1776	2	2	-	2
1777	1	4	-	-
1778	2	1	1	-
1779	2	2	-	1
1780	2	2	1	-
1781	2	1	1	-
1782	2	1	-	2
1783	-	-	-	1
1784	1	1	-	3
1785	-	-	-	4
1786	1	1	-	-
1787	1	1	1	2
1788	1	-	-	1
1789	-	-	1	-
1790	-	1	-	-
1791	-	1	-	1
1792	1	1	-	1
1793	-	1	-	1
1794	-	1	-	-
1795	-	-	-	1
1796	-	-	1	-
1797	-	1	-	1
1798	-	-	-	-
1799	-	-	-	1
1800	-	-	1	1
1801	1	-	-	-
1802	-	-	1	-
1803	-	-	1	1

accounts, his travelling expenses between 1773 and 1782 came to around £840.[30] The number of journeys he undertook were, therefore, all the more remarkable. He was wealthy enough to be able to spend quite lengthy periods of time between January/February and April/May in London, together with shorter spells in the summer months. He could, of course, cut down on expenses by staying in either his mother's house in Park Lane, at his mother-in-law's in Upper Brook Street, or at his brother-in-law's in Bond Street. Significantly, his accounts do not mention renting a house in London until 1776.[31] Of the seven children which Philip and Elizabeth Yorke had during the years 1771 to 1779, six were born and baptised in London. The first three were born between 1771 and 1774 in Lady Cust's home where Philip and Elizabeth Yorke lived during this period,[32] the fourth in 1775 in Sir Brownlow Cust's home in Bond Street, the fifth in 1776 at a house rented by Philip Yorke in George Street, and the sixth in another rented house in Conduit Street in 1777. All six were baptised in St. George's, Hanover Square.[33] Records of Philip Yorke's expenditure on his social engagements in the capital are very sparse, perhaps because he chose to obey Lord Chesterfield's injunction not to worry about keeping accounts of "the shillings and half-crowns which you may spend in chair-hire, operas etc.".[34] From 1774 to 1781 he would have had his parliamentary duties to attend to. A few accounts for March 1781 provide some clue to his social life apart, that is, from the usual round of visits, parties and balls which constituted a large part of the engagements of the London season.

Ranelagh (5 visits)	1/13/6
Oratorio	1/1/-
Opera	4/6
Museum	16/- [35]

There is no other evidence in his letters or elsewhere to suggest that Philip Yorke's presence at oratorio and opera performances was motivated by anything beyond a desire to participate in the fashionable activities of his day.

The number of visits to London became much rarer after his second marriage in 1782. He made only four visits between that year and 1790 when he let the house in Park Lane which he had inherited from his mother.[36] Apart from one visit in 1792 when he was the member for Grantham, and another to collect two of his sons in 1801, he did not go to the capital again. There is no record either of further visits to Overstone after his first wife died, but he did continue his visits to Lincolnshire; in 1792 for the parliamentary election in Grantham, and at other times, probably, because his sister-in-law, Mrs. Reynardson, had taken charge of his young daughters after Elizabeth Cust's death in 1779.[37] From the early 1780s onwards Philip Yorke's journeys, though still frequent, became more localised (see map on p.89).[38]

His visits to spa and seaside resort were one of the most interesting features of his social activities. Spa towns and, later, seaside resorts developed in the eighteenth century to cater for the entertainment and therapeutic needs of the relatively affluent. The "spa habit was fostered by the improvements made to the roads, coaches and other transport facilities of the period."[39] Visitors went in search of 'a cure' and for recreation. Gradually, as the century advanced, the seaside resort came increasingly to rival the inland spa in popularity. The reputation of the former was promoted by Dr. Russell of Brighton who prescribed the drinking of sea water for a variety of diseases.[40] Sea-bathing was also advocated, first as a cure and then as a pleasure. By the early nineteenth century the seaside resorts were overtaking the spas as centres of entertainment and recuperation.

In common with other aristocratic and gentry families, the Yorkes of Erthig naturally visited Bath but, in addition, they also spent time at a number of seaside places on the Welsh coast which were becoming popular at the latter end of the eighteenth century. Philip Yorke paid many visits to Abergele and the occasional one to Prestatyn, Flint and Aberystwyth.

The earliest recorded visit was to Prestatyn which in Philip Yorke's day would not have been very different from the tiny settlement of small, thatched cottages and a few more substantial houses which Edward Lluyd saw on his visit in 1699.[41] It has been suggested that the inability of the fashionable ladies of Dyffryn Clwyd to visit the continent during the French wars caused them to turn their attention to their own local scenery and seashore. This development, together with the growing mania for sea-bathing, was responsible for the growth of Prestatyn and Abergele into possibly the oldest holiday resorts in North Wales.[42] Philip Yorke sent the Earl of Hardwicke a most striking description of the former, an apparently depressing place, after a stay there in October, 1776.

To establish mine (i.e.my health) again, the next Winter, and to remove some Scorbutick Eruptions in my hand,[43] I have had recourse to this place, where we have very good Conveniences for bathing. I use the sea-water externally, and internally. It is not a pleasant draught, but I find it best to admit no distinction of this sort, in my constitution. This is not a beautiful part of Wales. I consider myself as under Quarantine, shut up from mankind on three sides, by Rocks, and Mountains, and open in the (northern)Front, by an endless tract of sea. We are distant from it, about half a mile, and in the foreground look on mounds of sand, blown into heaps, and inhabited by Rabbitts. The shore is also marked with Shakespeare's Image of Solitude, and melancholy – a lone House on a Warren.[44]

Apart from the view, bathing in October on a north-facing coast would hardly be conducive to a favourable opinion of Prestatyn. Perhaps it is little wonder that his correspondence contained no further reference to this resort, or that this was his only visit! A few years later, Prestatyn's most prestigious visitor, Mrs. Thrale (Mrs. Piozzi) of Brynbella, Tremeirchion, expressed, in doggerel verse, similar sentiments, couched in the familiar Romantic vein of the period.

> To rude Prestatyn's sea-beat shore,
> And Salutary Gale,
> The Muse of Health her Pow'rs restore,
> Or Gratitude prevail.
> Should lend at least one artless Rhyme
> To celebrate the Place
> Where savage nature's wild Sublime
> Presents an awful Face.[45]

Another of her verses, *Invitation to the Ladies*, denigrated the social amenities of the place:

> There shall you see no Bond Street Beaux,
> Nor Belles in Silk and Sattin,

But you may save your own best clothes
By living at Prestatyn.

No Conversation with Wise Men
Except in Greek, in Latin;
But you may use a Book or Pen
At pityful Prestatyn.

If then you languish with Ennui
And Hope begins to flatten,
Come, bathe in our bold Irish Sea
That roars around Prestatyn.[46]

Another bathing-place patronised by Philip Yorke was Parkgate on the Wirral which was the principal port for Ireland in the eighteenth century. Thousands of passengers and large quantities of goods were transported from here to Dublin. After 1750 it became fashionable as a seaside resort, regarded as a great rival to Abergele. The settlement grew to cater for both passengers and visitors. The proprietor of *The George Inn* advertised that he had purchased "an additional Bathing Machine on an entirely modern construction in which ladies may bathe with the utmost ease and Secrecy".[47]

On June 27th, 1778, Philip Yorke paid £10/8/6 expenses for a stay at Parkgate[48] and in 1781 he planned another visit there for his children, though by this time their mother had died and he himself was on service with the Militia. On August 15th, 1781, he wrote to John Caesar from Warley camp:

So soon as the High Sheriff has left Erthig, and things are set in their places again, I wish the Children to go for three weeks to Parkgate; and to accommodate them in that matter, you must first go over there, and agree proper Board and Lodging ... Besides sufficient Bed-Room, (and a very cooling diet), the Children should have the use of a lower Room, in which they may play, and change the Air.

Following his detailed instructions about the transportation of the children to Parkgate, he wrote: "I wish now the children to get there as soon as they possibly can consistent with what I before mentioned, tho' I think that Bathing in reasonable cool weather, is much better than when the season is exceedingly Hot."[49] It is significant, in the light of the above, that Philip Yorke himself preferred the early autumn for his visits to the seaside, not the middle of August.

After his marriage to Diana Meyrick in 1782, when he took up residence for lengthy periods at Dyffryn Aled, Llansannan, it is not surprising that the nearby coastal settlement of Abergele became a favourite resort. His account books show that in ten out of the eighteen years 1783 to 1800 the family stayed there during the summer and early autumn.[50] The accounts themselves offer fascinating glimpses of what staying at a seaside resort involved in the late eighteenth century. The family lodged at one of the inns, *The Cellar* or *The Bee*, which can both still be seen.[51] In 1787, for instance, he paid £4/10/- at *The Cellar* and £6/7/4 at *The Bee* in 1800, but without any indication of the length of stay or the number of people involved it is impossible to calculate the weekly cost of accommodation. In fact, the actual payments for the hiring of horses were higher than those for the lodging of the family, since his horse bills in June 1784 and July 1791 were £4/15/8 and £11/15/9 respectively (though the slight difference in dates may have had some effect). It seems he felt it necessary to supplement the inn fare by paying £1/5/- (half-a-crown a week for 10 weeks in 1791) for a cow to ensure the family an adequate supply of milk! The Yorkes must have taken to the sea since, in 1787, a "little house" (presumably a bathing machine) was hired for 1/-, with an attendant bathing woman who was paid 15/-.[52]

Abergele, it would appear, could boast of several attractions to entertain the visitor. An advertisement in *The Chester Courant* on September 30th, 1777 for the sale of a farm near Abergele recommended it as having "a most delightful Sea Prospect" and "At a very moderate and convenient Distance to walk there is as good a shore for sea bathing as on any Part of the North Wales Coast", adding that "by many Persons of Judgement, Abergele is esteemed a superior situation to Parkgate for that Purpose ..." Writing somewhat later, Samuel Lewis extolled

> The salubrity of the air, the pleasantness of its situation, and the decided superiority of its seabathing, (which) have rendered Abergele a favourite resort for invalids, and made it the most fashionable watering-place in North Wales; during the summer season it is frequented by numerous families, for whose accommodation every requisite arrangement has been made...[53]

Joseph Hucks was plainly perturbed about another of Abergele's attractions. He was shocked to see men and women bathing in a state of nature.

> The inferior orders of people commonly bathe, without the usual precautions of machines or dresses; nor is it singular to see ten or a dozen of both sexes promiscuously enjoying themselves in the lucid element, regardless, or rather unconscious, of any indecency. Not being myself accustomed to the mode, I chose to retire farther up ...[54]

The attractions of Abergele encouraged Philip Yorke's literary pursuits. On October 8th, 1792, he wrote to John Lloyd, Hafodunos, "I have been on the shore here, near a fortnight, and as I find bathing sufficient exercise, so I sit still the rest of the morning, and the Tribes are advanced ..."[55] The scene also inspired another flight of poetic fancy:

> Abergele entreats
> You would point her receipts,
> And give her a chance
> In this maritime dance,
> With Parkgate and Hoylake,
> The very great cry make,
> When their sea's but a fool,
> To our wider pool;
> *Here*, whenever you strip,

At all times, you may dip;
There, like oyster, or crab,
As a cockle, or dab,
Your mouth open'd wide
You gasp for the tide.

It was rather short of peers of the realm, but well supplied with squires and

...of ladies we boast,
As fine, as your Coast

and

To finish our bill
Physician of skill,
Who joins to his art,
Much goodness of heart,
And to this situation,
Gives recommendation.[56]

Flint was another settlement on the North Wales coast which was beginning to attract visitors, but Philip Yorke obviously did not entertain any great opinion of its amenities. On his way home from attending the Assizes he had, it would seem, stayed overnight in Flint. This stirred him to produce a verse, "Written at breakfast, at Flint, August 21st, 1766".[57]

Having little Enjoyment,
And much less Employment,
In this dreary scene
I took up the Pen
To lament the Transition
From Ruthin, to this Town...

Nevertheless, he was happy to pay for one of his workers, Daniel the Lodgeman, to stay there to improve his health. He wrote to John Caesar on June 28th, 1778, on his way to join the militia at Whitehaven:[58]

I write at this time more particularly on account of Daniel the Lodgeman; If that Fellow takes to drink he will lose his Eyes. I hope he does not love it, better than his Eyes. The common applications externally will be of little use to him. I would spare him one week, and allow him his pay notwithstanding, if he would go over to Flint in the full tides and bathe, and drink the water. You should send a note with him to say who he is; perhaps you may know some body at Flint to consign him to ...

If he could not go, a really grim fate lay in store for him:

If it is not possible for him to go, I desire that in that case, he may take four doses of salts; an ounce to each dose. I would have Richardson mix the salt in plain water, and buy it pure at the apothecary's. The mornings he takes the salts, he must stay at home till they have done working. It would be dangerous to go into the dews or heat himself till they have done working ...[59]

The change in the pattern of Philip Yorke's travels over the years is quite marked. In the 1770s, in spite of his wife's frequent pregnancies, the family travelled a good deal, spending considerable time in visits to both the Cust and Yorke families, and especially in protracted stays in London, even when he was not a Member of Parliament. Presumably the young couple were enjoying the social and cultural life of their circle and of the capital. In these years, too, Philip Yorke explored his own locality, with at least three tours of North Wales (and possibly a fourth), two visits to the races in Oswestry and one each to Parkgate and Prestatyn. It is somewhat surprising that all this travelling took place during the very years in which his cherished schemes for the improvement of his estate were being implemented – schemes which he had consequently to direct, in spite of his enthusiasm, largely by correspondence with his steward at Erthig.

From the early 1780s onwards, however, though he continued to travel frequently, he tended to do so within a more restricted field. With his second marriage in 1782 to Diana Meyrick, he began to spend considerable periods at Dyffryn Aled, the estate in west Denbighshire which she had brought him. It may have been that which reinforced his interest in the nearby coast. As we have seen, he had previously used Parkgate on the Wirral as a resort for his first hatch of children, but from 1783 Abergele became the favourite for reasons we can only conjecture. It is possible that Diana Yorke influenced the choice; she may have been less willing than her predecessor to combine lengthy journeys with frequent pregnancies, or, possibly, she was less interested in the social life of the capital, as indeed Philip Yorke himself may have become as he grew older. In any case, Abergele had obvious advantages. It was conveniently situated, only seven miles from Dyffryn Aled, and this involved no long and uncomfortable journeys with a brood of small children which may have weighed with Diana Yorke and, to judge by the accounts, it was inexpensive, always a consideration with her husband. Above all, perhaps, it consorted well with the over-riding interest of his later years, his investigation of the Tribes of Wales. This he pursued wherever he was, but from Abergele it was relatively easy for him to maintain his contact with Thomas Pennant, Walter Davies and the other assistants in his research.

The only other place he visited at all consistently in these later years was Bath and even that only intermittently. Bath was the prime example of that other noteworthy feature of the growing eighteenth century leisure industry - the development of the spa town. It has been described as "a magnet second only to the metropolis for those seeking pleasure, fortune and fashion".[60] A century-long programme of rebuilding and extending the old town and creating a more favourable environment for visitors through improving its social and recreational facilities received a great impetus when the Bath Improvement Act was passed in 1789. The aristocracy and gentry, the higher clergy, army officers and distinguished foreigners, all came to the city in their hundreds, and over the years "a ritualized leisure industry developed under the aegis of the Master of Ceremonies".[61] Perhaps, in a sense, Bath was, for Philip Yorke, a substitute for London. It seems likely that his first visit was in 1770. A letter of his, dated May 17th, was despatched from there and he could well have been staying with his mother. Dorothy Yorke, a hypochondriac, spent a good deal of her time there and she kept a spare room for him at her lodgings in Millsome Street.[62] Philip Yorke does not appear to have kept detailed financial accounts before 1772, however, and his letters provide no further information on the matter. He did not visit the city again for seventeen years and then paid two visits, one in 1787 and the other in 1789. After a second gap he returned in 1796 and then again in 1801 and 1802. Information on the earlier visits is confined to a few details of payments for the journey and lodgings,[63] but for those in 1801 and 1802 two letters to the Earl of Hardwicke provide some insights into his activities. On July 3rd, 1801, he wrote that "Bath is very empty, and garrisoned by its invalids, and inhabitants only". He appeared to spend his time gossiping and reading the latest publications, such as "my countrywoman Piozzi's retrospection" which he found entertaining, "but not grave history", and Mr. Bingley's *Tour of North Wales* which he thought was "... but an abridgement of my old friend Thomas Pennant, from whose bones, Bingley has picked two Octavo Volumes". He hoped that they had paid better than his own *Tribes of Wales*.[64]

His letter of December 15th, 1802 showed that his powers of observation and description were undimmed. The third Earl of Hardwicke was Lord Lieutenant of Ireland and Philip Yorke teased him about learning,

> to speak Irish, or Erse; the Gwyddelian is held by our best Antiquaries the most original Dialect, and the purest Celtic, and when I catch you, as I trust I shall, on your way back ... I expect you will beat us in our own language.[65]

> ... I have also seen Mr. Pitt in the Pump Room, looking very plump and well. I hope your ministerial cares, (of which he is now divested) do not dispose you to be otherwise. We have very full benches indeed at present here, but not filled with the first fashion. I see however among them, Lord Malmesbury and your Author, Cox, that I remember I once met at Wimple: Your Bishops Meath and Killala, are also among us. I passed the latter in the street the other day, whistling as he went. I escape just at present the evil of the place, the numerous Aesculapians (i.e. physicians). One of my daughters was unwell on my arrival, and I thought it right to resort to them to reconcile any mischief that might happen, tho' really none was to be expected. But Alas! it is so difficult to get rid of them again.

This reminded him of a passage from Horace. He then described a conversation with an old school friend who for many years had been the headmaster of 'the Free School' in Bath.

> We often quote Doctor Barnard of Etonian memory. My friend amused me with the advice that famous man gave him when he first began the roaring trade. "Nat," says he, "you are entering on a hard warfare, and it will be necessary often, as I have found it, to keep up a brisk fire. Put in then always a Double charge of powder, but very little shot ..."

After adding a few thoughts on the French war and war in general, he ended the letter with a reference to his favourite subject at this time, namely the Tribes of Wales, saying that it was time he should stop "scribbling for the Public", and that he had handed the task over to another (i.e. Walter Davies) together with the copyright to *The Five Royal Tribes* and the Fifteen Noble Tribes of Wales.[66]

Defoe had called Bath "the resort of the sound rather than the sick", while a modern historian has written that 'taking the waters' for medicinal reasons "was the excuse, but in reality it was a holiday spa".[67] There is some reason to question these assertions in so far as Philip Yorke's 1801 and 1802 visits to Bath are concerned. There were hints that 'taking the waters' was, perhaps, not an excuse in his case.

Years before, he had written to Jacky Caesar that the steward's father, who suffered from rheumatism, "has been a fellow sufferer with me".[68] In another letter to his steward he had written, "I thank God! I have recovered my Health, and the use of my hands, to be able to write a little."[69] Nimrod, referring to Philip Yorke's wretched horsemanship, remarked that he was no feather.[70] Though it may not be particularly significant, in one of his notebooks remedies for human and animal illnesses are intermingled with financial accounts.[71] Philip Yorke shared his contemporaries' obsession with remedies of all kinds for various ailments. However, any physical problems which he might have had were not sufficiently severe to prevent his being able to endure the discomforts of travel on the poor roads of that time, even in the year before he died.

Over thirty years earlier, Philip Yorke's mother had been a frequent visitor to Bath for reasons of health, and she had lived another nineteen years until 1787. While it is impossible to determine how ill Philip Yorke was or from what complaint he suffered, there are indications that all was not well with him in these last few years of his life. On May 18th, 1801, before setting out for Bath, he had written to the third Earl of Hardwicke about arrangements for his forthcoming visit to Erthig, and in the course of his letter mentioned that he was going to Bath in a week's time: "I thank God that my health has not required an earlier removal ..."[72] His lodgings were at 2, North Parade, within easy walking distance of all the main attractions of the city and advertised as such. In any case, chairs could be hired or ordered and brought to the door of a person's room.[73] Such amenities would have been of great service to someone who was not as mobile as he might have been. In the letter of July 3rd 1801, he wrote – "It will be five weeks tomorrow since we came here, and I am I thank God, the better for the waters which I only used internally".[74] On his final visit to Bath the following year, another letter, dated December 15th, 1802, stated, "... I have once more reached this place, I thank God, in sufficient health, to partake (in as much as I like) of its company and amusements."[75]

If he was debilitated physically, his mental powers do not appear to have diminished in any way, judging from the spate of correspondence on the *Tribes of Wales* with Walter Davies[76] and the letters to the Earl of Hardwicke. The latter, as we have seen, give some indication of how an ageing, intellectual and possibly physically incapacitated man spent his time in Bath.

There is, however, no similar information on Philip Yorke's stay in the Hot Wells, Bristol, in March and April 1803, and, apart from a few accounts, on his stay in Aberystwyth in July and August of the same year. Bristol, long a major port, had become by the mid-eighteenth century a crowded, fashionable resort, owing its popularity to its Hot Wells and its scenery, as well as to its good communications and its proximity to Bath. It had many fine houses and much accommodation for visitors and, by the time of Philip Yorke's visit, was enjoying a tourist boom, its Hot Wells thronged with scores of pleasure-seeking gentry and invalids of all ranks.[77]

Aberystwyth, the 'Brighton of Wales', had also become fashionable, its attraction resting on good facilities for sea bathing and its picturesque hinterland. The main source of entertainment was the theatre, while accommodation was cheap but hardly sumptuous.[78] In 1803, Philip Yorke's total bill for about a month came to £75/13/7.[79]

His letters to Walter Davies from these two places, as from Bath, were obsessed with his attempts to persuade the former to undertake the task of writing a book on the *Fifteen Noble Tribes of Wales*. The almost frantic tone of these letters, together with the visits, so near to each other, to two resorts he had never been to before, reinforces the suspicion that, with his visits to Bath in 1801 and 1802, he was seeking a cure for, or alleviation of some physical ailment. Of some significance, perhaps, is the fact that, after February 7th, 1803, Philip Yorke's accounts were written by someone else.

CHAPTER 13: Conclusion

On February 19th, 1804, Simon Yorke wrote to the Earl of Hardwicke,

> I am extremely concerned to inform your Lordship of my poor Father's decease which happened this morning at half past six. He had been for two months much indisposed with spasms on his chest,but they were relieved by proper remedies, and he appeared gaining ground towards amendment untill Friday last when the symptoms changed materially for the worse, altho' Dr. Currie of Chester who attended him was not aware yesterday, of immediate danger, but after his departure, he dozed and was delirious at times (the effects of laudanum) and expired without a groan or the smallest struggle..."[1]

A seemingly quiet end to a full and interesting life. What conclusions can be drawn from this study of Philip Yorke's career?

Luck was generally on his side. He was blessed with a lively and inquiring mind, a large fund of restless energy, boundless enthusiasm and tenacity of purpose, and a mischievous sense of humour. His two marriages and a substantial inheritance enriched the family coffers and furnished him with the financial resources to promote his various schemes of improvement. In the material sense, his fortunes were assisted by the fact that he did not have to provide portions for any of his daughters by his first wife. In the pursuit of his genealogical and antiquarian interests he was lucky to be able to enlist the services of friends who were also leading figures in the revival of historical and literary studies which was taking place in Wales in the closing years of the eighteenth century.

To portray him as merely a fortunate man would be to underestimate him, however. Even in his early years, at school and university, he appeared to seize his opportunities to make the most of the education he was offered, at a time when it was common to treat them very casually. As an adult, he showed the same initiative in embarking on the ambitious programme of extensions and improvements to house and estate which was largely completed in a few years in the 1770s. At times, his enthusiasm, his single-minded pursuit of the concern of the moment, led him to behave like a man possessed. This was evident in his youth not only in this promotion of improvements but also in his courtship of Elizabeth Cust and his attempts to secure the Hutton inheritance.

The fashion in which he pursued his genealogical investigations with the same relentless drive in later years shows that his mental vigour did not decline with age. At such times, this essentially amiable man became impatient and irascible, adopting a wily or badgering tone towards his employees or 'assistants'.

How far, then, does the evidence confirm the portraits of Philip Yorke by his contemporaries? Though that of the Rev. Samuel Strong was cast in the mould of a conventional obituary and Nimrod's in the form of reminiscences, in certain respects Philip Yorke fits the model well. That he was a cultivated man seems very clear. His love of the Classics and his interest in history were real and abiding. His own style, though often involved and convoluted in the manner of the period, was always lively, and he could produce the sharp and witty comment, the neat and vivid turn of phrase. There is little indication, however, that he was interested in the arts, though the evidence is so limited that one must be cautious. There is no mention of music in his letters, it appears that he visited the theatre only rarely, and his interest in the visual arts seems not to have extended beyond the fashionable commissioning of family portraits. A great deal of the furnishings added by Philip Yorke to what was already a fine collection at Erthig came from Newnham Manor, and it is impossible from the evidence to estimate the extent to which his first wife's taste prevailed in the decoration of the reconstructed rooms. Yet he seems genuinely moved by the beauty of landscape and to have been fully in sympathy with the contemporary vogue for travel in search of the romantic and awe-inspiring.

Again, his reputation as a benevolent family man and landowner seems to have been well-founded. Although he showed the usual prejudices of his class against the lower orders and distrusted workmen in general, his attitude to his own workmen could be rather different; he appreciated the services of some of them and he indulged in acts of kindness to individuals. Similarly, he revealed a strong sense of public duty, particularly towards the poor, and although at times he fulminated against his tenants and workers, there is no evidence that he actually carried out his threats.

As to his patriotism, there is no reason to doubt it; at the time of the American War of Independence he expressed his shock at the disloyalty of the colonists in the strongest terms. His attachment to England, however, pales somewhat in comparison with his love for Wales. Though he came of English stock, his father inheriting Erthig only ten years before his birth, Philip Yorke's identification with the family's adopted country is remarkable. The fact that his education, his family ties, his parliamentary seats and his social life in the years of his first marriage were all exclusively related to England makes this yet more striking. It is true that his second marriage linked him with Welsh society, but his interest in Welsh history and culture and his emotional involvement with Wales predated that and clearly was one of his major concerns.

Nimrod's portrayal of Philip Yorke as extravagant landowner (accepted on his authority by later writers) is too simplistic. The impetuous manner in which, with the exuberance of youth, he embarked on an almost ruinously expensive programme of wholesale improvements to his house and estate, contrasts sharply with his careful attention to every detail of expenditure, and continual insistence on economy. Generally speaking, the parsimonious Philip Yorke was much more evident than was the spendthrift squire.

He has been accused also of being a dilettante, a superficial trifler in intellectual matters. His verses were certainly trifles, tossed off as jokes, and he was the first to laugh at them as *Crude Ditties* indeed. Judged on his genealogical studies, it is obvious that Philip Yorke was a much more serious scholar than this charge would suggest. He showed the same meticulous attention to detail as he did in every other undertaking, learning to scrutinise his evidence critically and in some depth. This, of all his activities, became the all-absorbing passion of his later years.

In some respects, it is clear that he was a man of contradictions. There were, for example, a number of surprising omissions from his interests. Though he was an MP for a number of years, the great political and social upheavals of his time rate barely a mention in his correspondence – at least, in that which survives. Even the industrial developments which were taking place in his own neighbourhood did not stir him. Yet, as we have seen, in those areas which did arouse his interest, his enthusiasm could extend to obsession.

Some of the contradictions arose from his pragmatism and his predisposition to judge each situation on its merits. Thus, in his attempt to achieve a judicious blend of the aesthetic and utilitarian in the alterations to his house and garden, he adopted a solution which combined both radical and conservative features. On the other hand, where he thought change might lead to improvement he gave it his enthusiastic support. Thus he could well have led the field in north-east Wales by including husbandry covenants in his leases and in trying to enforce them. He participated eagerly in an experiment to improve the breed of sheep in the country. Similarly, he advocated a greater degree of professionalism and centralised control in an attempt to remedy the deficiencies of the traditional 'amateur' approach in local government. Again, the introduction of 'anecdotes' and close links with general history made his genealogical studies innovative, turning them, as it did, into much more substantial works than the familiar lists of names.

These were, perhaps, the main achievements of this enterprising man. For the historian, however, he has another significance; with vivid description, humour and often strong emotion, he had the ability to cast light in his letters on the people, events and concerns of his world. We are also left with the feeling of having encountered a man who speaks persuasively to us today; an amiable, idiosyncratic figure, performing conscientiously his duties towards family, estate and society.

NOTES

Introduction

1. DNB and Philip C. Yorke, *The Life of Lord Chancellor Hardwicke* (Cambridge, 1915). 3 vols. Vol. I, pp.25-27.
2. Geoffrey Holmes, *Augustan England* (London, 1983), p.152.
3. P.C. Yorke, op. cit., p.33.
4. Ibid., pp.24-26.
5. A.N. Palmer, *A History of the Thirteen Country Townships of the Old Parish of Wrexham* (Wrexham, 1903). p.233.
6. A.H. Dodd (ed.), *A History of Wrexham* (Wrexham, 1957), pp.67-68. Historians have long been divided about the nature of property exchanges in the period 1680-1740. H.J. Habbakuk argued that "the general drift of property in the 60 years after 1680 was in favour of the large estate and the Great Lord". 'English Landownership, 1680-1740' (*Ec. HR*. 2nd. Ser., vol. X, 1940, pp.1-2). This trend was seemingly apparent in Wales, too. (Geraint H. Jenkins, *Wales, 1642-1780*, Oxford, 1987, pp.92, 261). J.V. Beckett, however, in 'English Landownership in the Later Seventeenth and Eighteenth Centuries: the Debate and the Problems' (*Ec. HR*., 2nd. Ser., vol. XXX, 1, 1977) and 'The pattern of Landownership in England and Wales, 1660-1880' (*Ec. HR*., 2nd. Ser. vol. XXXVIII, 1, 1984, pp. l-22), and R.H. Holderness, 'The English Land Market in the Eighteenth Century: the Case of Lincolnshire', (*Ec. HR*., 2nd. Ser., vol. XXVII, 4, 1974, pp.557-576) have concluded, from research done in Cumbria, Lincolnshire, Devon and Glamorgan, that in these areas at least, the lesser gentry and the 'middling sort' purchased much of the land which came on to the market during this period.
7. Geraint H. Jenkins, op. cit., pp.264-270. See also M.J. Dowden, 'A Disputed Inheritance: the Tredegar Estates in the Eighteenth Century', *WHR*., vol. 16, no.1, June 1992, pp.36-47.
8. Geraint H. Jenkins, op. cit., pp.264-270.
9. CRO/DE 868.
10. Albinia Lucy Cust, *Chronicles of Erthig on the Dyke* (London, 1914), 2 vols. Volume I, p.253.
11. See for example CRO/DE 883.
12. See for example CRO/DE 875.
13. These novels were *The History of Lady Julia Mandeville* in 2 volumes, *The History of Betty Thoughtless* in 4 volumes, and *The Placid Man, or memoirs of Charles Beville* in 3 volumes.
14. Richard Hurd (ed.), *The Works of Joseph Addison* (London, 1954), p.303.
15. There is a good discussion of eighteenth century girls' education in Josephine Kramm, *Hope Deferred* (Methuen, 1965), chs. 7-10.
16. CRO/DE 888.
17. CRO/DE 868 .
18. *Victoria County History of Hertfordshire*, 1908, pp.355-356.

Chapter 1: School and University

1. For a full discussion of the debate see E.W. Griffiths, 'A Survey of British Educational Ideas, 1700-1750 (unpublished M.Ed. Thesis, Univ. of Leeds, 1964).
2. A.L. Cust, op. cit., vol. I, p.341.
3. CRO/DE 787.
4. Brit. Mus. Add. MSS., 35, 319.
5. CRO/DE 880.
6. CRO/DE 888. Dorothy Yorke to Philip Yorke, May 22nd, 1769.
7. DNB. Charles Yorke (1720-1770) was the second son of the first Earl of Hardwicke who, like his father, became Lord Chancellor.
8. Brit. Mus. Add. MSS., 35, 634.

9. CRO/DE 880.
10. Ibid.
11. A.L. Cust, op. cit. vol. I, p.346.
12. Ibid., p.343. Richard Woolfe to Simon Yorke, June 15th, 1749.
13. See for example CRO/DE 880. John Shepherd to Simon Yorke, May, 20th, 1750.
14. A.L. Cust, op. cit., vol. I, p.342. The only testimony seems to be the remark in John Shepherd's report of October 21st, 1749 (CRO/DE 880) to Simon Yorke that ". . . You, Sir, whatever Mrs.Yorke may do, will scarce know your son in two years time . . ."
15. CRO/DE 880. June 18th, 1754.
16. Ibid., John Shepherd to Simon Yorke, October 21st, 1749.
17. Ibid., June 22nd, 1749.
18. Brit. Mus. Add. MSS., 35, 634. Simon Yorke to Charles Yorke, January 24th, 1755.
19. A.L. Cust, op. cit., p.344.
20. George Harris, *The Life of Lord Chancellor Hardwicke* (London, 1847). 3 vols., Vol. 2, p.559.
21. CRO/DE 1542 (173).
22. Brit. Mus. Add. MSS., 35, 359. Only the year and month are given.
23. CRO/DE 879., Simon Yorke to Charles Yorke, February, 20th, 1766. Simon Yorke conveyed Matthew Wymondesold's request, not, for some reason, initially to the Lord Chancellor, but to his son Charles Yorke, citing his deep sense of obligation to Matthew Wymondeswold and John Shepherd's own merits, as his reasons for doing so (Brit. Mus. Add. MSS. 35, 634). Charles Yorke advised Simon to approach the Earl of Hardwicke directly. This he did without much delay, because on February 20th, Matthew Wymondesold informed him of the Earl of Hardwicke's "obliging proposal" of a choice of livings in the Lockinge area (CRO/DE 879). However, it was not until May 23rd, that Simon Yorke thought fit to inform Charles Yorke that he had written to the Earl of Hardwicke who had "returned him a very kind answer"(Brit. Mus. Add. MSS., 35, 634). On June 10th, Matthew Wymondesold wrote to thank Simon Yorke for his efforts and said that "John Shepherd will search out livings under the Great Seal available in the Lockinge area". (CRO/DE 879).
24. Nicholas Hans, 'New Trends in Education in the Eighteenth Century' (London, 1951), p.70.
25. Ibid., p.71.
26. Philip C. Yorke, op. cit., vol. I, p.101.
27. Thomas Pennant, *The Literary Life of the late Thomas Pennant, Esq., by Himself* (London, 1793), p.23. See p.206 n.15 for details about Thomas Pennant.
28. CRO/DE 880.
29. CRO/DE 1542(147).
30. Nicholas Hans, op. cit., ch. 3.
31. Ibid., p.62, and ch. 2. Doubts have been cast upon Professor Hans' conclusions, since they are based only on the biographies of those leading families included in the DNB.
32. This topic is discussed in full in E. W. Griffiths, op. cit., ch. 7.
33. Ibid., p.227
34. Nicholas Hans, op. cit., p.69.
35. DNB.
36. Nicholas Hans, op. cit., p.68.
37. Roy Porter, *English Society in the Eighteenth Century* (London, 1982), p.179.
38. Sir Lewis Namier and John Brooke, *The House of Commons, 1754-1790*, (H.M.S.O., 1964), 3 vols. Volume I, p.110.
39. Ibid., p.111.
40. A. L. Cust, op. cit., vol. I, p.249.
41. Nicholas Hans, op. cit., p.72.
42. CRO/DE 2500/2501. Dorothy was granted a portion of £6,000. There is a statement in a letter of John Shepherd's in May 1750 that James Hutton had paid for Philip's stay at Wanstead (CRO/DE 761) but there is no further evidence to support this.
43. CRO/DE 332.
44. CRO/DE 335.
45. CRO/DE 336.

46. Sir L. Namier and J. Brooke, op. cit., vol. l, p.110.

47; John Cannon, *Aristocratic Century* (Cambridge University Press, 1984), p.44.

48; John Lawson and Harold Silver, *A Social History of Education in England* (London, 1973), p.199.

49; *The Spectator.* no. 367.

50; Lionel Cust, *Records of the Cust Family:* 2nd. Ser. 1550-1779 (London, 1902), pp.234-235.

51; CRO/DE 1212.

52; Nicholas Hans, op. cit., pp.124-125.

53; DNB.

54. See p.41.

55. Another son, John, attended a preparatory school at Neston in the Wirral, possibly the one set up for ten boys at Great Neston in 1780 by a Rev. Corbar. (D. Robson, *Some Aspects of Education in Cheshire in the Eighteenth Century*, Manchester, 1966), p.81. He then went to Rugby, transformed into a very successful public school after 1780. (J. Lawson and H. Silver, op. cit., p.201). Two of Philip Yorke's sons, Brownlow from his first marriage and Piers from his second, attended Ruthin School, not far from Erthig, and then Eton. Philip, from his second marriage, was sent to Westminster school.

56; DNB. Philip Yorke(1720-1790) went to Bene't College in 1749, and Charles Yorke (1722-1770) in 1739.

57; Sir John Cust was at Bene't College from 1735 to 1739 - Sir L. Namier and J. Brooke, op. cit., Vol. l, p.290.

58; D. A. Winstanley, *Unreformed Cambridge: a study of Certain Aspects of the University in the Eighteenth Century* (C. U. P., 1935), p.54.

59. CRO/DE 887. January 25th, 1763.

60. Ibid.

61. Ibid.

62. CRO/DE 1210.

63. CRO/DE 887. December l9th, 1763.

64. Brit. Mus. Add. MSS., 35, 658. There is an almost identical version of the programme in CRO/DE 1205.

65. Ibid.

66. Ibid.

67. DNB.

68. John Rhys (ed.), Thomas Pennant, *Tours in Wales* (Caernarfon, 1883), Vol. I., Introduction, p. xxiii.

69. Roy Porter, op. cit., p.177. See also Derek Jarrett, *England in the Age of Hogarth* (London, 1976), p.168.

70. D. A. Winstanley, op. cit., p.49. For a full discussion of degree courses and qualifications see pp.41-91.

71. CRO/DE 1542(183).

72. Geoffrey Holmes, op. cit., pp.135-137, p.144.

73. Ibid., p.143.

74. Roy Porter, op. cit., p.90.

75. See p.120.

76. D. A. Winstanley, op. cit., p.79. Under the Elizabethan Code, privileged persons, meaning those related to the sovereign, could receive degrees without fulfilling the 'statutes'. This privilege was extended by Charles 11 to include barons and knights and, in the eighteenth century, even the grandsons and nephews of noblemen.

77. Ibid., p.86.

78. Sir L. Namier and J. Brooke, op. cit., vol. l, p.122. Also DNB.

79. CRO/DE 1172.

80 .J. A. Venn, *Alumni Cantabrigiensis* (Cambridge, 1954), part II, vol. II.

81. Brit. Mus. Add. MSS. 32, 967.

82. See ch. 9.

83. See for example CRO/DE 1396, and *Tracts of Powys*, pp.39-57.

84. C. J. Apperley, *My Life and Times* (London, 1842), p.302. C. J. Apperley (1779-1843) was born at

Plas Gronw on the Erthig estate. He wrote many books on sporting topics, mainly horse-racing and travel, under the pen-name 'Nimrod'.

85. Samuel Strong, Rector of Marchwiel, 1777-1816, and of Newtown, 1772-1775. Native of Poorstock in Devon. M. A., Trinity College, Cambridge. D. R. Thomas *The History of the Diocese of St. Asaph* (Oswestry, 1908), vol. l, p.362.

86. CRO/DE 422.

87. Jonathan Swift, 'Essay on Modern Education' in *The Works of Jonathan Swift*, ed. by Temple Scott (London, 1907), vol. XI, p.55.

88. CRO/DE 1205. Samuel Strong's obituary notice for Philip Yorke.

89. Ibid.

90. Henry Fielding, 'An Essay on Conversation', in *The Complete Works of Henry Fielding* (London, 1888), p.634.

91. James Forrester, 'The Polite Philosopher' (Edinburgh, 1734), printed in *Tracts on Manners* (Reading University Collection), p.233.

92. CRO/DE 1205.

93. C.J. Apperley, op. cit., p.302.

94. CRO/DE 1205.

95. CRO/DE 557. John Edwards to Philip Yorke, November 7th, 1767.

96. Quoted in *The Pelican Guide to English Literature*, vol. 4, 'From Dryden to Johnson', ed. Boris Ford, (London, 1957), p.34.

Chapter 2 Marriage and Inheritance

1. Brit. Mus. Add. MSS., 35, 638.

2. CRO/DE 336. The rents rolls for the years 1765 to 1767 are missing.

3. See p.63.

4. G.E. Mingay, *English Landed Society in the Eighteenth Century* (London, 1963), p.21. Nimrod's exaggerated claim that Philip Yorke was "a man of seven thousand a year" (C. J. Apperley, op. cit., p.300) has influenced later accounts. See for example, Richard Williams (ed.), *The Royal Tribes of Wales* (Liverpool, 1887), intro. p. xiii; A. L. Cust, op. cit., vol. 2, p.261; *The Dictionary of Welsh Biography down to 1940*(London, 1956); R. G. Thorne, *The House of Commons, 1790 -1820*, vol. V (London, 1986), p.676. Even in his later, more affluent years, and taking into account his income from his other properties and his investments, Philip Yorke's annual income would not have reached that figure.

5. H. J. Habbakuk, 'Marriage Settlements in the Eighteenth Century' (*TRHS*, 5th. Ser., vol. XXXII, 1950).

6. Ibid., p.28.

7. DNB. MP. for Grantham, 1743-1770; Speaker of the House of Commons, 1761-1770. The Custs had greatly increased their lands and prosperity with the acquisition of the Brownlow estates in the 1760s. R. H. Holderness, op. cit., p.573.

8. Lionel Cust, op. cit., p.20. John Cust's natural worry about Philip Yorke's modest means could have been exacerbated by the fact that he himself had met with opposition from his future wife's uncle, after her father had died, because he lacked the means to make any settlement on her equivalent to the large fortune she had inherited.

9. CRO/DE 889.

10 .Lionel Cust, op. cit., p. l. See also G. E. Mingay, *The Gentry* (London, 1976), pp.111-112.

11. CRO/DE 889.

12. Ibid.

13. Ibid.

14. Ibid. November 10th, 1767.

15. *Victoria County History of Hertfordshire*, p.356.

16. Reginald Hine, 'The Manor of Newnham' (*TEHerts. AS*, 1910), p.147.

17. A. L. Cust, op. cit., vol. ll, p.29.

18. CRO/DE 888.

19. Uncatalogued archive– Belton House: Philip Yorke to Sir John Cust, January 7th, 1768.

20. CRO/DE 1174.

21. CRO/DE 968. Also see p.73.
22..CRO/DE 787. In his will, James Hutton left £300 to James Chilton who was referred to as a friend.
23.. CRO/DE 889. Brownlow Cust to Philip Yorke, October 20th, 1768.
24. Ibid.
25. Ibid., November 16th, 1769.
26. Ibid.
27. Uncatalogued archive – Belton House: Philip Yorke to Brownlow Cust, January 6th, 1770.
28. He was buried at Newnham on August lst, 1770.
29. A. L. Cust, op. cit., vol. ll, p.143.
30. CRO/DE 787. See also A. L. Cust, op. cit., vol. ll, p.113, who mistakenly states that Newnham fell to Philip Yorke when his mother died in 1787.
31. CRO/DE 765.
32. H. J. Habbakuk, 'Marriage Settlements. '(*TRHS*, 5th. Ser., vol. XXX11, 1950) pp.21-22.
33 G. E. Mingay, *The Gentry*, p.133.
34. Quoted in H. J. Habbakuk, 'Marriage Settlements',(*TRHS.*, 5th. Ser. vol. XXX11, 1950), p.20. Much controversy has been aroused in recent years by competing interpretations of the terms 'strict', 'marriage' and 'family' settlements, and by whether such settlements favoured the interests of the eldest son or those of the younger members of the family. See Lloyd Bonfield, 'Affective Families, Open Elites and Strict Family Settlements in Early Modern England' (*Ec. HR.*, 2nd. Ser. vol. XXXIX, 3, 1986), pp.341-354; A. L. Erikson, 'Common Law versus Common Practice:the Use of Marriage Settlements in Early Modern England' (*Ec. HR.*, 2nd. Ser., vol. XLIII, l, 1990), pp.21-39; E. Spring, "The Strict Settlement: its Role in Family History '(*Ec. HR.*, 2nd. Ser., vol. XL, 3, 1988), pp.454-460.
35. G. E. Mingay, 'English Landed Society', pp.33-34. E. Spring, 'The Strict Settlement.' (Ec. HR., 2nd. Ser. vol. XLI, 3, 1988), pp.454-460.
36. H. J. Habbakuk, 'Marriage Settlements' (*RHS.*, 5th. Ser., vol. XXXII, 1950), p.29. See also CRO/DE 2525. In his will, dated March 14th, 1799, Philip Yorke left only £50 each to the surviving children of his first marriage, Brownlow and Dorothy, because they had been well provided for in his first marriage settlement.
37. See pp. 51-52. He had already concluded many lease agreements in the three year interval between his father's death in 1767 and his marriage settlement, when, before his estate was 'settled', he had enjoyed much greater freedom. See Lloyd Bonfield, 'Marriage Settlements and the Rise of Great Estates' (*Ec. HR.*, 2nd. Ser. . vol. XXXII, 4, 1979), p.493.
38. See G. E. Mingay, *The Gentry*, p. ll0.
39. CRO/DE 901.
40. C. J. Apperley, op. cit., p.411.
41. CRO/DE 901. May l9th, 1770.
42. See p.173
43. G. E. Mingay, *English Landed Society...* p.224.
44. CRO/DE 569.
45. See pp.13. It is difficult to draw any firm conclusion from such a casual reference.
46. See Geraint H. Jenkins, op. cit., pp.88, 258-259; G. E. Mingay, 'The Gentry', p.145.
47. CRO/DE 1212.
48. G. E. Mingay, *English Landed Society...* p.225.
49. CRO/DE 1417.
50. CRO/DE 1212.
51. CRO/DE 1417.
52. Ann Jemima, Philip Yorke's sister, who died in 1770, aged 16, and was buried in Marchwiel church.
53. CRO/DE 1215.
54. See p.180.
55. CRO/DE 563.
56. Ibid. August 15th, 1781.
57. Ibid.

58. CRO/DE 1212.
59. CRO/DE 563.
60. CRO/DE 1212;428.
61. Ibid.
62 .C. J. Apperley, op. cit., p.411c
63. CRO/DE 385.
64. CRO/DE 1212 and 428. Precise figures cannot be given for the education of any of Philip Yorke's sons because a number of entries in the accounts are ambiguous, John's accounts over 10 years at Neston and Rugby came to only £208. This may be because, due to his eye problems, he missed a great deal of school.
65. CRO/DE 912. Afterwards it came to be known as the 'Tribes Room'. See p.151.
66. CRO/DE 912.
67. Ibid.
68. See for example CRO/DE 2404. On June 9th, 1799, Philip Yorke informed Simon of a possible exchange of land with his neighbour, Sir Watkin Williams Wynn of Wynnstay, but said that he would "not enter on the matter till I saw you, and that I should leave it rather to you, than myself to determine for obvious reasons".
69. Ibid. Philip Yorke instructs Simon to carry out some research for him at the British Museum. See also pp. 151-152.
70. A. L. Cust, op. cit., p.210.
71. See pp.92-93.
72 .C. J. Apperley, op. cit., p.411.

Chapter 3: Landlord and Steward

1 .James Boswell, *London Journal* (F. A. Pottle, ed., London, 1950), p.153.
2. Daniel Defoe, *The Compleat English Gentleman*(1729; K. D. Buhlbring, ed., London, 1890), p.244-245.
3. C. J. Apperley, op. cit., p.302.
4. See pp.134-140.
5 . J. D. Chambers and G. E. Mingay, *The Agricultural Revolution, 1750-1880* (London, 1966), p.200. See also Joanna Martin, 'Estate Stewards and their Work in Glamorgan, 1660-1760; a Regional Study of Estate Management'(*Morg.*, XXIII 1979, pp.10-12, who states that this is a gross distortion of the truth as far as South Wales is concerned.
6 .G. E. Mingay, *The Gentry* , pp.87-88.
7. 2nd. ed., London, 1731. See CRO/DE 282. Philip Yorke compiled a catalogue of the books in the Erthig library and Laurence's manual is included in it.
8. John Laurence, *The Duty and Office of a Land Steward*. Preface.
9. Geraint H. Jenkins, op. cit., p.271. Joanna Martin, 'Estate Stewards and their Work in Glamorgan'(*Morg.* XXIII, 1979).
10. J. Laurence, op. cit., pp.7-8.
11. Philip Yorke himself confused matters by addressing both men as John Caesar in his letters. The ailing John Caesar was named as the tenant of Bryngolau until 1783, when he was succeeded by his widow. However, Philip Yorke's declared intention in December 1779 to pay Jacky Caesar £30 a year suggests that Jacky was in charge at Erthig some years before the death of his father. CRO/DE 1211.
12. Joanna Martin, 'Estate Stewards and their Work in Glamorgan' (*Morg.*, XXIII, 1979), p.18. G. E. Mingay, *The Gentry*, p.87.
13. Ibid., pp.15-16. See also E. M. Jancey, 'The Eighteenth Century Steward and his Work' (*TSh. Arch.S*, vol. LV1, 1957-1960), p.38.
14. J. Laurence, op. cit., p.7.
15. CRO/DE 563. January 6th, 1772.
16. There is no record of Jacky Caesar's date of birth in the local church records and the evidence for his youthfulness is therefore derived from the correspondence.
17. CRO/DE 335.
18. CRO/DE 563.

19. CRO/DE 559. March 20th, 1769.
20. CRO/DE 338.
21. See pp.41-42.
22. CRO/DE 341 and 342. The rentals show that the figures for rent were not just token payments as, for instance, they were for the Erthig demesne. See also CRO/DE 561.
23. J. Laurence, op. cit., p.12.
24. J. Martin, 'Estate Stewards and their Work in Glamorgan. . '(*Morg.*, XXIII, 1979), p.19.
25. CRO/DE 888.
26. Ibid.
27. Ibid.
28. Ibid., June llth, 1769.
29. Ibid., July 20th, 1769.
30. Ibid., May 19th, 1769.
31. See p.177.
32. CRO/DE 888, July llth, 1769.
33. Ibid., September 5th, 1769.
34. CRO/DE 384.
35. J. Laurence, op. cit., p.13.
36. J. Martin, 'Estate Stewards and their Work in Glamorgan.' (*Morg.*, XXIII, 1979), p.21. Geraint H. Jenkins, op. cit., p.271. On a large estate like Holkham, the steward in the 1760s could earn £300 a year. R. A. C, Parker, *Coke of Norfolk* (Oxford, 1975), p;63.
37. CRO/DE 1211.
38. CRO/DE 563
39. Ibid. (Undated fragment).
40. CRO/DE 1211.
41. CRO/DE 563, July 6th, 1772.
42. Ibid.
43. Ibid. May llth, 1771.
44. Ibid.
45. There is no evidence, as in the earlier period, of a careful perusal by Philip Yorke of the steward's accounts. It is, of course, possible that such evidence has disappeared.
46. CRO/DE 563.
47. Ibid., January 6th, 1772.
48. Ibid.
49. Ibid., June 6th, 1772.
50 CRO/DE 563. February 20th, 1772.
51.. Ibid. (Undated fragment).
52. Ibid.
53. Ibid.
54. Ibid., May 2nd, 1775.
55. CRO/DE 341;342.
56. C. J. Apperley, op. cit., p.303.
57. CRO/DE 1205.
58. CRO/DE 707.
59. CRO/DE 563. June 6th, 1772.
60. See p.177.
61. CRO/DE 563. July 31st, 1778.
62. Ibid.
63. Ibid., July 31st, 1778.
64. Ibid., June 22nd, 1775.
65. Ibid.
66. Ibid January 5th, 1787.
67. Ibid.
68. Ibid.
69. Ibid.

70. Ibid.

71. C. J. Apperley, op. cit., pp.302-303.

Chapter 4: Lease Agreements

1. Geraint H. Jenkins, op. cit., pp.280-281.

2. David W. Howell, *Land and People in Nineteenth Century Wales* (London, 1977), pp.25-26, 30.

3. A. H. Dodd, *The Industrial Revolution in North Wales* (Cardiff, 1933; Wrexham, 1990), pp.56-60.

4. Philip Yorke, *Tracts of Powys* (Druid Press, 1795), appendix B.

5. See for example A. H. Dodd, *The Industrial Revolution...*, p.37; John Davies, *Hanes Cymru* (London, 1992), p.320; D. Thomas(ed.), *Wales: A New Study* (Newton Abbot, 1977), p.97.

6. CRO/DE 968. Philip Yorke to Brownlow Cust, September 24th, 1768.

7. Ibid., This statement was preceded by: "I must consider my Farm this last year very advantageous to me. I have by me now two years Wheat, two years Barley, and near two years Hay, and a pretty good stock of Oats, and Peas – so I will well spare that large extensive demean for one year. Every Feild will be kept to the Culture I shall dictate".

8. G. E. Mingay, *English Landed Society. . ,* p.172.

9. J. A. Perkins, 'Tenure, Tenant Right, and Agricultural Progress in Lindsey, 1780-1850' (*Ag. HR.,* vol. 23, 1975), pp.1-2; G. E. Mingay (ed.), *Agrarian History of England and Wales* (Cambridge, 1989), Vol. VI, p.611; R. A. C. Parker, 'Coke of Norfolk and the Agrarian Revolution' (*Ec. HR.,* 2nd. Ser., vol. XIV, 1955), p.158.

10. R. A. C. Parker, (as previous note), p.158. See also Pamela Horn, 'An Eighteenth century Land Agent; the Career of Nathaniel Kent, 1737-1810' (*Ag. HR.,* vol. 30, 1, 1982), p.3.

11. J. Laurence, op. cit., p.14.

12. David W. Howell, *Patriarchs and Parasites* (Cardiff, 1986), pp.71-72; David W. Howell, 'The Economy of the Landed Estates in Pembrokeshire, c. 1680-1830' (*WHR.,* vol. 3, 1966-19673, pp.269-27; David W. Howell, *Land and People in Nineteenth Century Wales,* p.58.

13. J. Martin, 'Estate Stewards and their Work in Glamorgan' (*Morg.* XXIII, 1979), p.23.

14. Published in 1810; p.100.

15. C. Stella Davies, *The Agricultural History of Cheshire, 1750-1850,* vol. 4, 3rd. Ser. (Manchester, 1960), Ch. l, pp.13-53.

16. David W. Howell, ''The Economy of the Landed Estates...' '(*WHR.,* 3, pp.270-271. For the situation in England see J. D. Chambers and G. E. Mingay, op. cit., p.46.

17. For a brief summary of contemporary arguments see J. A. Perkins, 'Tenure, Tenant Right...', (*Ag. HR.,* vol. 23, 1975), pp.1-2.

18. CRO/DE 560. Only the year is given as the date of the letter.

19. Unfortunately, the rent rolls for 1765 and 1766 are missing.

20. CRO/DE 38; 206. Thomas Crew's 21 year agreement, for instance, allowed him to terminate it after 3, 7, or 14 years, while Edward Fabian's lease for 21 years permitted a termination "at the option of the tenant at Three or Seven Years End, and at the joint option of Tenant and Landlord at Fourteen years End".

21. See p.61.

22. J. D. Chambers and G. E. Mingay, op. cit., pp.46-47. See for example J. V. Beckett, 'The Lowthers of Holker; Marriage, Inheritance and Debt in the fortunes of an eighteenth century Landowning Family' (*THSLC,* 1978), p.53. He sees little evidence in the eighteenth century of progressive farming at Holker Hall and states that the few surviving leases do not indicate that the tenants were encouraged to use enlightened farming practices.

23. David W. Howell, *Land and People in Nineteenth Century Wales,* p.75. David W. Howell, *Patriarchs and Parasites,* p.73. See also Walter Davies, op. cit., p.99.

24 .Geraint H. Jenkins, op. cit., pp.282-284.

25. Francis Jones, 'A Squire in Anglesey: Edward Wynne of Bodewryd' (*TAAS,* 1940), pp.80-88, especially p.86.

26. A. H. Dodd, *A History of Caernarvonshire, 1284-1900* (Caernarvon, 1968), pp.232-233.

27. Geraint H. Jenkins, op. cit., p.282; A. H. Dodd, *The Industrial Revolution. . ,* p.37; G. Tegai Hughes and others(eds.), *Gregynog* (Cardiff, 1977), p.39.

28. R. J. Colyer, 'The Hafod Estate under Thomas Johnes and Henry Pelham, Fourth Duke of

Newcastle'(*WHR.*, vol. 8, June 1977), p.261. For other examples of 'improving' landowners in south-west Wales in the last quarter of the eighteenth century see David W. Howell, *Patriarchs and Parasites*, pp.77-80.

29. A. H. Dodd, *The Industrial Revolution...*, p.36.
30. David Thomas, *Agriculture in Wales during the Napoleonic Wars* (Cardiff, 1963), p.153.
31. J. Laurence, op. cit., pp.63; 66-71.
32. Philip Yorke, *Tribes of Wales* (Wrexham, 1799), p.48, note.
33. Pamela Horn, 'The Eighteenth Century Land Agent. .' (*Ag. HR.*, vol. 30, 1, 1982), p.3. Nathaniel Kent was invited by Sir John Cust to furnish him with an account of Flemish farming methods.
34. HRO/D/EX58/El. The only surviving record of a Newnham lease, dated July 13th, 1771, contains a husbandry clause.
35. He caused confusion by inserting an advertisement in the Chester newspapers to the effect that he had authorised the transfer of the clover seed market to a new location during the March fair and then, in answer to several complaints, inserting another announcing its return to the original site. CRO/DE 681.
36. CRO/DE 560. In 1769 (no other details of date given) Thomas Hayman promised Philip Yorke that he would have copies of the lease agreements ready against the time when he wished to execute them.
37. J. Laurence, op. cit., p.52, stipulated that "none of the Tenants do let any part of their Farms to Under-Tenants . . . who take the Heart out of the land".
38. The stipulations were more precise in some cases than in others as, for example, in that of Timothy Owens (20 out of 62 acres); Thomas Crew (40 out of 113 acres); Edward Fabian (24 out of 82 acres); Richard Davies (25 out of 95 acres); Daniel Owens (15 out of 46 acres).
39. J. Laurence, op. cit., p.35. "...great care ought to be taken, that none of the Tenants be allow'd to have much above a third part of the Farm in Tillage in any one Year, ...obliging them also to lay the same down, after a reasonable term of years with proper Grass-seeds; viz. after about four Crops taken, and two summer fallows given".
40. Walter Davies, *A General View of the Agriculture and Domestic Economy of North Wales* (London, 1810), p.108 See also J. Laurence, op. cit., p.36.
41. CRO/DE 38.
42. CRO/DE 707.
43. Ibid.
44. For the purchase and pre-1779 developments at New Sontley see pp.95-97, 110-112.
45. CRO/DE 54.
46. See pp.85.
47. R. A. C. Parker, 'Coke of Norfolk and the Agrarian Revolution' (*Ec. HR.*, 2nd. Ser., vol. XIV, 1955), pp.160-161.
48. R. A. C. Parker, 'Coke of Norfolk', pp.111-112.
49. G. E. Mingay(ed.), *The Agrarian History...*, vol. VI., pp.281-282. See also R. A. C. Parker, 'Coke of Norfolk', p.101.
50. J. D. Chambers and G. E, Mingay, op. cit., p.56.
51. J. Martin, 'Landed Estates in Glamorganshire, 1660-1760' (*Glam. H.*, 12, 1981), pp.17-18.
52. CRO/DE 547.
53. R. J. Colyer, 'Crop Husbandry in Wales Before the Onset of Mechanization' (*Folk Life*, vol. 21, 1983), p.50.
54. David Williams, 'The Acreage Returns of 1801 for Wales'(*BBCS.*, vol. XIV, Part 1, 1950), pp.66-68.
55. CRO/DE 563.
56. See pp.74-76.
57. CRO/DE 43.
58. CRO/DE 206.
59. CRO/DE 42.
60. CRO/DE 703.
61. Ibid.
62. David W. Howell, 'The Economy of the Landed Estates...' (*WHR.*, 3), p.271

63. CRO/DE 83. The lease for Pentreclawdd in 1756 contained a promise to "Ditch the wet meadows as soon as may be convenient either this Winter or next Summer, and Put the House and Out Buildings in good Repair next Summer". One lease is admittedly very slight evidence but it does suggest that Simon Yorke had set an example for his son to follow.
64. CRO/DE 707
65. Ibid, p.2.
66. Ibid., p. ll.
67. CRO/DE 703.
68. CRO/DE 149.
69. CRO/DE 707, p.17.
70. CRO/DE 559. John Caesar to Philip Yorke, January 23rd, 1769.
71. CRO/DE 563. July 22nd, 1775.
72. Ibid.
73. CRO/DE 707, p.12.
74. CRO/DE 1282.
75. Ibid.
76. Ibid.
77. Ibid.
78. CRO/DE 369
79. Ibid.
80. Ibid.
81. Ibid.
82. Ibid.
83. Ibid.
84. Ibid.
85. CRO/DE 369;1282. New Sontley formed part of the Erthig demesne at this time. See Ch. 6.
86. Walter Davies, op. cit., p. l00.
87. R. A. C. Parker, 'Coke of Norfolk', p. lll.
88. J. Laurence, op. cit., p.13.
89. Ibid., p.37.
90. G. E. Mingay, *The Gentry*, p.88. It was the custom for stewards on other estates to keep such records.
91. CRO/DE 707, p.3.
92. Ibid., pp.18-22.
93. Ibid., p.12.
94. Ibid., pp.15-16.
95. Ibid., p.36.
96. CRO/DE 42.
97. CRO/DE 338.
98. CRO/DE 39.
99. CRO/DE 707, p.23.
100. Ibid., p.40.
101. Ibid.
102. G. E. Mingay(ed.), *The Agrarian History...*, vol. VI, pp.609-610.
103. CRO/DE 39.
104. CRO/DE 707, p.23.
105. Ibid., p.44.
106. See also CRO/DE 83. Philip Yorke's father, Simon, in a 7 year lease for Pentreclawdd in 1766, allowed the tenant £5 towards marling.
107. CRO/DE 206.
108. CRO/DE 42.
109. CRO/DE 43.
110. CRO/DE 38.
111. CRO/DE 707, p.19.
112. CRO/DE 888. Dorothy Yorke to Philip Yorke, June 25th, 1769.

113. CRO/DE 563. April 6th, 1771.
114. CRO/DE 707, p.48.
115. Ibid., p.34.
116. See p65.
117. David W. Howell, *Land and People in Nineteenth Century Wales*, p.58.
118. See Chapter 5.
119. CRO/DE 2472. Contains a batch of yearly agreements for the period 1813 to 1860.
120. CRO/DE 625

Chapter 5: Rent Collection
1. G. E. Mingay (ed.), *The Agrarian History...*, vol. VI, pp.620-621. G. E. Mingay, *English Landed Society...*, p.52; David W. Howell, 'The Economy of the Landed Estates...' (*WHR.*, 3), p.274-275.
2. Geraint H. Jenkins, op. cit., pp.268-269.
3 CRO/DE 329.
4. CRO/DE 332.
5. CRO/DE 335.
6. CRO/DE 336.
7. CRO/DE 341. The acreage figures have to be treated with caution because not all properties have acreages attached to them in the rental accounts. However, since the rents in these instances are generally low, they appear to be small properties where the acreage, if it existed, could not be a great significance.
8. Ibid.
9. Ibid.
10. J. Laurence, op. cit., p.4.
11. CRO/DE 341.
12. CRO/DE 3348.
13. CRO/DE 336.
14. CRO/DE 329, 335, 336, 339, 341, 2355. The significance of the analysis in Table 3 should he assessed in the light of the comment in Note 7 above.
15. CRO/DE 337.
16. CRO/DE 337 and 341. Other examples of tenants who leased 'combined' holdings were: William Youd who leased "the old tenement" (148 acres) and "Ellis's late" (12 acres); Thomas Prichard who rented Caeclappiog (56 acres) and Avongoch (36 acres); Timothy Owens who leased Croesyglyn (43 acres), Pantyffrwd (7 acres and Francis's 10 acres); Edward Fabian who leased Porthwgan (28 acres) and Bentley's (54 acres); David Jones who leased Plas Drain (102 acres) and Caia (49 acres).
17. CRO/DE 2355.
18. CRO/DE 341, 342.
19. See p.76.
20. See pps 76,78. The sum of £600 is approximate because, while precise figures are available for the rents of the King's mill and New Sontley, there is no record of those for his other acquisitions which seem to have been leased as parts of other properties.
21. CRO/DE 2355. Philip Yorke died in February 1804 and the acreages have therefore been calculated as accurately as possible for the previous year.
22. See pp.101.
23. CRO/DE 342.
24. John Laurence, op. cit., p.33.
25. CRO/DE 888.
26. Ibid.
27. Ibid.
28. CRO/DE 563.
29. CRO/DE 568.
30. CRO/DE 559.
31. CRO/DE 559, April 30th, 1769.
32. CRO/DE 563.

33. CRO/DE 341.
34. See p.59.
35. Walter Davies, op. cit., p.94.
36. See pp.112-113.
37. There was a township and also a number of properties called Sontley. However, Philip Yorke's references in his letter to his steward, to Mr. Roberts and to his own offices and corn ricks, suggest that the transaction involving Mr. Lockitt concerned New Sontley which Philip Yorke had purchased from David Roberts in 1772. There still exists a plan(housed at Erthig) by William Emes of Intended Improvements at New Sontley, dating from 1766. David Roberts, who sold New Sontley to Philip Yorke for £7,879, had himself purchased the property from Matilda Hill in 1766 for £5,500. (CRO/DE 36) Whether the intended improvements were made and, if so, whether the £2,379 profit made by David Roberts was meant to recoup the cost, it is impossible to say. The allusion to the optional demolition of the house, however, and Philip Yorke's advertisement in *The Shrewsbury Chronicle* indicate that it was an earlier dwelling on New Sontley land.
38. CRO/DE 563.
39. CRO/DE 341. Because of a change in the method of recording payments of rent after 1782, calculations based on individual payments are not possible after that date, when annual estate totals only can be compared.
40. Ibid. January 7th, 1775.
41. Ibid.
42. Ibid. May 27th, 1776.
43. Ibid. April 24th, 1777.
44. CRO/DE 53. The mortgage was for £5,000.
45. CRO/DE 1212.
46. Ibid.
47. See p.101. The £5,000 mortgage was included in the £9,000 which Simon Yorke had to repay.
48. CRO/DE 563. September 15th, 1778. Philip Yorke had written to John Caesar from Maryport where he had been encamped with the Denbighshire Militia.
49. Ibid.
50. G. E. Mingay, *English Landed Society...*, p.52.
51. CRO/DE 563.
52. Ibid. August 9th, 1781.
53. Ibid. Undated.
54. See p. 85.
55. Calculated from the Rental Accounts. CRO/DE 342.
56. CRO/DE 563.
57. G. E. Mingay, *English Landed Society...*, p.271; Geraint H. Jenkins, op. cit., p.268; David W. Howell, *Patriarchs and Parasites...*, pp.87-8 Landowners in south-west Wales were also reluctant to grant abatements and reductions.
58. G. E. Mingay, *English Landed Society...*, p.52.
59. See p.48.
60. See pp.94, 95 and 101.
61. G. E. Mingay, *The Agrarian History...* , vol. VI, p.616; David W. Howell, *Patriarchs and Parasites. ..* pp.86-87.
62. Quoted in L. Stone and J. C. Fawtier Stone, *An Open Elite? England 1540-1880* (Oxford, 1986), p.300.
63. CRO/DE 563.
64. Since there is a gap in the records from 1789 until 1795, it is impossible to say how long he had Bryngolau on his hands. The 1795 rental account, however, shows that it was tenanted by that date.CRO/DE 342.
65. Ibid. The rental accounts for the period 1795 to 1804 do not give the acreages of farms. However, some assessment of unleased land can be made from the following figures: 1795-1797 Land worth £40 annual rental. 1798 Land worth £54/5/- annual rental. 1799 -1800 Land worth £81/5/- annual rental. 1801-1803 Land worth £41/5/- annual rental.

Chapter 6: The Home Farm
1. CRO/DE 558.
2. CRO/DE 968.
3. CRO/DE 558. January 29th, 1768.
4. CRO/DE 562.
5. Ibid.
6. Ibid.
7. CRO/DE 563. Philip Yorke to John Caesar, November 16th, 1770; June 22nd, 1775; July 31st, 1778; August 4th, 1780.
8. See pp.108-110.
9. CRO/DE 1282. £1,129/11/1 to be exact.
10. I am very much indebted for this and the following information on the King's mill to Derek Pratt's article on 'King's Mill, Wrexham' (*DHST*, vol. 29, 1980), pp. 115-159. He points out that there are two sets of accounts (CRO/DE 369 and DE 1282), one of which gives a total cost of £1,080/3/11^{1}/2 and the other £1,087/13/7^{1}/2. D. Pratt, op. cit. p.148.
11. G. E. Mingay(ed.), *The Agrarian History...*, vol. VI, pp.402-404.
12. D. Pratt, 'King's Mill. . (*DHST*, vol. 29), p.144.
13. G. E. Mingay (ed.), *The Agrarian History...*, vol. VI, p.406.
14. Ibid., p.407; D. Pratt, 'King's Mill' (*DHST*, vol. 29), p.149.
15. CRO/DE 369.
16. CRO/DE 559.
17. CRO/DE 559. May 19th, 1769.
18. John Caesar's letter of January 29th, 1769 mentions Mr. Lloyd's Quarry. This probably refers to William Lloyd, the squire of an estate to the west of Wrexham called Plas Power. (Ibid.)
19. Ibid.
20. D. Pratt, 'Kings Mill. .''(*DHst*, vol. 29), p.153.
21. CRO/DE 563.
22. Ibid.
23. In return for these acquisitions Philip Puleston of Hafod-y-Wern received Samuel's Meadow, 1^{1}/2 acres called Bryn-y-go-banau and Nagshead, a tenement in "the Street under the Churchyard". See D. Pratt, 'King's Mill' (*DHst*, vol. 29), p.150.
24. Ibid., pp.135-137.
25. G. E. Mingay, *The Agrarian History...*, vol. VI, p.399.
26. CRO/DE 341.
27. CRO/DE 342.
28. CRO/DE 968. Philip Yorke to Brownlow Cust, September 24th, 1768.
29. CRO/DE 141.
30. D. Pratt, 'King's Mill' (*DHst*, vol. 29), p.152.
31. CRO/DE 562.
32. CRO/DE 682. Letter quoted in full in D. Pratt, 'King's Mill' (*DHST*, vol. 29), pp.158-159.
33. See p.31.
34. CRO/DE 384.
35. See p.196, note 37.
36. CRO/DE 36.
37. CRO/DE 341.
38. CRO/DE 369; 1282.
39. CRO/DE 1212.
40. Ibid.
41. H. J. Habbakuk, 'Marriage Settlements...' (*TRHS.*, 5th. Ser., vol. XXXII, 1950), p.28.
42. J. V. Beckett, 'English Landownership in the Later Seventeenth and Eighteenth Centuries...' (*Ec. HR.*, 2nd. Ser., vol. XXX, 4, 1977), pp.567-581; p.577. On the basis of his research in Cumbria, J. V. Beckett, along with others, contends that many families did not use portions to buy land; p.581.
43. See p.30.
44. CRO/DE 385.

45. CRO/DE 563. John Caesar's reply is also included.
46. Ibid. July 2nd, 1772.
47. CRO/DE 204 and 251. See also A. N. Palmer, *A History of the Thirteen Country Townships...*, p.240.
48. CRO/DE 561.
49. CRO/DE 154. See also CRO/DE 1212. Philip Yorke paid the money for his new property in instalments of £56/3/-; £733/1/3; £30; £20; £80/8/5; £70/12/6; £200/3/6 and £100/17/-.
50. CRO/DE 707. Philip Yorke to John Caesar, November lst, 1772.
51. A. Goodwin (ed.), *The European Nobility in the Eighteenth Century* (London, 1967); see essay on the English gentry and nobility by H. J. Habbakuk, p.4. David W. Howell, *Patriarchs and Parasites...*, pp.52-54; David W. Howell, *Land and People in Nineteenth Century Wales*, p.35; David W. Howell, 'The Economy of the Landed Estates...' (WHR., 3), pp.267.
52. CRO/DE 386;387.
53. Ibid.
54. G. E. Mingay(ed.), *The Agrarian History. .* , vol. VI, p.399.
55. CRO/DE 386;387.
56. Ibid.
57. CRO/DE 411; 414; 419.
58. CRO/DE 411; 414; 415; 416; 417; 419.
59. CRO/DE 413.
60. Ibid.
61. Ibid.
62. CRO/DE 411. The accounts included oxen presumably because they performed the same functions on the farm as the horses.
63. CRO/DE 412.
64. CRO/DE 392.
65. CRO/DE 415.
66. CRO/DE 414.
67. CRO/DE 419.
68. CRO/DE 411.
69. CRO/DE., 414.
70. CRO/DE., 415.
71. CRO/DE, 416.
72. CRO/DE 386; 387.
73. See pp.97-100.
74. G. E. Mingay, *English Landed Society. .* , pp.168-169.
75. CRO/DE 707.
76. CRO/DE 341.
77. CRO/DE 391-402
78. A. H. Dodd, 'The North Wales Coal Industry During the Industrial Revolution' (*Arch. Camb.*, vol. LXXXIV, 1929), pp. 201-202. Also CRO/DE 369. There is a record of a pit worked by John Mellor which by 1724 employed sixteen men, but it mostly supplied the needs of the estate, and of three small pits which in 1728 produced coal which appears to have been sold locally.
79 .CRO/DE 1212 contains a reference for 1799 to "profit from Coal Mines of £26/7/- and CRO/DE 2482 refers to an agreement for 21 years with R. Kirk and W. and T. Jones (ironmasters), allowing them to dig for coal and ironstone 'under' Pentreclawdd, in return for a payment to the landowner of one-sixth of all ore raised.
80. J. R. Rhodes, *The London Lead Company in North Wales (1693-1792)* (unpublished Ph.D. Thesis, Leicester University, 1970). The Edisbury brothers began open-cast working after 1683 but the London Lead Company took over the mine in 1714. In 1781 the company accused of misconduct, had to wind up its affairs in Trelogan.
81. CRO/DE 428. In 1796 he did not have 5 full shares in the Company (i. e. £500) and was deprived of his right to vote. Shr. PL., Rail 827, 868.
82. For the road from Pool to Wrexham in 1788. Shr. PL. F25. 6.

Chapter 7: Peripheral Properties

1. See p.30.
2. CRO/DE 789. He left £300 each to W. M. Lally and James Chilton, and £1,000 to W. M. Lally for the education of William Smith, James Hutton's illegitimate child. If William Smith died before he reached the age of 21, the money was to go to Philip Yorke. Mrs. Catherine Lally received an annuity of £80 a year for life (Philip Yorke continued to pay this until 1783). Mrs. Barker had a £60 annuity for life; this was paid until 1781.
3. CRO/DE 616.
4. CRO/DE 1211.
5. CRO/DE 616. Mr. Crowther could have been Diana Meyrick's agent on her estate in Yorkshire, although there is no documentary evidence to support this.
6. CRO/DE 628.
7. CRO/DE 563.
8. Ibid.
9. CRO/DE 567. Elizabeth Ratcliffe to John Caesar, September 12th, 1771.
10. CRO/DE 563, July 22nd,1775.
11. CRO/DE 1211.
12. HRO/D/EX 58 El.
13. CRO/DE 1211.
14. HRO/D/EX 58 El.
15. CRO/DE 609.
16. Ibid. July 22nd,1784.
17. Ibid. September 10th,1784.
18. CRO/DE 628.
19. Ibid.
20. CRO/DE 609. William Simkins to Philip Yorke, November 7th,1784.
21. Ibid. December lst,1784.
22. Ibid.
23. Ibid.
24. CRO/DE 616.
25. CRO/DE 623. A letter written to Simon Yorke by a Mr. B. Loudon on behalf of John Festing, dated October 27th,1785.
26. CRO/DE 619.
27. Ibid.
28. CRO/DE 621. John Festing to Simon Yorke, July 22nd,1805.
29. CRO/DE 622.
30. L. Stone and J. C.F. Stone, op. cit.,p.300.
31. CRO/DE 616.
32. See J.E. Griffith, *Pedigrees of Anglesey and Caernarvonshire Families* (Horncastle,1914),pp.126-127; p.167 and J.Y.W. Lloyd, *The History of the Princes, the Lords Marcher and the Ancient Nobility of Powys Fadog* (London,1884),vol. IV, p.183.
33. He was a first cousin to Owen Rutland Meyrick who had inherited Bodorgan Hall in Anglesey in 1770. V. E. Mapp, 'The Rebuilding of Bodorgan Hall' (*TAAS.*,1983), p.47.
34. CRO/DE 2503.
35. Brit. Mus. Add. MSS.,35,619.
36. Diana Wynn Yorke (1748-1805). Portrait by Joseph Allen (1804). This comment suggests that the plainness of her attire in the portrait was not solely due to her widowhood as is generally believed.
37. C.J. Apperley, op. cit., pp.412-413.
38. The Yorkshire estate consisted of the freehold manors of Cudworth over Cudworth and Nether Cudworth, and the Leasehold rectory of Royston. No details are given of the income from the lands in Devon, Dorset and Wiltshire. CRO/DE 2503.
39. CRO/DE 346.
40. CRO/DE 2503; 776(a). The following arrangements were made: if there was only one son to provide for, £15,000; if only one daughter, £10,000. If there was no son and two or more

daughters, £5,000 for the eldest daughter at 21 and £10,000 for the other daughters at 21. If an eldest son and one or more younger children, £20,000 was to be raised, £10,000 for the eldest at 21 and £10,000 to be shared among the younger children, payable at the age of 21.

41. CRO/DE 2503 and 766(a).
42. He signed his letters W. M. Lally. He could have been the William Michael Lally left £300 by both Simon Yorke and James Hutton in their wills. He was one of the signatories of Philip Yorke's and Diana Meyrick's marriage settlement of 1782, where he was referred to as William Michael Lally of the Chancery Office, London.
43. See p.105.
44. Probably on Diana Meyrick's recommendation. He was also involved in the reconstruction of Bodorgan Hall which began in 1779. V. E. Mapp, op. cit., pp.46-47.
45. CRO/DE 577 gives details of the arrangements. Thomas Lloyd, *The Lost Houses of Wales* (London,1986),p.27.
46. CRO/DE 919.
47. Ibid.
48. CRO/DE 2503. Figures in other correspondence from William Lally differ from the ones quoted: for example, one undated letter put her debts at £16,000 and her annual income at £1,700, while another,dated October lst, 1780 gave her £1,300 a year to live on.
49. CRO/DE 919. (Letter undated).
50. CRO/DE 907.
51. Ibid.
52. CRO/DE 919. April 9th,1782.
53. CRO/DE 2503.
54. CRO/DE 1385.
55. CRO/DE 968.
56. CRO/DE 387.
57. R. Trow-Smith, *A History of Livestock Husbandry, 1700-1900* (London,1959), pp.284-285.
58. G. E. Mingay(ed.), *The Agrarian History...*,vol. VI, p.323.
59. R. Trow-Smith, op. cit., p.286.
60. H. B. Carter, *His Majesty's Spanish Flock* (Edinburgh,1964),Ch. 4.
61. H. B. Carter, op. cit., pp. 190 and 217. The King thought that improving "the Wool of this Country" was "a most national object".
62. Ibid., p. l91.
63. L. Twiston Davies and A. Edwards, *Welsh Life in the Eighteenth Century* (London, 1939), p.9.
64. Brit. Mus. Add. Mss., 42, 072. The estate referred to is Dyffryn Aled.
65. Quoted in H. B. Carter, op. cit., p.218.
66. October 3rd,1794; quoted in H. B. Carter, op. cit., p.218.
67. Brit. Mus. Add. MSS., 42, 072.
68. H. B. Carter, op. cit., p.218.
69. Philip Yorke to Sir Joseph Banks, February 18th, 1798.
70. Sir Joseph Banks to Philip Yorke, February 14th, 1799 quoted in H. B. Carter, op. cit., p.219.
71. See Chapter 11.
72. NLW.,1809E. June 27th, 1797.
73. A. H. Dodd, *The Industrial Revolution...* pp.39-41.
74. NLW., 1809E. Philip Yorke to Walter Davies, September 30th, 1797.
75. Ibid., Philip Yorke to Walter Davies, October 24th, 1797.
76. R. Trow-Smith, op. cit., p.209.
77. Walter Davies, op. cit., pp.327-328.
78. Philip Yorke to Sir Joseph Banks, December 17th, 1799, quoted in H. B. Carter, op. cit., p.219. See also G. E. Mingay (ed.), *The Agrarian History...*,vol. VI, pp.323-324.
79. H. J. Habbakuk, 'English Landed Families, 1600-1800' (*TRHS.*, vol 29, 1979), p.196.
80. CRO/DE 620.
81. CRO/DE 615.
82. CRO/DE 767.
83. CRO/DE 620.

84. CRO/DE 284.
85. CRO/DE 620.
86. CRO/DE 6.
87. See p. 45.

Chapter 8: The House and Park

1. Quoted in G. E. Mingay, *English Landed Society.* . p.160.
2. Ibid., pp.160, 209; G. E. Mingay, *The Gentry*, p.148; L. Stone and J. C. F. Stone, op. cit., p. 199; David W. Howell, *Patriarchs and Parasites…* , pp.177-178.
3. From a copy of a letter in the Cust archives kindly supplied by Andrew Baker, the Assistant Historic Buildings representative of the National Trust.
4. CRO/DE 563.
5. Ibid, see also *The Royal Tribes of Wales*, p.11, where he considered what he deemed the excesses of the Wynn memorial in Ruabon church to be "a mass and massacre of marble, ludicrous to look on".
6. G. Jackson-Stops, 'Erddig Park,Clwyd', l. (*Country Life*, April 6th, 1978), p.909.
7. L. Stone and J. C.F. Stone, op. cit., p.236.
8. Brit. Mus. Add. MSS., 35, 611.
9. Ibid.
10. Ibid.
11. CRO/DE 1211.
12. Ibid.
13. See G. Jackson-Stops, op. cit., p.909. The evidence for James Wyatt's involvement in the Erthig alterations is summarised on this page.
14. G.E. Mingay, *English Landed Society…* , p.209.
15. G. Jackson-Stops, op. cit., p.909. He suggests that Wyatt was the "master mind" behind Philip Yorke's alterations and that Joseph Turner acted as executant-architect.
16. J.M. Robinson, *The Wyatts: an Architectural Dynasty* (Oxford, 1979), p.60.
17. Mark Girouard, *Life in the English Country House* (London, 1979) p.211.
18. Ibid., pp.219-220.
19. CRO/DE 1282. See also CRO/DE 369 for another set of these accounts.
20. CRO/DE 1211.
21. Ibid.
22. Ibid.
23. Ibid.
24. Mark Girouard, op. cit., p.230; L. Stone and J. C. F. Stone, op. cit., p.245.
25. G. Jackson-Stops, op. cit., p.909.
26. CRO/DE 1211.
27. CRO/DE 1212.
28. G. Jackson-Stops, op. cit., p.909.
29. CRO/DE 284.
30. CRO/DE 563.
31. Ibid.
32. Ibid.
33. Ibid.
34. Ibid.
35. Brit. Mus. Add. MSS.,35,612. Philip Yorke to Lord Hardwicke, August 26th, 1774.
36. CRO/DE 563.
37. CRO/DE 1282.
38. Walter Wilde, 'Not Just a Pupil of Brown's' (*Country Life*, October 15th 1987), p.152.
39. G. and S. Jellicoe, P. Goode and M. Lancaster, *The Oxford Companion to Gardens* (Oxford, 1984), p.161.
40. W. Wilde, op. cit., p.156.
41. See pp.73-74.
42. CRO/DE 563.

43. Ibid.
44. Ibid.
45. Ibid.
46. Ibid.
47. G. and S. Jellicoe and others., op. cit., p.161.
48. Roger Miles, *Forestry in the English Landscape* (London, 1967), p.32.
49. CRO/DE 339.
50. See p. 112 below.
51. Roger Miles, op. cit., p.39.
52. CRO/DE 563.
53. Ibid.
54. Ibid.
55. Ibid.
56. CRO/DE 2355.
57. Andrew Ginger, *Country Houses of England Scotland and Wales: a Guide and Gazetteer* (London, 1991), p.21.
58. CRO/DE 563.
59. Ibid.
60. CRO/DE 1212.
61. Roger Miles, op. cit., p.33.
62. Ibid., p.26.
63. CRO/DE 563.
64. Ibid.
65. CRO/DE 708.
66. CRO/DE 709.
67. See pps. 69-70.
68. See p.106.
69. See pp.100-101.
70. CRO/DE 2431.
71. Merlin Waterson, *The Servants' Hall* (New York,1980), p.153.
72. L. Stone and J. C. F. Stone, op. cit., p.239.
73. David W. Howell, *Patriarchs and Parasites...*, p.181.
74. CRO/DE 1542 (219).
75. G. E. Mingay, *The Gentry*, p.121.

Chapter 9: Public Life

1. Sir Lewis Namier, *The Structure of Politics at the Accession of George III* (2nd. ed.,Oxford,1957),p.61.
2. Sir L. Namier and J. Brooke, op. cit.,vol. III, p.387.
3. Philip C. Yorke, op. cit., vol. I, p.211; Lionel Cust, op. cit., 3rd. Ser., p.41.
4. CRO/DE 1542/192.
5. Brit. Mus. Add. MSS., 35,609.
6. Sir L. Namier and J. Brooke, op. cit.,vol.III, p.387; DNB (entry for Philip Yorke, 2nd Earl of Harwicke), and note 54 below.
7. Sir L. Namier and J. Brooke, op. cit., vol. II, p.229.
8. Frank O'Gorman, *Voters, Patrons and Parties* (Oxford, 1989), p.143.
9. Sir L. Namier and J. Brooke, op. cit.,vol. II, p.229.
10. Journals of the House of Commons, 1774-1776, vol. XXXV, p.187.
11. For the details, see Sir L. Namier and J. Brooke, op. cit., vol. II, pp.229-230.
12. Ibid., p.230.
13. Ibid., pp.288-290.
14. *Journals of the House of Commons,1774-1776*, vol. XXXV, pp.187-189.
15. Ibid., and Sir L. Namier and J. Brooke, op. cit., p.179.
16. For the detailed legal arguments see 'The Case of the Borough of Helstone on the Petitions of Philip Yorke and Francis Cust Esqrs, and of divers Electors of the said Borough, Against the

Election and Return of the Marquis of Carmarthen and Francis Owen Esq, Before a Committee of the House of Commons March llth, 1775'. (Uncatalogued item in the library at Erthig).
17. Sir L. Namier and J. Brooke, op. cit., vol. I, p.180.
18. 'The Case of the Borough of Helstone...' pp.5-8.
19. Journals of the House of Commons, vol. XXXV, pp.194-195.
20. Sir L. Namier and J. Burke, op. cit., vol.II, p.230.
21. 'The Case of the Borough of Helstone...', p.14.
22. CRO/DE 1212.
23. Brit. Mus. Add. MSS., 35, 612.
24 . Sir L. Namier and J. Brooke, op. cit., vol.II, p.229.
25. Ibid., p.368.
26. Brit. Mus. Add. MSS., 35, 622. He says much the same thing in his letter of February 2nd, 1784.
27. C.J. Apperley, op. cit., p.312.
28. CRO/DE 1212.
29. Sir L. Namier and J. Brooke, op. cit., vol. I, p.463. The Wynns of Wynnstay had exercised the dominant interest in Denbighshire but, during the long minority after the death of Sir Watkin Williams Wynn in 1749, representation had been decided by an arrangement between the heads of the other leading families, the Myddletons of Chirk Castle and the Cottons of Lleweni. This arrangement persisted until 1774, when Sir Watkin Williams Wynn, now of age, became the MP.
30. Sir L. Namier and J. Brooke, op. cit., vol. I , p.5.
31. CRO/DE 1306.
32. P.D.G. Thomas, *Society, Government and Politics*, pp.19-20, in *Wales in the Eighteenth Century*, D. Moore (Ed.) (Llandybie, 1976).
33. Geraint H. Jenkins, op. cit., p.302.
34. Robert Watkin Wynn actually held the seat until 1796. Sir L. Namier and J. Brooke, op. cit., vol. III, pp.672-673.
35. T. W. Pritchard, 'Sir Watkin Williams Wynn, Fourth Baronet (1749-1789) (*DHST*, vol. 28. 1979), p.58.
36. Sir L. Namier and J. Brooke, op. cit., vol. I, p.325.
37. R. G. Thorne, *The House of Commons...*, vol. V. pp.675-676.
38. Sir L. Namier and J. Brooke, op. cit., vol. I, pp.214-215.
39. Ibid., p.217.
40. Ibid., vol. ll, p.681.
41. CRO/DE 563.
42. P.D.G. Thomas, *The House of Commons in the Eighteenth Century* (Oxford, 1971), p.229.
43. Ibid.
44 . CRO/DE 1205.
45. C.J. Apperley, op. cit., p.415.
46. Ibid., p.411.
47. P.D.G. Thomas, *The House of Commons...*, p.231. See also Geraint H. Jenkins, op. cit., pp.306-307.
48. P.D.G. Thomas, *The House of Commons...* pp.231-232.
49. CRO/DE 1396, May 4th. and 5th, 1768. See also CRO/DE 1394.
50. Brit. Mus. Add. MSS. 35, 608.
51. P.D.G. Thomas, op. cit., pp.150-151.
52. Information on this topic has been gleaned from A. Aspinall, 'The Reporting and Publishing of the House of Commons Debates, 1771-1834' in R. Pares and A. J. P. Taylor, *Essays presented to Sir Lewis Namier* (London, 1956), pp.227-256.
53. Brit. Mus. Add. MSS., 35, 613 and 35, 614.
54. W. Cobbett (ed.), *The Parliamentary History of England from the earliest period to 1803* (London, 1814), vol. 19, pp.241-273; 775-815; 834-867.
55. Brit. Mus. Add. MSS., 35, 613.
56. Ibid.
57. Ibid., 35, 614.
58. CRO/DE 563 (Undated).
59. Ibid.

60. Ibid.
61. CRO/QSD/JQ/2.
62. CRO/DE 1306.
63. CRO/DE 1307.
64. Keith Williams-Jones (ed.), *A Calendar of the Merioneth Quarter Sessions Rolls*, vol.I, 1773-1765 (Merioneth County Council, 1965), Introduction, pp. lx, lxi; David W. Howell, *Patriarchs and Parasites*, p.140.
65. The information is based on Quarter Sessions Minute and Order Books in Clwyd Record Office (Reference numbers of individual examples are cited below).
66. K. Williams-Jones, op. cit., p. lxxxiv on the situation in Merionethshire
67. CRO/QSD/SO/1/7. Quarter Sessions Order Book, pp.285-286.
68. Ibid., p.454.
69. Ibid., pp.328-329.
70. CRO/QSD/AB/1/332.
71. CRO/QSD/AB/1/333, 334.
72. CRO/QSD/AB/1/502, 520.
73. CRO/QSD/SO/1/7, pp.63-64.
74. Ibid., p.106.
75. CRO/QSD/AB/1/358.
76. Ibid., p.371.
77. See p. 148.
78. NLW., 12422 D.
79. CRO/QSD/AB/1/453.
80. CRO/QSD/SO/1/7, p.259.
81. Ibid., p.278.
82. A. H. Dodd(ed.), *A History of Wrexham*, pp.87-88.
83. 'A Table of Parochial Assessment and Expenditure in the Parish of Wrexham', p.893.
84. A. H. Dodd(ed.), *A History of Wrexham*, p.86.
85. CRO/DE 683. This is a copy, in another hand, of Philip Yorke's letter, with his own signature appended.
86. S. and B. Webb, *English Poor Law History: part 1, The Old Poor Law* (London, 1963), pp.120-121.
87. Ibid., pp.121-125. Also SR0/83/1/309.
88. S. and B. Webb, op. cit., pp.116-120.
89. CRO/DE 683.
90. CRO/PD/101/1/260.
91. A. H. Dodd(ed.), *A History of Wrexham*, p.90.
92. CRO/PD/101/1/260.
93. Ibid.
94. Ibid., and A. H. Dodd(ed.), *A History of Wrexham*, p.91.
95. A. H. Dodd, op. cit., p.91.
96. CRO/P0/101/1/326, 327, 328.
97. Geraint H. Jenkins, op. cit., p.334.
98. CRO/QSD/SR/340.
99. CRO/QSD/SM/2.
100. CRO/DE/1212.
101. CRO/PD/101/1/260.
102. Ibid.
103. Ibid. Also A. N. Palmer, *A History of the Parish Church of Wrexham* (new ed. Wrexham, 1984) p.45.
104. CRO/PD/101/1/260.
105. CRO/DE 50, 54.
106. CRO/DE 563.
107. D. R. Thomas, op. cit., vol. I, p.362.
108. See Geraint H. Jenkins, op. cit., pp.343-347.
109. NLW., SA/RD/26.

110. See pp.21-22.
111. See for example CRO/DE 563. Philip Yorke to John Caesar, September 15th, 1778.
112. Ibid.
113. CRO/DE 1212. Philip Yorke noted: "Painted window at M. £37/2/6."
114. NLW., SA/RD/26.
115. CRO/PD/81/1/13.
116. Ibid., January lst, 1774.
117. Ibid.
118. Ibid.
119. D.R. Thomas, op. cit., vol. l, p.454. See also NLW., SA/QA/5: Queries and Answers for Archbishop's Visitation, 1753.
120. CRO/PD/81/1/13.
121. NLW., SA/RD/28.
122. C.J. Apperley, op. cit., p.413.
123. CRO/DE 1366, 1396.
124. CRO/DE 1365.
125. CRO/DE 1396. December 29th, 1781.
126. CRO/DE 1366.
127. CRO/DE 1368.
128. CRO/DE 369.
129. C. J. Apperley, op. cit., p.409.
130. J. R. Western, *The English Militia in the Eighteenth Century* (London, 1965), Appendix. pp.448, 450.
131. CRO/DE 1316.
132. Brit. Mus. Add. MSS., 35, 616.
133. CRO/DE 1229.
134. Waterson, M., op. cit. pps. 101-102.
135. J.R. Western, op. cit., p.407.
136. Ibid., pp.430-434.
137. Ibid., p.340.
138. D. Jarrett, op. cit., pp.37-38.
139. PRO/W0/146/34.
140. CRO/DE 563. Letters to John Caesar from Garstang (on his way to Whitehaven), Cockermouth, Boroughbridge, Workington and Maryport.
141. CRO/DE 563. Letter to John Caesar from Maryport, September 15th, 1778.
142. Brit. Mus. Add. MSS., 35, 616.
143. Brit. Mus. Add. MSS., 35, 614. Philip Yorke to Earl of Hardwicke, July 30th, 1778.
144. CRO/DE 563.
145. J.R. Western, op. cit., pp.397-399.
146. CRO/DE 563. September 12th, 1778.
147. CRO/DE 1399. Philip Yorke, *Crude Ditties* (Wrexham, 1862), pp.3-9. For comments on Philip Yorke's verses and further examples, see pp.141-143.
148. A. L. Cust, *Chronicles of Erthig on the Dyke*, vol. 2, p.216.
149. J. R. Western, op. cit., p.341. For a detailed discussion, see Ch. Xlll.
150. Ibid., pp.388-389.
151. CRO/DE 563.
152. J.R. Western, op. cit., p.344.
153. CRO/DE 1212.
154. Brit. Mus. Add. MSS., 35, 617. Philip Yorke to the Earl of Hardwicke, October 20th, 1780.
155. See J. R. Western, op. cit., pp.388-397.
156. CRO/DE 563.
157. Ibid.
158. Brit. Mus. Add. MSS., 35, 642. Philip Yorke to the Earl of Hardwicke, November 22nd, 1801.
159. Ibid., December 15th, 1802.
160. J.R. Western, op. cit., p.388.

161. CRO/DE 563. Philip Yorke to John Caesar, October 5th, 1781.
162. PRO/WO. 27/483. The five companies consisted of 64, 64, 62, 65 and 65 men each. See also PRO/W0/13/422.
163. PRO/W0/146/34.
164. J.R. Western, op. cit., pp.419-420.
165. See below.
166. PRO/W0/72/9. Lieutenant-General Lane Parker to Sir Charles Gould, June 21st, 1781.
167. PRO/W0/72/9. From the address, it appears that the letter was written by Sir Charles Gould to a Captain Hunt on July 27th, 1781.
168. See below, Philip Yorke's letter to the Earl of Hardwicke; and PRO/W0/272/9, letters of July 17th, of Captain Hunt to Sir Charles Gould.
169. PRO/W0/72/9. The Earl of Hardwicke to Sir Charles Gould, August 4th, 1781.
170. Brit. Mus. Add. MSS., 35, 618.

Chapter 10: Literary Pursuits

 1. See pp.22-23.
 2. See below note 20.
 3. See p.153.
 4. C.J. Apperley, op. cit., p.411.
 5. Rev. John Evans, *The Beauties of England and Wales* (London, 1812), vol. XVII, part 1, p.590.
 6. Quoted on p136.
 7. Rev. John Evans, op. cit., p.519.
 8. Tudur Aled, c.1485-1525.
 9. The examples are from Philip Yorke's collection, *Crude Ditties* (Wrexham. 1802).
10 . CRO/DE 1396.
11. CRO/DE 1212. His accounts contain an item for August 24th, 1772: "£6/6/- . . Tour of Wales in part. "
12. CRO/DE 1211. As well as the tour he actually made in 1776, he planned another with his friend Mr. Casamajor, starting in Oswestry and visiting Pistyll Rhaeadr, Chirk Castle, Llangollen, Corwen, Bala, Drws-y-nant, Dolgelley, Barmouth, Harlech, Penmorfa, Pontaberglaslyn, Caernarfon, the summit of Snowdon by Llyn Cwellin and back to Caernarfon, to Bangor (by water), Conway, Llanrwst, Rhaeadr y Wennol, back to Llanrwst, Llansannan, Denbigh, Ruthin, Wrexham – a total of 225 miles. There is no evidence that this tour was ever undertaken.
13. Brit. Mus. Add. MSS., 35, 611.
14. See pp.174-175.
15. DNB. Thomas Pennant (1729-1798), traveller and naturalist; born at Downing, near Holywell, Flintshire; matriculated at Queen's College, Oxford, but left without taking his degree, 1754, elected F.S.A., but resigned in 1760. 1767, elected R.R.S. 1771, received degree of D.C.L. from Oxford University. He published, amongst other works, *British Zoology, History of Quadrupeds, Arctic Zoology,* accounts of his Tours in Wales, Scotland and of *The Journey from Chester to London, The History of the Parishes of Whiteford and Holywell* and *The Literary Life of the late Thomas Pennant, Esq., by Himself.*
16. Prys Morgan, *The Eighteenth Century Renaissance* (Llandybie, 1981), pp.119-120.
17. Brit. Mus. Add. MSS., 35, 613.
18. WRO/CR2017/TP22/5/1
19. Ibid.
20. DNB. John Lloyd, Hafodunos and Wigfair (1749-1815). Member of the Cymmrodorion Society, F.R.S., F.S.A., F.L.S., D.C.L., of Oxford. M.P. for Flintshire, 1797-1799. His library was reputed to contain 10,000 items. He also possessed a valuable collection of scientific instruments.
21. Author of *The Historie of Cambria,* 1584.
22. Author of *Britannia* (ed. E. Gibson, London, 1695).
23. NLW., 12, 422 D.
24. CRO/DE 385.
25. R. Paul Evans, *Thomas Pennant's Writings on North Wales* (unpublished M. A. Thesis, University

of Wales), pp.16-17, states that Sir Cyril Fox claimed that Thomas Pennant was the first to identify Wat's Dyke as a distinct entity, separate from Offa's Dyke. Up to 1778 the two earthworks had been classed as a single creation. Thomas Pennant claimed that John Evans, the cartographer, was the source of this revelation. Might one suggest that Philip Yorke, perhaps, has a claim to at least a share of the glory!

26. NLW., 15423.
27. WRO/CR2017/TP23/4.
28. WRO/CR2017/TP401/2/1.
29. See for example, Donald Moore, 'Cambrian Antiquity: precursors of the Historians' in *Welsh Antiquity* (George C. Boon and J. M. Lewis, eds., Cardiff, 1976), pp.193-220; Geraint H. Jenkins, op. cit., pp.239-249; E. Hobsbawn and T. Ranger, *The Invention of Tradition* (Cambridge, 1983), Ch. 3, pp.45-46.
30. See pp.32-35.
31. R. Paul Evans, *Thomas Pennant's Writings on North Wales*, p.7.
32. CRO/DE 383.
33. R. Paul Evans, *Thomas Pennant's Writings on North Wales*, p.7.
34. Philip Yorke, *Tracts of Powys* (Wrexham, 1795): Preface.
35. R. Paul Evans, 'Reverend John Lloyd of Caerwys(1733-1793): Historian, Antiquarian and Genealogist'. (*JFHS.*, vol. 31, 1983-1984), pp.109-124; DWB. John Lloyd was born in Llanarmon-yn-Ial and nicknamed 'Blodeu Llanarmon' (the flower of Llanarmon). Philip Yorke used the plural 'blodeu' (flowers) instead of the correct 'blodyn' (flower); see *Royal Tribes of Wales* p.122. In 1757, John Lloyd graduated from Jesus College, Oxford. He was Appointed Curate at Caerwys in 1761, Rector of Nannerch in 1771 and Rector of Caerwys in 1778.
36. Thomas Pennant, *The Literary Life of the late Thomas Pennant, Esq., by Himself*, p.26.
37. C.J. Apperley, op. cit., p.414.
38. CRO/DE 1394, 1396.
39. NLW., 27817D, July 3rd, 1787.
40. NLW., 12422D, Philip Yorke to John Lloyd, Hafodunos, September 17th, 1791.
41. CRO/DE 563. June 22nd, 1775.
42. Thomas Pennant, *A Tour in Wales, 1770* 2 vols. (London, 1784), vol. l, Advertisement.
43. R. Paul Evans, *Thomas Pennant's Writings on North Wales*, p.9.
44. CRO/DE 1294. See E. D. Jones, 'Robert Vaughan of Hengwrt' (*JMHRS.*, vol. l, part 1, 1949), pp.21-30. b. 1592, d. 1667. (Philip Yorke was incorrect in saying that Robert Vaughan died in Charles I's reign) Robert Vaughan was a historian, antiquarian and collector; the Hengwrt manuscripts, together with later accretions formed the core of the National Library of Wales in 1909. *British Antiquities revived* was his only publication. CRO/DE 1394 contain a copy of Robert Vaughan's work, as does Thomas Pennant's *Tours in Wales*, (Caernarvon, 1883 ed.) vol. 3, appendix XXVIII, pp.421-453
45. WRO/CR2017/TP 401/5. July 19th, 1791.
46. Philip Yorke, *The Royal Tribes of Wales*, to which is added *An Account of the Fifteen Tribes of North Wales* (ed. Richard Williams, Liverpool, 1887); Preface, p.VIII.
47. Ibid.; and WRO/CR 2017/TP 576, undated letter to Thomas Pennant.
48. NLW. 1809E. Philip Yorke to Walter Davies, October 21st, 1803.
49. WRO/CR 2017/TP 401/5. July l9th, 1791.
50. WRO/C 2017/TP 56. Undated letter.
51. See for example , *DWB. down to 1940* (London, 1959); Meic Stephens(ed.) *A Companion to Welsh Literature* (Cardiff, 1986), p.649.
52. *Arch. Camb.*, (vol. I, 4th. Ser., 1870), p.186.
53. *DNB.* Moses Griffith (1749-1809). Draughtsman and engraver, a native of Lleyn. Born of humble parents, poor education, but showed exceptional skill in drawing. He was taken into service in 1769 by Thomas Pennant, who helped him to study drawing. He became Pennant's constant companion on his tours and excursions, and made the drawings and engravings for Pennant's many works. He performed similar service for others, like Philip Yorke. Thomas Pennant described him as "that treasure". See *The Literary Life of the late Thomas Pennant, Esq., by Himself* (London, 1793), p.10.

54. NLW., 4857D.
55. Ibid.
56. CRO/DE 1542(246).
57. NLW., 4857D.
58. NLW., 1565C.
59. NLW., 12422D. June 28th, 1791.
60. Ibid.
61. WRO/CR 2017/TP 401/5.
62. Presumably the British Museum which opened in 1759.
63. NLW., 12422D.
64. Ibid. October 28th, 1792.
65. WRO/CR 2017/TP 576.

Chapter 11: The Royal Tribes of Wales

1. *Bygones*, (1878-1881), p.218. *Bygones* consisted mainly of anecdotes and news items relating to Wales and the Border Counties.
2. Prys Morgan, op. cit., p.93.
3. Philip Yorke, *The Royal Tribes of Wales*; Preface, p. vii.
4. Walter Davies, whose bardic name was 'Gwallter Mechain', was a graduate of Trinity College, Cambridge. After serving as a curate at Meifod and Ysbyty Ifan, he obtained the livings of Llanwyddelan in 1803, Meifod in 1807 and Llanrhaeadr ym Mochnant in 1837.
5. John Thomas Owen, *Gwallter Mechain, ei hanes, ei waith a'i safonau* (M.A. Thesis, University of Wales), pp.46-54.
6. Williams, Richard, 'Montgomeryshire Worthies' (*Mont. Colls.*, vol, 9, 1876), pp.378-383.
7. William Warrington, *History of Wales* (3rd. ed., London, 1788). In the Preface he acknowledged his debt to, among others, John Lloyd of Caerwys, William Owen Pughe and Philip Yorke, "whose gentleness of manners and benevolent spirit, render him an amicable friend and a valuable man". Thomas Pennant, in his *Tours in Wales*, vol. I, pt. V., acknowledged his debt to John Lloyd of Caerwys, Philip Yorke and several others.
8. NLW., 1809E.
9. Philip Yorke, *Tracts of Powys*. p.37.
10. NLW., 1809E. Philip Yorke to John Painter, March 2nd, 1803.
11. Philip Yorke, *The Royal Tribes of Wales*, p.134.
12. Thomas Pennant for instance, had a poor grasp of Welsh, see Prys Morgan, op. cit., p. 92. Very little is known about William Warrington. Apparently he was the son of George Warrington from Aigburth in Lancashire who settled in Wrexham in the early or mid-eighteenth century. William Warrington became vicar of Old Windsor (*Arch. Cam.* 6th Ser., vol. 4, 1904), pps. 176-177; see also A. N. Palmer, *A History of the Town of Wrexham* (Wrexham, 1893), pps. 61, 91. His local residence was Rhyddyn Hall, Caergwrle. (*JFHS.*, vol. 31, 1983-4), p.123; see also E. Hubbard, *The Buildings of Wales: Clwyd* (London, 1986), pps. 354-355. For William Warrington's own comment on his knowledge of Welsh see his *History of Wales*, Preface, p.vii.
13. Philip Yorke, *The Royal Tribes of Wales*, pp.67-69.
14. Philip Yorke, *Tracts of Powys*, p.6.
15. Prys Morgan, op. cit., p.41.
16. NLW., 1809E.
17. Ibid. Philip Yorke to Walter Davies, October 7th, 1798.
18. Discussed in several accounts, for example, Glanmor Williams, *Religion, Language and Nationality in Wales* (Cardiff, 1979), pp.1-7.
19. Geoffrey of Monmouth (c. 1090-1155), in his *History of the Kings of Britain* (c.1136).
20. DNB. Polydore Vergil (c1470-c1565), born in Urbino; came to England as collector of Peter's Pence in 1501 or 1502; wrote a history of England (*Anglia Historia*), published in 1534.
21. Geraint H. Jenkins, op. cit., pp.223-224; 246-248.
22. NLW., 4857D. March 21st, 1791.
23. Philip Yorke, *Tracts of Powys*. pp.39-57.
24. Philip Yorke, *The Royal Tribes of Wales*, pp.45-46: Footnote.

25. NLW., 1809E. April 3rd, 1802.
26. Ibid., October 31st, 1803.
27. Ibid. Philip Yorke to Walter Davies, September, 1796.
28. Ibid., October 26th, 1796.
29. Ibid., December 3rd, 1796.
30. Ibid., December 29th, 1796.
31. Ibid., December 9th, 1797.
32. Ibid., February 20th, 1797.
33. Ibid.
34. CRO/DE 1396. Walter Davies to Philip Yorke, February l9th, 1798.
35. Ibid.
36. Ibid. (Undated).
37. NLW., 1809E.
38. CRO/DE 1396. I. Owen to Philip Yorke, October 12th, 1796.
39. Ibid. David Thomas to Philip Yorke, October 22nd, 1799.
40. Philip Yorke, *The Royal Tribes of Wales*, (ed. Richard Williams), Preface, p. ix.
41. NLW., 1809E. June 27th, 1797.
42. Ibid., March 5th, 1797.
43. NLW., 1809E. March 14th, 1798.
44. NLW., 1809E.
45. Ibid.
46. Ibid.
47. Ibid. The date on the first letter is given as June l9th. This must be wrong since Philip Yorke stated that he would send the horses to Meifod on the 18th, and thanked Walter Davies in a letter dated the 17th, for agreeing to visit Erthig.
48. Ibid.
49. Ibid.
50. Ibid.
51. Ibid.
52. This appears to be a careless mistake. Surely he meant Davies of Llansilin.
53. NLW., 1809E.
54. Ibid.
55. CRO/DE 1396. December 25th, 1798.
56. NLW., 1809E. May 27th, 1799.
57. Ibid.
58. John Painter, a leading Presbyterian in the town, set up as a printer and stationer in Wrexham's High Street at the beginning of the nineteenth century. A.H. Dodd(ed.), *A History of Wrexham*, pp.225-226.
59. NLW., 1809E.
60 . Ibid., January 9th, 1802.
61. Ibid., January 31st, 1802.
62. Ibid., March 16th, April 3rd, 1802.
63. Ibid., December 10th, 1802.
64. Ibid.
65. Ibid., April 12th, May 31st, July l9th, 1803.
66. Ibid., July l9th, 1803.
67. Ibid., October 21st, 1803.
68. Ibid., December 10th, 1803.
69. Ibid., July 3rd, 1801.
70. Brit. Mus. Add. MSS., 35, 642. December 15th, 1802.
71. See Ch. 12
72. CRO/DE 1396. Undated.
73. Philip Yorke, *The Royal Tribes of Wales*, pp.102-104.
74. Ibid., p.49.
75. See p. 162.

76. See p. 153.
77. CRO/DE 1396.
78. Philip Yorke, *The Royal Tribes of Wales*, p. l.
79. W. Warrington, op. cit., Preface.
80. Benjamin Heath Malkin, *The Scenery, Antiquities and Biography of South Wales*, London, 1807; republished 1970), Ch. l.

Chapter 12: Leisure Activities
1. G. E. Mingay, *English Landed Society. . ,* p.205.
2. CRO/DE 385. Evidence suggests that Philip Yorke's own conveyances during the 1770s and 1780s were confined mainly to a coach and a two-wheeled chaise (CRO/DE 352 – undated fragment) on which he paid annual duty varying from £4 to £7 on the former and £2 to £2/12/6 on the latter. (CRO/DE 384)
3. CRO/DE 1211.
4. CRO/DE 1212.
5. CRO/DE 888.
6. CRO/DE 1212.
7. C.J. Apperley, op. cit., p.411.
8. CRO/DE 1212.
9. CRO/DE 383.
10. CRO/DE 428.
11. C.J. Apperley. op. cit., p.303.
12. CRO/DE 563.
13. Ibid., July 30th, 1771.
14 . CRO/DE 1542 (242).
15. C.J. Apperley, op. cit., p.414.
16. CRO/DE 563. Philip Yorke to Jacky Caesar, September 15th, 1778. The venison came from Wynnstay. He instructed Jacky Caesar: "I would have you send forthwith for the Wynnstay venison to be brought to Erthig, and from thence sent by a labourer with my respects to Mr. Strong of Marchwiel".
17. CRO/DE 563.
18. Cecil Price, *The English Theatre in Wales* (Cardiff, 1948), p.61.
19. The following advertisement appeared in *The Chester Courant* for February 6th, 1781:

Wrexham Theatre
by Desire of
W. Lloyd Jun. of Plas Power
To-Morrow Evening, Wednesday, February 7th, 1781,
The School for Scandal, and a Farce call'd
Cross Purposes
And, on Friday Evening
By Desire of the Rev. Bennett Dorset,
The (undecipherable) Daughter
The New Highland Laddie, and Vauxhall Echo
between the Acts with
High Life Below Stairs

20. For a full account of the Wynnstay Theatre see Cecil Price, op. cit., Ch. X, and T.W. Pritchard, 'The Architectural History of the Mansion of Wynnstay' (*DHst*, vol. 29, 1980), pp.24-30.
21. In the *Chester Courant*.
22. C.J. Apperley, op. cit., p.298.
23. T.W. Pritchard, 'The Architectural History of the Mansion of Wynnstay', pp.24-25.
24. CRO/DE 888. May 9th, 1770.
25. WR0/1542/217. Amongst the local gentry and their wives in the production were Mr. Apperley as the Duke, Mrs. Lloyd as Jessica and Mrs. Puleston as Nerissa.
26. WRO/CR2017/TP597/14. Mr. Pennant was Bardolph.
27. CRO/DE 1542(215). Undated.
28. CRO/DE 1399, p.13. Also quoted in M. Waterson, op. cit., pp.58-59.

29. The material for this table was derived from Philip Yorke's account books CRO/DE 1212 and CRO/DE 428, and from references in his letters. His accounts for the period 1767 to 1772 are too fragmentary to serve as a basis for any firm conclusions about his visits. However, from the slight evidence available, it would seem that he paid several visits to London and Belton House during the period of his courtship of Elizabeth Cust, and after their marriage in 1770, and one visit to Bath in 1770.

30. CRO/DE 1212.

31. Ibid. £117 paid on June 19th, and £147 on June 26th, in 1777.

32. A.L. Cust. op. cit., vol. II, p.180.

33. CRO/DE 1417.

34. G.E. Mingay, *English Landed Society. . ,* quoting from Lord Chesterfield's letters, p.205.

35. CRO/DE 1422.

36. See p.101.

37. See p.34.

38. CRO/DE 1211.

39. Roy Porter, op. cit., pp.245-246.

40. Ibid., p.246.

41. D.W. Harris, *History of Prestatyn* (Chester, 1939), p.29.

42. Ibid.

43. G.E. Mingay, *English Landed Society. . ,* p.221. Anaemia and scorbutic symptoms could have been the result of an inadequate consumption of butter and fresh vegetables which caused some deficiency in the intake of vitamins and iron. See J. Pearson, *Neston and Parkgate* (Birkenhead, 1985), pp.16-17. In 1784, Mrs. Emma Hart, later to becaome the famous Lady Hamilton, visited Parkgate to treat a skin complaint from which she was suffering, by bathing in sea water.

44. Brit. Mus. Add. MSS., 35, 613. Philip Yorke to the Earl of Hardwicke, October 7th, 1776.

45. CRO/DE/NT/83. From 'Verses written September 22nd, 1804 in Prestatyn, Flintshire, ' by Mrs. H. Thrale.

46. Ibid.

47. J. Pearson, op. cit., pp.15-19.

48. CRO/DE 1212.

49. CRO/DE 563.

50 . The actual dates were 1783, 1784, 1785, 1787, 1788, 1791, 1792, 1795, 1797 and 1800.

51. *The Cellar* is now *The Harp Inn.* William Davies, *Handbook for the Vale of Clwyd* (Ruthin, 1856, repr. 1988), pp.37-41. *The Bee* was known as 'the Queen of Hotels', while *The Cellar* is reputed to be the oldest inn in Abergele.

52. CRO/DE 1212.

53. Samuel Lewis, *Topographical Dictionary of Wales* (London, 1840), 2 vols.

54. Joseph Hucks, *A Pedestrian Tour Through North Wales, 1795* (Alun R Jones and W. Tydeman, eds., Oswestry, 1979), p. ix.

55. NLW., 12422D.

56. CRO/DE 1399. Philip Yorke, *Crude Ditties,* pp.20-21.

57. CRO/DE 1205.

58. For Philip Yorke's Militia activities see pp.134-140.

59. CRO/DE 563.

60 . Phyllis Pembry, *The English Spa(1560-1815): A Social History* (London, 1990), p.129.

61. Ibid., p.135.

62 . CRO/DE 1211.

63. CRO/DE 1212. For example:

1789 November 27th. Journey back to Bath	£3/3/
December 12th. Petty expenses at Bath	£6/3/6
Master of the Ceremonies	£2/2/-
Journey from Bath, myself to Erthig	£2/12/6
Hostler and Barber at Bath	£1/13/-

64. Brit. Mus. Add. MSS., 35, 644.

65. Ibid.

66. Ibid.
67. Roy Porter, op. cit., p.245.
68. CRO/DE 563. July 31st, 1778.
69. CRO/DE 563. Undated.
70. C.J. Apperley, op. cit., p.409.
71. CRO/DE 1211.
72. Brit. Mus. Add. MSS., 35, 644.
73. John Haddon, *Portrait of Bath* (London, 1982), pp.82-83.
74. Brit. Mus. Add. MSS., 35, 644.
75. Ibid.
76. See pp.159-163.
77. P. Pembry, op. cit., pp.245-249.
78 . I. Gwynedd Jones(ed.), *Aberystwyth, 1277-1977* (Llandysul, 1977), pp.114-115.
79. CRO/DE 1212.

Conclusion
1. Brit. Mus. Add. MSS., 35, 644.

BIBLIOGRAPHY

1 Manuscript Sources

A. BRITISH MUSEUM, Additional MSS: Hardwicke, Newcastle, Greville papers.

B. NATIONAL LIBRARY OF WALES, Wynnstay, Chirk Castle, Pennant, Wigfair, Lloyd of
Caerwys collections; Walter Davies ('Gwallter Mechain') papers; St. Asaph Diocesan
records (Rural Dean's reports).

C. PUBLIC RECORD OFFICE, War Office records.

D. CLWYD RECORD OFFICE, Erthig papers; Plas Power estate records; Wrexham and
Marchwiel Church records; Denbighshire Quarter Session Minute and Order Books.

E. HERTFORDSHIRE RECORD OFFICE, Newnham and Radwell estate papers.

F. SHROPSHIRE RECORD OFFICE, Quarter Sessions General Order Book (Shrewsbury) and
Minute Book (Whitchurch).

G. SHREWSBURY PUBLIC LIBRARY, Turnpike Trust and Canal records.

2 Printed Sources Pre-1840

Cobbett, W. (ed.),*The Parliamentary History of England from the earliest period to 1803*
(London,1814).

Davies, W. *A General View of the Agriculture and Domestic Economy of North Wales*
(London,1810).

Evans, J.C., *The Beauties of England and Wales* (London,1812).

House of Commons Journals, vol. XXXV, 1774-1776.

Hucks, J., *A Pedestrian Tour through North Wales, in a Series of Letters*, (1795), eds. A.R. Jones
and W. Tydeman (Cardiff,1979).

Laurence, J., *The Duty and Office of a Land Steward* (London,1731).

Lewis, S., *A Topographical Dictionary of Wales* (London,1840).

Malkin, B.H., *The Scenery, Antiquities and Biography of South Wales* (London,1807; republished
1970).

Pennant, T., *Tours in Wales*, ed. J. Rhys. 3 vols. (Caernarvon,1883 ed.).

Pennant, T., *The Literary Life of the Late Thomas Pennant Esq. by Himself* (London,1786).

*The Case of the Borough of Helstone on the Petitions of Philip Yorke and Francis Cust Esqrs., and of
divers Electors of the said Borough, Against the Election and return of the Marquis of Carmarthen
and Francis Owen Esq., before a Committee of the House of Commons, March 11th., 1775.*

A Table of Parochial Assessment and Expenditure in the Parish of Wrexham, 1795.

Warrington, W, *History of Wales* (London, 1786).

Yorke, P., *Crude Ditties* (Wrexham,1802).

Yorke, P., *The Royal Tribes of Wales* (Wrexham,1799).

Yorke, P., *Tracts of Powys* (Wrexham,1795).

3 Secondary Sources

Addison, J., *The Works of Joseph Addison*, ed. R.Hurd (London, 1954).

Apperley, C.J., *My Life and Times* (London, 1842).

Boon, G.C. and Lewis, J.M. (eds.), *Welsh Antiquity* (Cardiff, 1976).

Boswell, J., *London Journal*, ed. F.A. Pottle (London, 1950).

Cannon, J., *Aristocratic Century* (Cambridge, 1984).

Carter, H.B., *His Majesty's Spanish Flock* (Edinburgh, 1964).
Chambers, J.D. and Mingay, G.E., *The Agricultural Revolution, 1750-1880* (London, 1966).
Cust, A.L., *Chronicles of Erthig on the Dyke*. 2 vols. (London, 1914).
Cust, L., *Records of the Cust Family*, 2nd. Ser., 1550-1779. (London, 1902).
Davies, C.S., *The Agricultural History of Cheshire, 1750-1850* (Manchester, 1960).
Davies. J., *Hanes Cymru* (London, 1992)
Davies, L.T. and Edwards, A., *Welsh Life in the Eighteenth Century* (London, 1943).
Davies, W., *Handbook for the Vale of Clwyd* (Ruthin, 1856).
Defoe, D., *The Compleat English Gentleman* (1729), ed. K.D. Buhlbring (London, 1890)
Dodd, A.H., *The Industrial Revolution in North Wales* (Cardiff, 1933; new ed., Wrexham, 1990).
Dodd, A.H. (ed.), *A History of Caernarvonshire, 1284-1900* (Caernarvon 1968; new ed., Wrexham, 1990)
Dodd, A.H. (ed.), *A History of Wrexham* (Wrexham,1957; 2nd. ed., 1989).
Fielding, H., 'An Essay on Conversation' in *The Complete Works of Henry Fielding* (London, 1888).
Ford, B. (ed.), *The Pelican Guide to English Literature* ,vol. IV (London, 1957).
Forrester, J., *The Polite Philosopher* (Edinburgh, 1734).
Ginger, A., *Country Houses of England, Scotland and Wales - A Guide and Gazetteer* (London, 1991).
Girouard, M., *Life in the English Country House* (London, 1979).
Goodwin, A. (ed.), *The European Nobility in the Eighteenth Century* (London, 1967).
Griffith, J.E., *Pedigrees of Anglesey and Caernarvonshire Families* (Horncastle, 1914; new ed. Wrexham 1985).
Haddon, J., *Portrait of Bath* (London, 1982).
Hans, N., *New Trends in Education in the Eighteenth Century* (London, 1951).
Harris, D.W., *History of Prestatyn* (Chester, 1939).
Harris, G., *The Life of Lord Chancellor Hardwicke*, 2 vols. (London, 1847).
Hobsbawm, E. and Ranger, T., *The Invention of Tradition* (Cambridge, 1983).
Holmes, G., *Augustan England* (London, 1983).
Howell, D.W., *Land and People in Nineteenth-Century Wales* (London, 1977)
Howell, D.W., *Patriarchs and Parasites: the Gentry of South-West Wales in the Eighteenth Century* (Cardiff, 1986).
Hubbard, E. *The Buildings of Wales: Clwyd* (London, 1986)
Hughes, G.T., Morgan, P. and Thomas, J.G. (eds.), *Gregynog* (Cardiff, 1977)
Jarrett, D., *England in the Age of Hogarth* (London, 1976).
Jellicoe, G.and S., Goode, P., and Lancaster, M., *The Oxford Companion to Gardens* (Oxford, 1984).
Jenkins, G.H., *Wales,1642-1780* (Oxford, 1987).
Jones, I.G. (ed.), *Aberystwyth, 1277-1977* (Llandysul, 1977).
Jones-Mortimer, H.M.C., *A List of the Names and Residences of all the High Sheriffs of the County of Denbigh* (Aylesbury, 1971).
Kramm, J., *Hope Deferred* (London, 1965).
Lawson, J. and Silver, H., *A Social History of Education in England* (London, 1973).
Lloyd, J.Y.W., *The History of the Princes, the Lords Marcher and the Ancient Nobility of Powys Fadog* (London, 1884).
Lloyd, T., *The Lost Houses of Wales* (London, 1986).
Miles,R., *Forestry in the English Landscape* (London, 1967).
Mingay, G.E., *English Landed Society in the Eighteenth Century* (London, 1963).
Mingay, G.E.,*The Gentry* (London, 1976).
Mingay, G.E. (ed.), *The Agrarian History of England and Wales*, vol. VI, 1750-1850 (Cambridge, 1989).
Moore, D. (ed.), *Wales in the Eighteenth Century* (Llandybie, 1976).

Morgan, P., *The Eighteenth Century Renaissance* (Llandybie, 1981).

Namier, Sir L., *The Structure of Politics at the Accession of George III* (2nd. ed., Oxford, 1957).

Namier, Sir L. and Brooke, J., *The House of Commons, 1754-1790* (London, 1964).

O'Gorman, F., *Voters,Patrons and Parties* (Oxford, 1989).

Palmer, A.N., *A History of the Parish Church of Wrexham* (new ed., Wrexham, 1984).

Palmer, A.N., *A History of the Thirteen Country Townships of the Old Parish of Wrexham* (Wrexham, 1903).

Palmer, A. N., *A History of the Town of Wrexham* (Wrexham, 1893).

Pares, R. and Taylor, A.J.P. (eds.), *Essays presented to Sir Lewis Namier* (London, 1956).

Parker, R.A.C., *Coke of Norfolk* (Oxford, 1975).

Pearson, J., *Neston and Parkgate* (Birkenhead, 1985).

Pembry, P., *The English Spa, 1560-1815: a Social History* (London, 1990).

Pennant, T., *Tours in Wales*, ed. J.Rhys (Caernarvon, 1883).

Porter, R., *English Society in the Eighteenth Century* (London, 1982).

Price, C., *The English Theatre in Wales* (Cardiff, 1948).

Robinson, J.M., *The Wyatts: an Architectural Dynasty* (Oxford, 1979).

Robson, D., *Some Aspects of Education in Cheshire in the Eighteenth Century* (Manchester, 1966).

Stephens, M. (ed.), *A Companion to Welsh Literature* (Cardiff, 1986).

Stone, L. and Stone, C.F., *An Open Elite? England,1540-1880* (Oxford, 1986).

Swift, J., *The Works of Jonathan Swift*, ed. T.Scott (London, 1907).

Thomas, D., *Agriculture in Wales during the Napoleonic Wars* (Cardiff, 1963).

Thomas, D. (ed.), *Wales: a New Study* (Newton Abbot, 1977).

Thomas, D.R., *A History of the Diocese of St. Asaph* (Oswestry, 1908).

Thomas, P.D.G., *The House of Commons in the Eighteenth Century* (Oxford, 1971).

Thorne, R.G., *The House of Commons,1790-1820* (London, 1986).

Trow-Smith, R., *A History of Livestock Husbandry, 1700-1900* (London, 1959).

Venn, J.A., *Alumnii Cantabrigiensis* (Cambridge,1954). *Victoria County History of Hertfordshire,*1908.

Waterson, M., *The Servants' Hall* (London, 1980).

Webb, S. and Webb, B., *English Poor Law History: Part 1, The Old Poor Law* (London, 1963).

Western, J.R., *The English Militia in the Eighteenth Century* (London, 1965).

Williams, G., *Religion, Language and Nationality in Wales* (Cardiff, 1979)

Williams-Jones, K.(ed.), *A Calendar of the Merioneth Quarter Sessions Rolls: 1, 1733-1765* (Aberystwyth, 1965).

Winstanley, D.A., *Unreformed Cambridge: a study of certain aspects of the University in the Eighteenth Century* (Cambridge, 1935).

Yorke, P.C., *The Life of Lord Chancellor Hardwicke*, 3 vols. (Cambridge, 1915).

4 Articles

Beckett, J.V., 'English landownership in the later seventeenth and eighteenth centuries: the debate and the problems' (*Ec.HR.*, 2nd. Ser. vol. XXX, 1, 1977).

Beckett, J.V., 'The Lowthers of Holker: marriage, inheritance and debt in the fortunes of an eighteenth century landowning family' (*THSLC*, 1978).

Beckett, J.V., 'The pattern of landownership in England and Wales, 1660-1780' (*Ec.HR.*, 2nd. Ser., vol. XXXVIII, 1, 1984).

Bonfield, L., 'Affective families, open elites and strict family settlements in early modern England' (*Ec.HR.*, 2nd. Ser., vol, XXXIX, 3, 1986).

Bonfield, L., 'Marriage settlements and the rise of great estates: the demographic aspect' (*Ec.HR.*, 2nd. Ser., vol. XXXII, 4, 1979).

Colyer, R.J., 'Crop husbandry in Wales before the onset of mechanisation (*Folk Life*, vol. 21, 1983).

Colyer, R.J., 'The Hafod estate under Thomas Johnes and Henry Pelham, Fourth Duke of

Newcastle' (*WHR.*, vol. 8, June 1977).

Dodd, A.H.,'The North Wales coal industry during the Industrial Revolution' (*Arch.Camb.*, vol. LXXXIV ,1929).

Dowden, M.J., 'A disputed inheritance: the Tredegar estates in the eighteenth century' (*WHR.*, vol. 16, no.1, June 1992).

Erikson, A.L., 'Common law versus common practice: the use of marriage settlements in early modern England' (*Ec.HR.*, 2nd. Ser., vol. XLIII, 1, 1990).

Evans, R.P., 'The Reverend John Lloyd of Caerwys (1733-1793): historian, antiquarian and genealogist' (*JFHS.*, vol.31, 1983-1984).

Habbakuk, H.J., 'English landed families, 1600-1800' (*TRHS.*, vol. 29, 1979)

Habbakuk, H.J.,'English landownership, 1680-1740' (*Ec.HR.*, 2nd. Ser., vol. X, 1940).

Habbakuk, H.J.,'Marriage settlements in the eighteenth century' (*TRHS.*, 5th. Ser., vol. XXXII, 1950).

Hine, R.,'The manor of Newnham' (*TEHerts. AS.*, 1910).

Holderness, R.H.,'The English land market in the eighteenth century: the case of Lincolnshire' (*Ec.HR.*, 2nd. Ser., vol.XXVII, 4, 1974).

Horn, P.,'An eighteenth century land agent: the career of Nathaniel Kent 1737-1810' (*Ag.HR.*, vol. 30, 1, 1982).

Howell, D.W., 'The economy of the landed estates in Pembrokeshire, c.1680-1830' (*WHR.*, vol. 3, 1966-67).

Jackson-Stops, G., 'Erddig Park, Clwyd. I' (*Country Life*, April 6th., 1978).

Jancey, E.M.,'The eighteenth century steward and his work' (*TSh. Arch.S .*, vol. LVI, 1957-1960).

Jones, E.D.,'Robert Vaughan of Hengwrt' (*JMHRS.*, vol. l, part 1, 1949).

Jones, F., 'A squire in Anglesey: Edward Wynne of Bodewryd' (*TAAS.*, 1940).

Mapp, V.E.,'The rebuilding of Bodorgan Hall' (*TAAS*, 1983).

Martin, J., 'Estate stewards and their work in Glamorgan,1660-1760: a regional study of estate management' (*Morg. XXIII*, 1979).

Martin, J., 'Landed estates in Glamorgan,c.1660-1760' (*Glam.H.*, 12, 1981).

Parker, R.A.C., 'Coke of Norfolk and the Agrarian revolution' (*Ec.HR.*, 2nd. Ser., vol. XIV, 1955).

Perkins, J.A., 'Tenure, tenant right and agricultural progress in Lindsey, 1780-1850' (*Ag.HR.*, vol. 23, 1975).

Pratt, D., 'King's mill, Wrexham' (*DHST.*, vol. 29, 1980).

Pritchard, T.W., The architectural history of the manor of Wynnstay' (*DHST.*, vol. 29, 1980).

Pritchard, T.W., 'Sir Watkin Williams Wynn, Fourth Baronet (1749-1789)' (*DHST*, vol. 28, 1979).

Spring, E., 'The strict settlement: its role in family history' (*Ec.HR.*, 2nd. Ser., vol. XLI, 3, 1988).

Wilde, W., 'Not just a pupil of Brown's' (*Country Life*, October 15th, 1987).

Williams, D., 'The acreage returns of 1801 for Wales' (*BBCS.*, vol. XIV, part 1, 1950).

Williams, R., 'Montgomeryshire worthies' (*Mont.Colls.*, vol. 9, 1876).

5 Unpublished Theses

Evans, R., *Thomas Pennant's writings on North Wales* (M.A., University of Wales, 1985).

Griffiths, E.W., *A survey of British educational ideas 1700-50* (M.Ed., University of Leeds, 1964).

Owen, J.T., *Gwallter Mechain, ei hanes, ei waith a'i safonau* (M.A., Prifysgol Cymru, 1928).

Rhodes, J.R., *The London Lead Company in North Wales* (Ph.D., Leicester University, 1970).

6 Newspapers & Periodicals

Bygones

Chester Courant

Shrewsbury Chronicle

Index

Numbers in italics indicate a reference to a picture.